Ancient

Egyptian

Magic

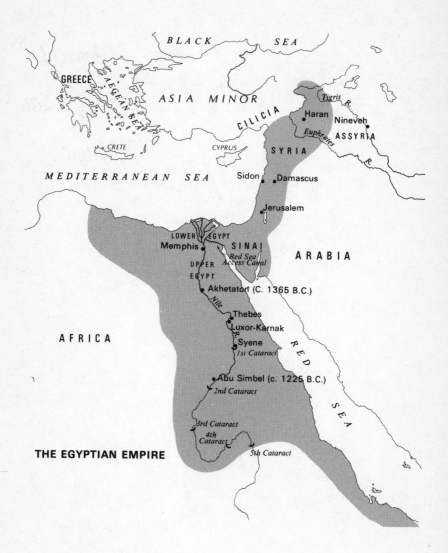

THE EGYPTIAN EMPIRE

BLACK SEA

GREECE
AEGEAN SEA
ASIA MINOR
CILICIA
CRETE
CYPRUS
SYRIA
Tigris R.
Haran
Nineveh
Euphrates
ASSYRIA
Sidon
Damascus
MEDITERRANEAN SEA
Jerusalem
LOWER EGYPT
Memphis
SINAI
ARABIA
UPPER EGYPT
Red Sea Access Canal
Akhetaton (C. 1365 B.C.)
AFRICA
Nile
Thebes
Luxor-Karnak
Syene
1st Cataract
Abu Simbel (c. 1225 B.C.)
2nd Cataract
RED SEA
3rd Cataract
4th Cataract
5th Cataract

Ancient Egyptian Magic

Bob Brier

QUILL

New York 1981

Grateful acknowledgment is made for permission to reprint Chapter 17 from *Ancient Egyptian Literature* by William K. Simpson, Yale University Press, New Haven, copyright © 1972 by Yale University, with permission of Yale University Press.

Library of Congress Cataloging in Publication Data

Brier, Bob.
    Ancient Egyptian magic.

    Bibliography: p.
    Includes index.
    1. Magic, Egyptian. I. Title.
[BF1591.B75   1981]   133.4′3′0932   81-11224
ISBN 0-688-03654-6   AACR2
ISBN 0-688-00796-1 (pbk.)

Printed in the United States of America

20 19 18 17 16 15 14 13

BOOK DESIGN BY BERNARD SCHLEIFER

Contents

Acknowledgments

THERE ARE MANY people on three continents who have helped me to prepare this book. In Africa there are my Egyptian friends and colleagues who helped me gain access to the materials and information I needed. I should like to thank Ms. Chah Mafouz for being so willing to take me to her numerous friends who had the keys to the locked tombs. At the Cairo Museum there is Dr. Dia Abu el Ghazi who so often worked her magic to get things done quickly. I should also like to thank Dr. Gamal Mokhtar, the former president of the Egyptian Antiquities Service, for his kind invitation to come to Egypt to do my research. In Luxor there are Naguib and Mustafa with whom I spent many pleasant hours drinking tea in front of Hassani's shop, talking about Egyptology and always benefitting from their knowledge.

In Europe there is Dr. T.G.H. James of the British Museum, who was so helpful in obtaining photos of the museum's collection.

On this continent there are almost too many to name. The C. W. Post College Research Committee assisted in the preparation of the manuscript with a generous grant. Dr. Virginia Lee Davis read several chapters and made important suggestions. Russell Rudzwick was always willing to photograph magical objects at any time of the night. At the Brooklyn Museum Drs. Bernard Bothmer and Robert Bianchi were extremely helpful in obtaining photos as was Dr. Christine Liliquist at the Metropolitan Museum of Art. Judith Turner did the line drawings for the Amulets chapter. A special thanks must go to my colleague Hoyt Hobbs who put aside the writing of his own book on Egypt to help me ready this book for publication. I cannot praise highly enough the advice of my editor, Eunice Riedel. She was always willing to deal with problems ranging from the organization of the manuscript to the intricacies of transliterating hieroglyphs into English. She has contributed a great deal to whatever intelligibility this book has. Thanks are also due to Carol Conklin, who helped with the translation of the Brooklyn Magical Papyrus; Diane Guzman, the librarian of the Brooklyn Museum's Wilbour collections; and Mary Chipman for her help in restoration of the *menyet*-necklace shown on page 161.

Finally, I should like to thank my second editor, my wife Barbara. She put aside her own writing projects to edit the very rough copy which I produced, often typed late at night, and was ready the next morning to discuss the manuscript. More important than her help on the manuscript, she was able to tolerate its author.

Introduction

WHILE WE ALL USE "magic" in our vocabularies, it is a difficult word to define. In the 1920s Lynn Thorndike, the Columbia University scholar, began publishing his monumental eight volumes on the *History of Magic and Experimental Science*. Despite the wealth of information, nowhere in the eight volumes is there a clear definition of "magic." There are two reasons the word is so difficult to define. First, "magic" has had numerous meanings over the last four thousand years. Second, religion, magic's sister discipline, is in many ways indistinguishable from it.

In our common speech, "magic" implies falsity, or trickery. A magician is one who uses deceit. This association of magic with falsity is a relatively new development. The word derives from *magi*, the Greek word for the wise men of Persia and Babylonia. These men were considered powerful, but their powers were foreign to the Greeks. The concept of magic as foreign, then, was at first essential to the definition of the word, and to this day there is a holdover of this belief. Whenever occult or supernatural powers are discussed, people are more willing to believe in them if they are attributed to a swami in India or a holy man in Tibet than if the claim is for a neighbor in the Bronx. Eventually, this notion of magic as something efficacious but foreign changed to something still efficacious but essentially evil. Finally, there evolved the modern view of magic as impotent foolishness.

Magic is often difficult to delineate from religion because both involve belief in the supernatural and deal with the realm of the unseen. Undeniably, the ancient Egyptians had both religious and magical practices, and sometimes it is almost impossible to decide in which category a particular act belongs. Yet two characteristics do seem to delineate magic from religion, magicians from priests.

In magic there is an immediacy lacking in religion. When the magician says an incantation, it is *he* who brings about the desired effect; whereas, when a priest prays for something, it is not he, but a deity, who brings about the effect. In magic the magician is the agent; in religion the priest is only the intermediary between the mundane world and the supernatural agent. This leads to a second difference between magic and religion.

In religious ritual, such as prayer, there is often an ultimate goal in sight, but the goal is not essential. It is possible to worship a god just for the sake of worshiping the god. The worshiper does not have to be asking for something. In magic this is not possible. A magician never recites a spell for its own sake—magic is never an end in itself, it is always a means to an end. Magic is a direct attempt by the practitioner to control supernatural forces to achieve a specific goal.

Three elements are essential to the magical act: the spell, the ritual, and the magician. The spell is what must be said for the act to have its desired effect. It may be crucial that the words be uttered properly, with a certain intonation. To the ancient Egyptian, words were extremely powerful: The word was the deed; saying something was so made it so. This is why names were so important in Egypt. When one pharaoh overthrew another, usually the first thing he did was obliterate the name of his predecessor on all monuments. If the name no longer existed, the predecessor no longer existed. For this reason ancient Egyptians had several names, only one of which was the *real* name. This real name was never revealed, so that, if someone tried to work a spell on you by using the name you commonly went by (which was not your real name), the spell could have no effect on you. In ancient Egypt if someone wanted to indicate that a person was extremely powerful, he would say, "Even his mother does not know his name." *No one* could work magic against such a person.

The second essential element in the magical act, ritual, is the action the magician performs while reciting the spell. Frequently, this part of the magical act was quite elaborate, as in the *heb-sed* festival in which the pharaoh had to run, wrestle, jump, and dance so that he would be magically rejuvenated. Sometimes the ritual involved making effigies or holding magical amulets. It was in the ritual that the apparatus of the sorcerer was employed. There were wands to be waved, wax images to be formed, incense to be burned, and potions to be drunk—all an essential part of the magical act.

The magician, the last element in the magical act, usually came from the ranks of the priests of the temples. He was a man who kept his knowledge of occult practices secret, so that he was held in awe by the commoner. For a fee he could write a spell for the diseased, interpret a dream for the perplexed, or fashion a charm for the young man in love. The ancient Egyptian believed that, with the proper combination of spell, ritual, and magician, virtually anything was possible. This book is about the spells and incantations the magicians of Egypt used for more than thirty centuries.

The last popular book on Egyptian magic was by E. A. Wallis Budge, the Keeper of Egyptian and Assyrian Antiquities in the British Museum, and appeared in 1895. While Budge is an almost inexhaustible source of information, much of what was then believed about magical practices has been revised, the knowledge of the language has increased greatly, and even the concept of magic has changed. This book is intended to present recent research on Egyptian magic. At times some of the older translations of spells have been used when others were not available in the hope that, while they are far from perfect, they will give the reader a feeling for how the ancient Egyptians practiced a particular kind of magic.

1. Egypt

WHEN FRENCH TROOPS were preparing for the Battle of the Pyramids, Napoleon told them that forty centuries of history looked down upon them. Napoleon was considering only the recorded period of Egyptian history; even so, he was underestimating its duration. It is difficult to conceive how far back in time ancient Egyptian civilization goes, but for example, when Stonehenge was being completed in England, the pyramids already were more than a thousand years old.

To date, no one has written an adequate book on the history of Egypt. Aside from the time span, one of the difficulties is that there are so many approaches to the subject: from the point of view of the philologist, dealing primarily with the written texts; from the point of view of the art historian, emphasizing the masterpieces of art; from the point of view of the archaeologist, chronicling the major discoveries and excavations; and countless others. If a writer selects just one approach, he is bound to leave out important information; if he tries to tackle them all, he sooner or later finds himself in a muddle of mechanical difficulty. This is why you will not find here a comprehensive history of Egypt, only enough background to understand and appreciate the practice and development of magic in ancient Egypt.

Because we are dealing with almost incomprehensible periods of time, it is best to divide Egyptian history into manageable units. Even these are formidable. The three major periods are Old Kingdom (2664–2181 B.C.), Middle Kingdom (2134–1786 B.C.), and New Kingdom (1570–1075 B.C.). There are numerous important events

13

before the Old Kingdom and after the New Kingdom, but these units make assimilating them a more feasible task.

We know very little about the earliest inhabitants of the Nile Valley because no human remains have been found from that period. We do know that the area was first inhabited around 500,000 B.C. by settlers who had as their only tool the hand ax. This marked the beginning of the Paleolithic, or Stone Age, Period. By modern standards change was slow. When we think of the changes in our civilization in the last hundred years, it is almost inconceivable that in the first 450,000 years of Egyptian civilization the only improvement was a better hand ax! When the Egyptians developed different tools, during the Middle Paleolithic Period, Egypt must have been moister than it is now. We assume this because, although tools are found in regions that are now desert, there had to have been water available then for habitation. Man of this period was Neanderthal, a term that today connotes a savage; but Neanderthal man buried his dead with ritual, practiced simple surgery, and cared for the injured and old.

By around 30,000 B.C., the Late Paleolithic Period, Neanderthal had been replaced by modern man, Homo sapiens sapiens. Because the level of the Nile was declining during this period, these people probably were forced to live near swamps. They lived on mollusks and fish and made clay hearths on which they cooked and grindstones on which they ground wild cereal grains and pigments. Sometime around 15,000 B.C. they began using the bow and arrow. Between 10,000 and 5,000 B.C., when the Nile reached its lowest level and most of the land had become desert, they used ostrich eggshells as cooking pots and vessels. Survival became a difficult matter, and at this time the population was probably not more than a few thousand.

Around 5,000 B.C. the Fayoum Lake, Egypt's only major lake, which had dried up millennia earlier, began reappearing, facilitating survival and the growth of population. Also around this time, pottery was developed and the Egyptians began farming and raising cattle. After farming began, the history of Egypt became so closely associated with the Nile that to understand the civilization one must understand the river.

The Nile is the only major river of the world that flows from south to north. It is an indication of how vast Africa is that even in the middle 1800s the river's source was not known. Actually, the Nile has two sources. One is Lake Victoria in East Central Africa, which becomes the White Nile; the other is the Blue Nile, which originates in Ethiopia and joins the White Nile at Khartoum several hundred miles south of the Egyptian border. It was the Blue Nile, swollen by spring monsoons and the run-off of melting snow and ice in Ethiopia, that caused the river to overflow its banks each year.

Although Egypt is a large country, covering nearly 400,000 square miles, the vast majority of it is uninhabited desert. The ancient Egyptians were not desert dwellers. They viewed the desert as inhospitable. Since all life clustered close on the banks of the Nile, the annual rising of the river determined the fate of the country for the year. Each year it overflowed its banks, depositing topsoil it had brought from the south. First it turned red (because of the soil suspended in it), then green (because of the vegetation on top). Then it rose twenty feet, spilling over the land for miles. If it was a good year and the river was high, crops were abundant. If it was a bad year and the river was low, when the Nile overflowed, it would not cover as much of the land, and crops would be reduced. In times of extremely low river, famine was a reality. So valuable was the topsoil that the Egyptians did not build their houses on cultivatable land, the "black" land, but lived on its edge, on the "red" land of the desert.

Two factors enabled Egypt eventually to become the dominant country of the Near East. One was geography. While the Nile was bountiful and provided ample food supplies, the desert on either side protected Egypt from invasion on its borders. Any foreign army attempting to enter Egypt from the east or west would have to confront a most hazardous journey. The second factor was a strong central government. In any country, it is much more productive if a single leader focuses national resources on joint projects than if each village leader works separately. The conversion of Egypt from divided political segments to a centralized government may have been the work of one man, the famous Narmer. The records we have of this king are few, and it is possible that more is made of him than should be. The most important document is in the Cairo Museum and has become known as the Narmer Palette.

The Egyptians used small slate palettes to grind various ingredients for eye paints. To commemorate important events, they fre-

1a.   1b.

FIGURE 1a. The Narmer Palette probably commemorates the unification of Upper and Lower
Egypt. On this side Narmer, wearing the white crown of Upper Egypt, strikes an enemy.

FIGURE 1b. The other side of the palette shows the king, wearing the red crown of Lower
Egypt, walking in a procession. Cairo Museum

quently carved scenes in relief on palettes about twice the normal
size. The Narmer Palette is carved on both sides (Figures 1a and 1b).
One side shows Narmer wearing the traditional white crown of
Upper Egypt and striking an enemy he holds by the hair. The other
side shows him walking in a procession and wearing the red crown
of Lower Egypt, suggesting that he is now king of both the north
and south. The event commemorated on the palette may be no less
than the unification of the two politically distinct sections of Egypt
and the beginning of centralized government. Narmer is thus considered by many to be the first king of the First Dynasty. Unification probably took place around 3100 B.C., approximately the time

that hieroglyphic writing began in Egypt. Narmer's name is given on the palette in the form of two pictures, a fish and a chisel—*nar* and *mer*.

The combination of geographical endowment and centralized government made Egypt great. With survival assured, the Egyptians could devote energy to major agricultural projects, such as the creation of an extensive system of irrigation canals to channel and control the overflow of the Nile. With increased farm production came surplus crops to trade for foreign goods. (So important was the system of irrigation that, in some versions of the *Book of the Dead,* the deceased was instructed to tell the gods judging him that he never diverted the flow of water in the ditches.) In addition, the pharaoh was able to marshal manpower into an efficient standing army. Not only could invasions be repulsed easily, but also new lands could be conquered and taxed.

From the time of the unification of the north and south, Egypt began to grow steadily and rapidly until, by the end of the Third Dynasty, its technology was sufficient to undertake what was then the greatest building project in the history of the world—the construction of the first pyramid. This growth continued throughout most of the Old Kingdom, resulting in the development of two large and important classes of people: priests and artisans. At this time art became the handmaiden to religion: Artistic styles and religious conventions were fused and formalized into patterns which would remain virtually unchanged for two thousand years.

The prosperity of the Old Kingdom continued only until the Sixth Dynasty, or 2181 B.C. Its abrupt decline is still not fully understood. One intriguing possibility is that the pharaoh Pepi II— whose ninety-four-year reign is the longest in the history of the world—outlived his effectiveness as a ruler. In ancient times the pharaoh was not only the political leader of the country but, in time of war, its general as well. It may be that Pepi became too old and feeble to lead the country or the army or even to oversee their maintenance, with the result that the strong centralized government became weak. Pepi II's longevity cannot be the only cause of the fall of the Old Kingdom, but it was probably one of the factors that plunged Egypt into an anarchistic period from which we have no records, not even the names of some of the pharaohs. This period is known as the First Intermediate Period—intermediate between the Old Kingdom and the Middle Kingdom—and lasted for about fifty years. There was such turmoil that the priest-historian Manetho says that, at one point, there were seventy kings in seventy days. The nomearchs, the governors of the states into which Egypt was divided, battled for power until eventually Egypt emerged once more as a nation with centralized government.

This second period of stability and consolidation, the Middle Kingdom, is an important period of Egyptian history often overlooked by historians because the pharaohs are not memorable as individuals and the art is not so beautiful as the art of the Old Kingdom. This period does reflect, however, the country's ability to recover from almost total chaos and to reestablish itself as the dominant power in the Near East. By Egyptian standards, it was a short period of prosperity, lasting only three hundred years before a second collapse.

The cause of turmoil during the Second Intermediate Period (1786–1575 B.C.) is also not fully understood. Frequently, it is attributed to a single event, the invasion of a people known as the Hyksos, or "foreign kings." There is no doubt that the Egyptians were ruled by these foreigners (Thirteenth through Seventeenth Dynasties), but the country must have been in an already weakened state to have been conquered. The fact that, at the time of the Hyksos invasion, the horse had not yet been introduced into Egypt leads to the theory that the Hyksos' use of chariots gave them a great advantage over the Egyptian foot-soldiers, but there is not much evidence to support this.

The Hyksos left few written records of their occupation, so we still are uncertain who they were. They were content to remain in the Delta in the north, while the Egyptians in the south seem to have ruled themselves from Thebes. We do have some documentation of the events that supposedly led to the Hyksos' expulsion. From the Delta the Hyksos king, Apophis, sent a letter to the Egyptian ruler in Thebes, Sekenenre, telling him that the hippopotami in the pools at Thebes disturbed his sleep and that they had to be silenced. Since the Hyksos capital, Avaris, and Thebes were several hundred miles apart, the complaint may be viewed as somewhat inflammatory. The goad seems to have worked. Sekenenre's mummy was discovered in 1881 in a cache of royal mummies and, judging from the holes in his skull, he died in battle. His son Kahmose recorded on a stela, found in the Temple of Karnak in 1954, that he, Kahmose, stormed the city of Avaris. Apophis, however, had walled himself in and could not be reached. He sent a messenger to Cush (Nubia) asking for reinforcements and promising the king of Cush a division of Egypt between them. The messenger was intercepted by the Egyptians, and the Cushite king never sent troops. The final routing of the Hyksos was completed by Kahmose's brother and successor, Ahmose.

With the expulsion of the Hyksos, Egypt began a new period of expansion and glory. The New Kingdom, which lasted for five hundred years, was ruled by only three dynasties, the Eighteenth, Nineteenth, and Twentieth. That the kingship remained in only a few families for hundreds of years is a sign of order and prosperity. The pharaohs most associated with the greatness of Egypt—Tuthmose III, Amenhotep III, Tutankhamen, and Ramses II—ruled during this period. It was a time of expansion and building. One of the ways a pharaoh could demonstrate his greatness was to attack other countries and "expand the borders of Egypt." With increased revenues from conquered countries, the pharaohs were able to build to an extent not seen since the days of the pyramids. Most of the Temple of Karnak, Luxor Temple, Ramses II's huge temples at Abu Simbel, and Hatshepsut's fantastic mortuary temple at Deir el Bahari—all were built during the New Kingdom, and it was then that the pharaohs began carving their tombs in the Valley of the Kings at Thebes.

It was also then that the priesthood of the god Amun accrued great power. The pharaohs had successively given more and more land to the temples until the holdings of the priesthood were almost as great as those of the pharaoh. At this point Amenhotep IV broke with the priesthood, changed his name to Akhenaten and attempted to change the religion of Egypt from polytheism, with the major god being Amun, to monotheism and the worship of the solar disk, the Aten. The change was never really effected, and with Akhenaten's death, Tutankhamen and his successors returned the religion to its previous state. (This brief break between the pharaoh and the priesthood was a prefiguring of a break two hundred years later.)

The Twentieth Dynasty ended with a succession of pharaohs named Ramses (Ramses III–Ramses XI). With the exception of

Ramses III, who ruled for more than thirty years, most of these kings had short and relatively weak reigns. By the end of the Twentieth Dynasty the kingship was so weakened and the priesthood so strong that the high-priest of Karnak, Hrihor, was able to call himself a king and begin a succession of priest-kings.

From the Twenty-first Dynasty on, Egypt slowly declined. The next half millennium was spent fighting off invaders, including the Nubians, Assyrians, Persians, and finally the Greeks. There were many reasons for this long period of decline. One, frequently mentioned, is that Egypt was not the first in the Near East to develop iron. When its enemies were armed with iron weapons, the Egyptians' softer bronze weapons were no match. This was undoubtedly a factor, but if one cause is to be singled out, it should be the rise of centralized governments around Egypt. Egypt had been, literally, the first nation in the world. When it alone could call up a great army, it was unbeatable. With that advantage gone, Egypt could no longer dominate the Near East.

Egypt was conquered for the last time by Alexander the Great in 332 B.C. The Greeks had always revered Egyptian civilization and were proud to trace their religion and architecture back to Egypt. They did not seek to impose their culture on the vanquished Egyptians. The situation was unique: Alexander wanted to be crowned pharaoh, son of the sun. After his death, when Egypt was ruled by his general, Ptolemy, and by a succession of pharaohs of that name, no attempt was made to eradicate the culture of Egypt. The Ptolemaic temples, while distinct from temples of the New Kingdom, certainly were Egyptian in form, and their inscriptions were written not in Greek, but in hieroglyphs.

The death of the ancient Egyptian civilization was a long process. During the Ptolemaic period the Greeks ran Egypt much as a business, placing troops throughout the country to keep order and instituting oppressive taxes. There was no longer the possibility of a large priesthood or of a large number of artisans supported by wealthy patrons. Egyptian art declined in quality greatly during this period, but more important, so did the priesthood. With the reduced number of priests and the introduction of the Greek language, the number of Egyptians who could read hieroglyphs dwindled. By the time of the Roman occupation of Egypt, there were few priests alive who could read the inscriptions of the temple walls that told of the glory of Egypt.

The long and many-faceted history of Egypt has always fascinated the masses. People are not intrigued by the Hittites, Babylonians, or Assyrians the way they are by the ancient Egyptians. The wide appeal is probably the result of the fact that Egyptian civilization has so many aspects. For the art lover, there are innumerable true masterpieces; for the romantic, there are awesome heroes: for the armchair adventurer, there are exciting archaeological discoveries; for the lover of languages, there are the hieroglyphs and the saga of their decipherment. This book is for those who have always wondered about the occult and essentially hidden aspect of ancient Egyptian man—his magic.

2. Hieroglyphs

TACITUS, THE HISTORIAN, tells us that when the Roman emperor
Germanicus visited the ruins of Thebes he was puzzled by the
meaning of the hieroglyphic inscriptions on the walls of the tombs
and temples. He found an old man wandering through the crum-
bling buildings and asked what the carvings said. The old man told
Germanicus that he was the last man alive who could read the
writings of the Egyptians, and he pretended to translate the hieroglyphs. Undoubtedly the old man lied to Germanicus. In the early
first century A.D., when Germanicus visited Egypt, few could read
hieroglyphs, and soon any knowledge of the sacred script was to
die. Because the Egyptians had been conquered by the Persians,
Greeks, and Romans, only a small vestige of the priestly caste remained who could read ancient Egyptian and finally even these
remnants were gone. Then, for almost fifteen hundred years scholars wondered what the carvings of birds, feet, animals, and other
symbols meant.

Many of their speculations were based upon the belief that the
inscriptions were mystical or magical in nature, a guess not far
from correct. When the Greeks first came into Egypt they called
the writings "hieroglyphs," or "sacred carvings," since only the
priests could read them. When the knowledge of how to read the
hieroglyphs had died, this association with the priests remained,
and hieroglyphic writings were thought to be religio-magical.

Numerous attempts were made to decipher the hieroglyphic
inscriptions. Interestingly, they all failed because they were based
on the false assumption that hieroglyphs were basically picture
writing. If there was a carving of a foot, that represented the con-

22

cept of a foot; if there was the carving of a duck, the text was discussing a duck.

Horapollo of Nilopolis, a writer of the third century A.D., did much to foster this erroneous belief. Writing in Coptic, the language of the Egyptian Christians, he says that the vulture was used to denote a mother ". . . because in this race of creatures there is no male." Aside from the bad biology, the philology is poor. While it is true that the ancient Egyptians did use the vulture to denote *mother*, this has nothing to do with the qualities of vultures. The sign represented the sound "mut," which was the ancient Egyptian word for *mother*. Here the hieroglyph does not really represent a concept, but a sound, which in turn denotes a concept.

In the fifteenth century Horapollo's text was translated from the Coptic into Greek, and with the availability of his writings, scholars went farther and farther from the truth. In the seventeenth century the Jesuit scholar, Athanasius Kircher, came across a volume of engravings of the obelisks that had been erected in Rome. Convinced that the inscriptions contained answers to mysteries of the universe, he studied the engravings and wrote a book entitled *Sphinx Mystagogia*. This contained Kircher's imagined translations of the hieroglyphs, based on the principles set down by Horapollo.

Not until the eighteenth century did modern linguists begin to suggest that the ancient Egyptian language was not mere pictograms, but was also composed of signs that had phonetic value— they represented sounds. But while some suggested that the signs represented sounds, no one knew which signs represented which sounds, or what concepts those sounds stood for. Finally, with a combination of brilliant scholarship and good fortune, the hieroglyphs could once again be read. The good fortune was the discovery of the Rosetta Stone.

When Napoleon went to Egypt, he took with him a large corps of savants to study its architecture, measure its monuments, and copy the inscriptions and art works, all with the goal of increasing man's understanding of ancient Egyptian civilization. The most significant discovery of the expedition was an accidental one, one which none of the savants could have expected.

Toward the end of Napoleon's campaign it was evident that the British forces were too strong for the French, and Napoleon and his men would soon have to flee. By the summer of 1799 Napoleon's army was defending the northern coast of Egypt. In August of that year the French were digging in a few miles from the town of Rosetta. In the course of the digging, a large black stone was discovered. The Rosetta Stone was covered with writing in three different scripts (Figure 2). The scientists present immediately realized that the top script was hieroglyphs and the bottom was Greek. Later it was realized that the middle script was demotic, a late form of Egyptian writing. The stone contained the same message written in three scripts. Basically, it was a "thank-you" note from the priests of Memphis to Ptolemy V for gifts which the pharaoh had donated to the temple.

The stone was taken to Cairo, where Napoleon had established an institute to study ancient Egyptian civilization. There copies of the stone were made and sent to France. Then the stone was sent to the house of General de Menou in Alexandria for safekeeping. In 1801, when the French surrendered to the British, all Egyptian antiquities collected by Napoleon's expedition were confiscated. By 1802 the stone was in the British Museum, where it remains.

Ancient Egyptian was written in four different scripts. Two scripts developed at approximately the same time, hieroglyphic and hieratic. Hieroglyphic corresponds to our printed letters and hieratic to our handwriting. The hieroglyphic script was used on Egyptian temples and monuments and wherever else artistic value was important. It is the script most people think of when they hear of Egyptian writing. The signs used are representations of clearly identifiable objects with which the Egyptians were familiar. In a hieroglyphic text, an owl is clearly identifiable as an owl.

Because it took a scribe or artist considerable time to form each sign in a hieroglyphic script, hieratic, the more cursive form of writing, was used for such mundane needs as letters, receipts, inventories, and other business matters. While derived from the hieroglyphs, the objects that the signs represent are not clearly identifiable (Figure 3). For example, the hieroglyphic sign, 𓃀 , became the hieratic 𐌆 .

In a later form of ancient Egyptian writing, demotic, the hieratic was transformed into an even more cursive form with the objects still less recognizable. While the Rosetta Stone had two of the three Egyptian scripts on it (hieroglyphic and demotic), it was the third, the Greek, which was the crucial element in the decipherment of the other two. It alone could be read by the nineteenth

FIGURE 2. The Rosetta Stone is a proclamation written in three scripts: hieroglyphs at the top, demotic in the middle, and Greek at the bottom. Reproduced by courtesy of the Trustees of the British Museum

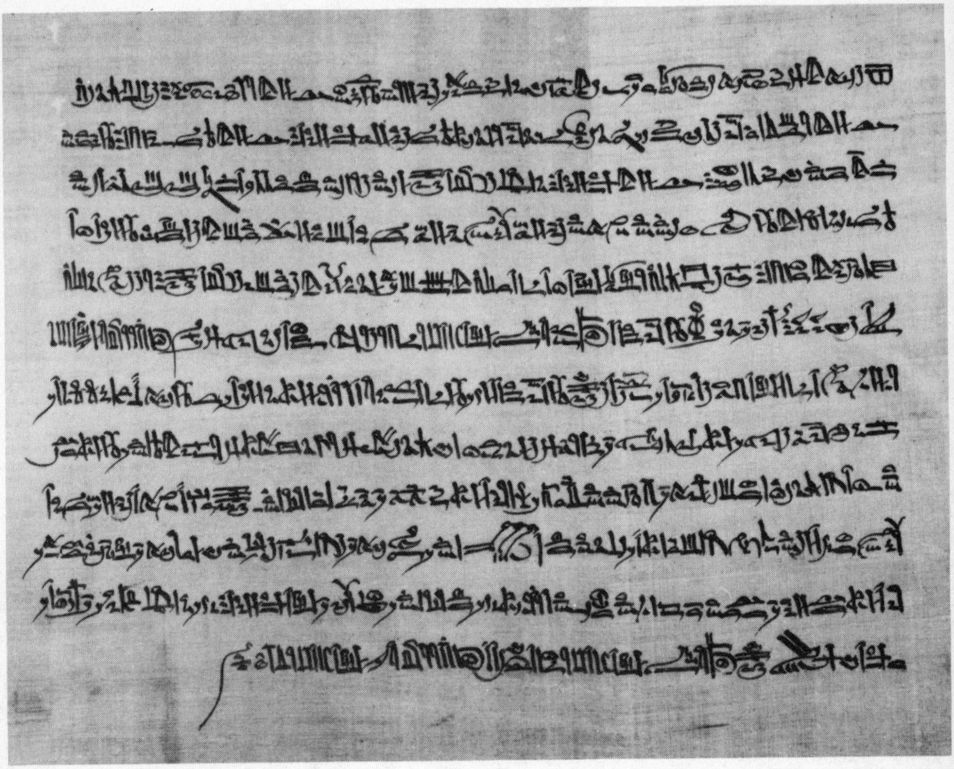

FIGURE 3. The Great Harris Papyrus, written in hieratic, is more than 135 feet long. Reproduced by courtesy of the Trustees of the British Museum

century linguists who attempted to decipher the Rosetta Stone's inscriptions.

One of the most important early decipherers of the stone was the brilliant English physicist Thomas Young. Young, a physician and scientist by training, had made ancient languages his avocation, and the Rosetta Stone was just the kind of challenge he loved. By decoding it, he hoped to open the door to discovering the sciences of the ancient Egyptians. He decided to work on the demotic text first.

Young quickly realized that groupings of signs in the demotic inscription corresponded to names of the pharaoh and queen in the Greek text. Soon he deduced that the demotic signs were basically phonetic, but more important, he began to see similarities between the demotic-sign groups and groups of signs in the hieroglyphic text. This meant that the hieroglyphs were phonetic also. By 1818 he had determined with *some* accuracy the hieroglyphic alphabet. After this start at deciphering the Rosetta Stone, Young lost interest in the project and left it for Jean François Champollion to complete.

As a youth, Champollion demonstrated a unique ability to learn languages. Since his father was a librarian, Champollion was accustomed to playing among books written in various languages. He studied Latin, Greek, Arabic, Syriac, Chaldean, and Hebrew. But the language which was of most use to him in translating the Rosetta Stone was Coptic.

Coptic, the language spoken in Egypt during the late period, was written in the Greek alphabet with seven special characters added. It is called "Coptic" because the Copts were the Egyptian Christians who used this script. Coptic is the connection between written hieroglyphs and how the words were pronounced. For example, the hieroglyph ♀ meant *life.* The later Coptic word for life was *onch.* When we see the sign ♀ , therefore, we can be reasonably sure that it was pronounced *onch.*

In 1808, while still a teenager, Champollion obtained a copy of the Rosetta Stone and began his relentless pursuit of its meaning. He first realized that there were three Egyptian scripts—hieroglyphic, demotic, and the hieratic (which was not represented on the stone). He deduced this by comparing hieratic papyri with hieroglyphic and demotic inscriptions. Champollion then began comparing the hieroglyphic inscription of the Rosetta Stone with its Greek counterpart. The key was the name "Ptolemy." It had long been known that the pharaohs wrote their names in ovals called "cartouches." The oval represented a rope showing the pharaoh's dominion over all that the sun encircles. Since the Greek inscription mentioned Ptolemy, the name in a corresponding cartouche in the hieroglyphic text had to be Ptolemy. The cartouche

read: ⬭. Here the ▢ = P, ⌒ = T, 𝔉 = O, ⫯ = L, ⌒ = M, ⎮⎮ = I, and ⎮ = S. (Ptolmis was the Greco-Egyptian way of writing the name.) With these letters established, he went on to other names.

From an inscription on an obelisk found on the island of Philae, he had the name Cleopatra. (He knew it was Cleopatra's name because the base of the obelisk had an inscription in Greek mentioning her.) Her cartouche read:

With the letters from Ptolemy's name he knew that the lion (⚬) was "L," the reed ( ) something close to "I," the loop ( ) an "O," and the square (□) a "P." That gave him:__ L __ O P __ __ __ __ __. The first blank had to be the hard "C" or "K" sound, and the second blank an "E." The bird that appeared twice was obviously the "A," and the hand the "T." (In earlier times, the hand was closer to the "D" sound.) The mouth sign was an "R." Thus Champollion was left with CLEOPATRA. Champollion had seen the two extra signs at the end of the name after names of other queens. The loaf, ⌒ , is the ending "T," appended to Egyptian names and words that are feminine. The egg is the sign indicating that a name is that of a woman.

Champollion's work on the hieroglyphic alphabet is the basis of what we know today. The Egyptians omitted vowels but did have what are called semi-vowels. Also, for a good part of their three thousand years of written history they did not have signs for the sounds "L" or "O," which appeared in Ptolemy's and Cleopatra's names.

Below is the Classical Egyptian alphabet, the alphabet used in Egypt for approximately three thousand years. While the Egyptians did not write the vowels, some of the signs may be used in place of vowels in writing modern names. Thus the Egyptian vulture may be used in place of the sound "a," the arm in place of the "e," etc.

Classical Egyptian Alphabet

HIEROGLYPH	OBJECT DEPICTED	SOUND
	vulture	a
	foot	b
	placenta	ch
	hand	d
	arm	e

Classical Egyptian Alphabet (continued)

HIEROGLYPH	OBJECT DEPICTED	SOUND
	horned viper	f
	jar stand	g
	twisted flax	h
	reed leaf	i
	snake	j (dj)
	basket	k
	owl	m
	water	n
	mat	p
	hill	q
	mouth	r
	folded cloth	s
	pool of water	sh
	loaf of bread	t
	tethering ring	tch
	quail chick	u or w
	two reed leaves	y
	door bolt	z

You might try writing your name in hieroglyphs. Replace the letters of your name with the hieroglyphic signs that represent the same sound. For example, the name BARBARA is written:

Where a particular letter is lacking in the Egyptian alphabet, you can leave it out. In William, the "L" is omitted:

In some cases you can substitute a sign that is similar in sound. In EUNICE, the "C" can be replaced by an "S" to give: . It should be noted that this is not *translating* but *transliterating*, or representing sounds written in one script with the characters of another script.

On the Rosetta Stone were quite a few signs other than those of the alphabet. Another of Champollion's discoveries was that some signs were "determinatives." That is, after a word was spelled out phonetically, there was sometimes a sign at the end of the word that indicated the object denoted by the word. For example, in the

word ⬚ , the hieroglyphs ⬚ ,   ⬚ ,   and   ⬚   told
how the word was pronounced *(dpt*—we don't know the vowels).
The last sign showed that the word meant boat.

Champollion's 1822 paper on deciphering hieroglyphs enabled
future Egyptologists to read inscriptions that had been silent for
fifteen hundred years. Throughout his dedicated undertaking,
Champollion was plagued by an extremely weak constitution. He
was often incapacitated and lay in bed exhausted for days. Even
after he published his paper, "Lettre à M. Dacier, Relatif à l'Alphabet Des Hiéroglyphes Phonétiques," he continued to improve the
knowledge of hieroglyphs and traveled to Egypt to copy inscriptions for further study. A letter written from Abu Simbel on New
Year's Day, 1829, shows his dedication. After spending two and a
half hours inside the temple in ovenlike heat, he wrote:

> We regained the entrance and went out. As soon as I emerged I put
> on two under-waistcoats of flannel, threw on a large woolen blanket,
> and covered myself with my cloak; and there sitting by one of those
> columns in front of the temple whose huge sides completely shel-
> tered me from the north wind, I reposed half an hour, till the heavy
> perspiration had passed off. I then immediately regained the boat
> where I passed more than two hours upon my bed.[1]

Three years later Champollion was dead at the age of forty-one.
With his death a new group of scholars began to translate texts, and
the magical nature of the hieroglyphs became evident.

To the ancient Egyptians, the message conveyed by the hieroglyphs was not the only concern. The configuration and shape of
the hieroglyphs were also of great importance. For this reason,
hieroglyphic writing had to be extremely flexible, capable of being
molded to suit the needs of the priests. To achieve maximum flexibility, rules for writing hieroglyphs were developed which permitted inscriptions to be written from either left to right, right to left,
or top to bottom. Below is the same sentence, "Magic is everywhere," written three different ways:

(1) [hieroglyphs]   (3) [hieroglyphs]

(2) [hieroglyphs]

In (1) the sentence reads from left to right, and in (2), from right to left. The indicator as to which way to read the sentences is the way the birds, animals, people, or objects face. The hieroglyphs are always read toward the mouths. The third version of the sentence reads from top to bottom. When two signs are on the same line they read from left to right.

The freedom to write hieroglyphs in any direction desired gave the Egyptians added artistic freedom. For example, they often covered the walls of a tomb with a magical inscription. If there was a door in the center of the wall, the inscription might read from the center of the doorway toward the end of the wall.

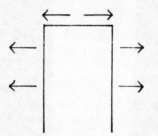

This would give the wall a symmetry that would be lacking if the inscription began on the right and read toward the left.

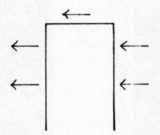

Not only the arrangement of the hieroglyphs was important, but also the way they were inscribed. When we write a letter, the most important thing is that each letter be recognizable, so that the meaning of the message will be conveyed. To the Egyptians not only the meaning was important, but the hieroglyphs themselves were too. Since the hieroglyphs were ends in themselves, scribes and artists practiced for years to learn how to make beautiful hieroglyphs.

At one point in Egyptian history people believed that the hieroglyphs, by magic, could become real. Thus the hieroglyph for the
sound "M," which was an owl, might become a real owl and leave
the wall! This belief in the magical reality of hieroglyphs led to a
rather bizarre practice in writing. An example was found in the
pyramid of the princess Neferuptah.

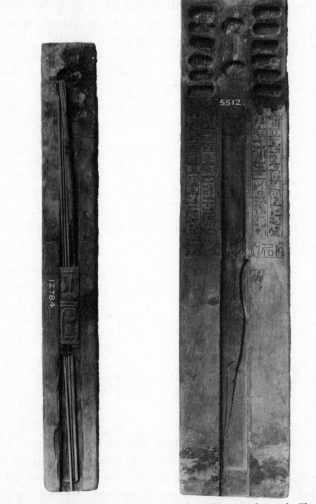

FIGURE 4. The scribe's palette on the left holds reeds in the central trough. The ends of the
reeds were chewed to make a brush. At the top of the palette are two pits, one for black ink,
the other for red. The more elaborate palette on the right has pits for several colors, probably
for illustrating papyri. Reproduced by courtesy of the Trustees of the British Museum

The pyramid of Neferuptah is unique in all of Egyptian archaeology. It is the only royal pyramid found unrobbed, with the
mummy still in it. Neferuptah was the daughter of the Pharaoh
Amenemhet III, who ruled in the Middle Kingdom. When the pyramid was discovered, it was found that, unfortunately, water had
seeped into the burial chamber, and most of the contents of the
tomb had been destroyed. Enough fragments of the sarcophagus
were recovered, however, to show that the hieroglyphs were
formed in a most unusual way. All the animals were drawn mutilated. The owls and chicks were drawn without legs: ✎ and
✎ . And the viper was without a tail: ⌐ . This was probably
done so that the animals would not escape and spoil the text.

The *Book of the Dead* even has a spell intended to assure that
the deceased will have the tools of the scribe in the next world. The
hieroglyph for "writing"   (𓏞)   depicts these tools (Figure 4):
the water bowl, the reed pen, and the palette that held the brushes
and two circular blocks of dry ink—one red and one black. The
scribe would dip the brush in the water bowl and then touch it to
the ink. If the deceased had these tools in the next world, he would
know all the magical secrets contained in the writings of Toth. The
spell to obtain these tools instructs the deceased to say:

> O Eldest who looks upon his Father, secretary of Thoth, behold, I
> am come blessed, possessed of a soul, mighty, equipped with the
> writings of Thoth. I have purified myself while [I] tarried [with]
> Sokar. Bring me water-bowl, bring me palette, even this outfit of
> Thoth, and the secrets that are in them, [the secrets of] the Gods.
> Behold, *I* am a scribe. Bring me the putrid effluent of Osiris, that I
> may write therewith. "Do [what] the great God says," says Re,
> "[every day,] namely the good things that Harakhte commands
> thee." [I] do righteousness, that I may go [to] Re every day.[2]

For the ancient Egyptian, hieroglyphs were not mere signs used
to convey messages. They were objects bound by the rules of
magic, just as all other objects in their world.

3. Magicians

IT WOULD BE INTERESTING to know what the daily life of an Egyptian magician was like—what he did, what his powers were, who his clientele were, and so forth. But no magician has left such a record, so we must reconstruct the life of a magician from papyrus fragments, brief inscriptions on temple walls, and actual tools of the trade which have survived the ages.

Egypt had two kinds of magicians. There were trained priest-magicians who were from established temples and who were part of the orthodox hierarchy. Then, there were what we might call "lay" magicians, untrained men who practiced magic but who were not attached to any institution. The second type was closer to our faith healers, or occultists. However, by far the great majority of magicians in ancient Egypt was of the first type—priests of the establishment. Therefore, to know what a magician's life was like, we first will have to know his life as a priest.

Today, we expect our clergy to have entered into their profession because of a deep religious commitment. In ancient Egypt, however, being a priest was merely a job, a means to making a good living and having status in the community. This may strike us as odd and perhaps even missing the whole point of a religious life, but there was a crucial difference between the function of a priest in ancient Egypt and that of a modern cleric. In our society a minister or priest is thought of as having a close one-to-one relationship with God. If he does not have strong religious convictions, the relationship is vacuous. This was not the case with the Egyptian priest. His job was primarily to be a stand-in for the pharaoh.

Egypt was a theocracy—its political ruler was a god. As a god, the pharaoh ultimately was responsible for maintaining the divine order throughout Egypt. Obviously, the king could not be present for all the ceremonies at the various temples in Egypt. He needed delegates who could take his place at temple functions. As the functions became more and more numerous—sometimes several ceremonies each day at each temple—the delegates became more and more numerous. This was the origin of the priesthood.

Since ancient Egyptian priests were not a group of men set apart from the rest of the community by their religious commitments, they dealt with mundane matters of life much as laymen did. For instance, it was common for a priestly office to be hereditary. The father who held a particular office could pass that position down to his son, regardless of the son's religious beliefs or moral conduct. Herodotus recorded the practice:

> They led me into the inner sanctuary, which is a spacious chamber, and showed me a multitude of colossal statues, in wood, which they counted up, and found to amount to the exact number they had said; the custom being for every high-priest during his lifetime to set up his statue in the temple. As they showed me the figures and reckoned them up, they assured me that each was the son of the one preceding him. . . .

> Herodotus, Book II, 143

Eventually, the priesthood became a tremendous bureaucracy numbering thousands of men. There were hundreds of temples dedicated to the various gods, and each temple was somewhat autonomous, having its own hierarchy and division of labors. However, all temples had similar offices with extreme specialization of services.

Perhaps one of the most important functions of the priests was caring for the cult statues of the gods, or "oracles." (See Chapter 13, "Oracles.") Only a select few of the priests were permitted to enter each temple's holy of holies and care for the oracle (Figure 5). This involved presenting food before the god several times a day, clothing him in the morning, sealing the chamber in the evening, and so forth. These priests were called the *stolists* by the Greeks, because they were in charge of the clothing of the god.

While no great religious conviction was required for the job, the priest did have to purify himself before he came in contact with

FIGURE 5. This view from one of the "holy of holies" in the Temple of Karnak was originally blocked by an ornate door, sealed every day, to keep out all but the high-priests. Photograph by Barbara Benton

the god. Even the hieroglyphs for the most common order of priest, the *wab*-priest, illustrate this notion of purity. They were written 𝌆 𝌇 , first showing water of purification being poured from a vessel (this part of the word means pure) with a man behind it. So, a priest was depicted as a pure man, or one who purifies.

To be pure, or clean in a religious sense, the priest had to shave off all hair on his body. This was because lice were a common problem in Egypt and shaving removed the nesting areas. On temple reliefs and tomb paintings, priests are always depicted as shaven-headed. Washing also was an important part of purification. Herodotus tells us that the priests bathed four times a day, twice during the day and twice in the evening. Many of the temples had sacred lakes where purification was performed.

These artificial pools also had another function. On festival days the cult statues, in their shrines, or barks, would be carried out of the temples on the shoulders of the priests and floated on the sacred lake (Figure 6). At temples without lakes, the priests would perform their ablutions in basins placed in special locations.

FIGURE 6. The sacred lake at Karnak lies in a basin formed by stonework, visible in this photograph taken in the early 1920s.

In addition to shaving and washing, the priests were circumcised and prohibited from eating certain foods. The forbidden foods varied from nome to nome. (A nome was equivalent to a state in the United States.) Variations also depended upon the temple. Included were cow's meat, pigeon, and garlic, but the most universally proscribed food seems to have been fish. There are numerous references to fish being considered unclean, and frequently, before entering a temple, the supplicant would have to say, "I am clean. I have not eaten fish. . . ." This prohibition held only for the priests, as fish was a staple of the commoner.

It is clear that the food regulations were taken seriously by the Egyptians. In the Oxyrinchus Nome, the fish of that name was sacred, and no one was permitted to eat it. (*Oxyrinchus* means long-nosed, and the fish does have an extremely long nose.) The inhabitants fought a civil war over the prohibition when they learned that the citizens of neighboring Cynopolis were eating the fish. They retaliated by capturing some dogs and cooking and eating them! Fighting broke out and soldiers had to be called in to restore peace.

There were also clothing restrictions. Priests were not permitted to wear wool, since wool came from animals, and animals obviously were unclean. They wore only fine linen, stored in special rooms of the temples and cared for by other priests whose function it was to assure their cleanliness. It seems contradictory that, while priests were forbidden to wear clothes made from wool because it came from animals, the *sem*-priest, or high-priest, wore a leopard skin at important occasions as the sign of his office (Figure 7).

Yet another condition of purity for the priests was sexual abstinence. This might seem like a severe rule for a job requiring no religious conviction, but the priests adhered to it for only the short time they were in service. In all the temples there was a system of rotation. The priests were divided into corps called "phylai," each unit serving the temple for only one month three times a year. That is, a priest would serve the temple for one month, during which he lived a restricted life in the temple. Then he would have three months off, during which he lived in the lay community in a way no different from the average layman.

After all the conditions of purity were met, a priest had to undergo an initiation rite for the higher temple offices. Although

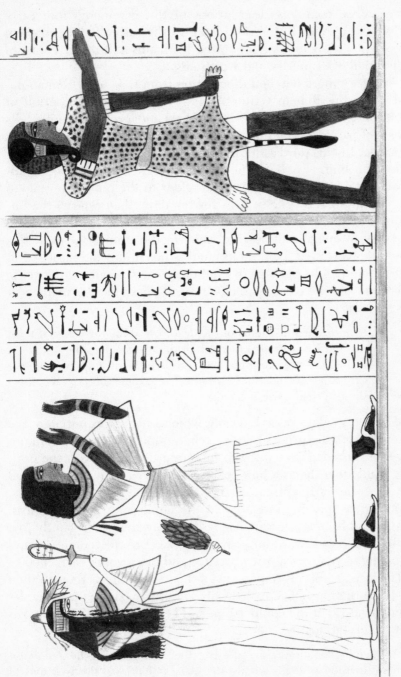

FIGURE 7. A priest dressed in leopard skin leads the deceased, Ani, and his wife to the next world. This unusual portrait of a priest, copied from the Papyrus of Ani, shows him with the sidelock of a youth. Drawing by Dorothy Spano

there are no complete descriptions of this ceremony from early periods of Egyptian history, we do know the basics. Before entering the temple, the candidate anointed his hands and made a solemn declaration of his purity and worthiness.

We get a more detailed description from the Greco-Roman period when the Roman writer Apulius describes the initiation of Lucius into the Temple of Isis. One of the elders of the temple tells Lucius of papyri in the library that reveal what he must do for his initiation. Lucius purifies himself in the sacred lake and has water poured on him as part of the cleansing ceremony. When he approaches the cult statue of Isis, the elder of the temple reveals to him cosmic secrets. Lucius fasts for ten days, then repeats the initiation ceremony. Finally, the ultimate secrets are revealed to him.

One can imagine the mental state of the young Lucius at this point. He has fasted for ten days and is taken into the most secret part of the temple, perhaps in total darkness. Undoubtedly incense is burning and the priests are chanting. He describes his feelings at this moment:

> I approached the limits of the dead; I trod the threshold of Proserpine, and I was carried beyond all the elements; in the middle of the night I saw the sun shine with a brilliant light; I approached the gods from below and from on high, I saw them face to face and I worshipped them near at hand.[1]

Even in the late period, during which Lucius was initiated, the system of rotating priests between the temple and the lay community still existed. This tended to integrate the priest with the ordinary man rather than set him apart. For this reason it is not unusual to hear stories of Egyptian priests who behaved quite scandalously. One papyrus tells the sad story of the family of a priest, Pet-Isis. Pet-Isis had been a priest in Thebes but moved with his family to a small town. As a reward for previous services to the temple, he and his family were given a priestly office and the revenues attached to it. The local priests of Amun viewed the new family as rivals. When Pet-Isis turned his office over to his son-in-law, Horoudja, they decided to get rid of the competition and keep his share. The papyrus tells the brutal details.

> When in the morning the priests gathered together at the temple for the division of grain among the classes of priests, the two sons of Horoudja appeared saying: "Come on, let the fifth be measured." At

this moment, the young priests drew out their sticks, surrounded the sons of Horoudja and began to beat them. The two young sons fled to the sanctuary, but they were followed there and alas! caught in the very entrance of the sanctuary of Amon, they were killed by the force of the blows.[2]

The story does not end here, but chronicles over a century during which the family and descendants of Pet-Isis were terrorized by the priests of Amun. Our first reaction is to be incredulous of such behavior by priests, but when we remember that no divine calling or high ethical standard was required for the ranks of the ordinary priests, the situation is not so strange.

Besides these, there were many priests whose jobs were merely clerical, involving such duties as supervising lands belonging to the temples, overseeing artists who decorated the temple walls, or recording temple stores. Almost certainly the magicians would not be among these, but among the strictly religious personnel, and they would probably be the most learned of their class.

At the top of the hierarchy of priests was the high-priest, the *sem*-priest, or "First Prophet of the God." He would have been an extremely learned man, an elder of the temple, a man with considerable administrative ability and political sense. He would have been in charge of seeing that the temple and all its holdings ran smoothly, and officiating at the most important ceremonies. While normally such a man would have risen to his position through the ranks, it was the pharaoh's prerogative to place whomever he wanted in that office.

Beneath the high-priest was a whole cadre of priests with specialized training. Among these were the "horologers," or "priests of the hours," whose job it was to determine as precisely as possible the hours of the day and night. This was crucial to the functioning of the temple, since various rituals had to start at precise times. These priests, through watching the progress of the sun or stars across the sky, determined when the rituals should begin.

Closely akin to the horologers were the astrologer-priests. These were not like our modern astrologers. That is, they did not watch the procession of the stars and planets across the sky in order to predict what would happen on earth. Instead, these priests were the custodians of a mythological calendar that told earthly mortals how to behave. In ancient Egyptian mythology there is an event for each day of the year which determines whether the day will be good or bad and upon which the advice for each day was based. The most famous of these calendars is the Cairo Calendar, reproduced in Chapter 15.

But the magicians did not come from the ranks of even these learned priests. To find the magicians we must look to an institution associated with almost all of the large temples—the House of Life. The House of Life was written with two hieroglyphic signs: ⊔̣ . The ⊏⊐ sign was pronounced *per* and meant *house*. The ♀ sign was pronounced *ankh* and meant *life*. The House of Life was a building, or perhaps a small group of buildings, where the library of the temple was kept and where the custodians of the knowledge of the temple studied. Here the layman would come if he had a problem and needed a magic spell or charm. The priests could interpret dreams, supply incantations to make someone fall in love, cure an illness, dispense magic amulets, or counteract malevolent influences. To maintain their powers, the priests kept their books away from the few laymen who could read. Indeed secrecy was an important part of their business. In the *Book of the Dead* prepared for the priest Nebseni, one of his titles is given as "presiding over the secrets of the temple." Perhaps Nebseni was in charge of the temple library. Indeed these papyri were considered so powerful that the commoner had to be kept away from them or he could become extremely dangerous by misusing the power. A good example of this occurred during the reign of Ramses III.

During this period a unique episode took place which later became known as "The Harem Conspiracy." Several officials of Ramses' court intended to overthrow their sovereign. They plotted in a typically political manner and eventually took into their confidence several ladies of the harem, probably to obtain information about the pharaoh. Eventually, the overseer of the royal cattle, a high official in the government, became involved and enlisted the help of the man in charge of the royal library. From him the overseer obtained a papyrus of magical formulae, which he attempted to use to cast spells over Ramses. He made wax figures and magical amulets and had them smuggled into the palace. All this conspiring, however, was fruitless. The plot was discovered and the conspirators severely punished. The point of the story is that it tells of papyri in the king's library that were kept from the common man.

No doubt, these papyri originated in the House of Life, but for whom were they intended? Most probably, they were written by and intended for the priests of the House of Life.

Etymological evidence for this comes from the Coptic word for "magician": "seshperonch." This is derived from the hieroglyphs 𓏞𓉐𓋹, "sesh per ankh," which mean "scribe of the House of Life." There is even a papyrus, Papyrus Westcar, that tells the story of a high-priest who was cuckolded. For revenge he fashioned a crocodile of wax, recited magical words over it, and instructed his servant to place the effigy in the river. When his wife's lover came down to the river to bathe, the figure came to life and devoured him. From this story it is clear that there was nothing extraordinary about a priest, even a high-priest, using magic.

There is another, better-known tale of a magician-priest which has come down to us in a somewhat distorted form. The ancient writer Lucian tells the story of Eucrates, who traveled to Egypt to study with the scribes and priests of the temples. Eucrates journeyed south to Thebes to see the two colossal statues of Memnon. In his day, one of the two colossi could be heard at dawn uttering sounds. Apparently his trip was a success, for he says that the statue spoke to him—seven oracular verses, no less! These words must have been quite potent because Eucrates said that it would not be appropriate to repeat them. (When restoration was done on the statue in ancient times, the sounds stopped.)

On the boat returning north, Eucrates met one of the sacred scribes of Memphis. This man was very learned, having spent twenty-three years in the underground sanctuaries (House of Life?), where Isis herself taught him magic. This man was clean-shaven and dressed in linen, so he was almost certainly a priest. On the boat Eucrates saw the magician work numerous miracles on the creatures of the river. He could ride crocodiles and command everything in the water. Eucrates was much impressed and wanted to become more acquainted with the magician; so when the boat trip came to an end at Memphis and the magician invited him to stay with him, he eagerly accepted.

Eucrates had a retinue of servants with him. The magician had none and he told Eucrates to dismiss his, as they would not be needed. When they arrived at where they would be staying, Eucrates could see that the magician had no servants at all, but clearly he needed none. When there was a chore to be done, he would put clothing on a door bolt, pestle, or a broom. Then, when he said magic words, the object would come alive and do his bidding. When the service was done, the magician said another few words to turn the servant back into an inanimate object.

Eucrates was eager to learn this trick, but the magician was extremely secretive. One day, while the magician was saying the incantation over a pestle, Eucrates overheard him and learned the magic word. (The story specifies that the word had three syllables, but does not give the word.) When the magician went out, Eucrates tried out his new power by instructing the pestle to fetch water. When the pestle had brought the water, Eucrates told it to stop and become a pestle again, but it did not obey because Eucrates had not learned the words to make it stop. It just kept bringing water. In desperation, Eucrates cut the pestle in two, but then both halves took up vases and continued bringing water. Finally, just as the house was being inundated, the magician returned to restore order.

The story is best known to us through Walt Disney's *Fantasia*. The sorcerer's apprentice becomes Mickey Mouse, the pestle is a broom, and the water vases are buckets, but the story is basically that of an Egyptian magician-priest. The tale also indicates the ancient Greeks' belief in the ability of Egyptian magicians.

The learned scribes of the House of Life are not to be confused with the mere copyists who duplicated the *Book of the Dead* for sale to the nobility. The primary jobs of the more learned scribes were to clarify religious and magical texts, to supply missing gaps in papyri, and to develop new texts and spells when events called for them. They were also responsible for determining the texts to be carved on the walls of newly erected temples. One can imagine these priests arguing for hours over some theological point or over the wording of an incantation.

Their treasured papyri were kept in a secluded section of the House of Life, often in niches dug into the walls of the temple (Figure 8). There was an important House of Life at Edfu, a great temple dedicated to Horus. Edfu is the best preserved temple in all of Egypt, as it was covered in sand until recent times. On one of the walls of the temple is engraved a list of the sacred books kept in the House of Life. Along with the books on rules of the temple, inventories of the temple holdings, and religious calendars, there were

FIGURE 8. The Temple of Edfu, dedicated to the god Horus, had one of the most important Houses of Life, where priests were trained in magic.

numerous books on magic. These give us an idea of the powers supposedly possessed by priest-magicians of ancient Egypt:

The Book of Appeasing Sekhmet
The Book of Magical Protection of the King in His Palace
Spells for Warding Off the Evil Eye
The Book of Repelling Crocodiles
The Book of Knowledge of the Secrets of the Laboratory
The Book of Knowing the Secret Forms of the God

From these titles, it is evident that the priests of the House of Life were considered powerful men. They were entrusted with the responsibility of protecting the king by magic, warding off malevolent forces, protecting fishermen from crocodiles, and numerous other functions. "The Book of Appeasing Sekhmet" is an interesting title. Appeasing the lioness-headed goddess Sekhmet affected the fate of all of mankind. There is an Egyptian myth involving the near destruction of mankind by Sekhmet, who became angry because men were not respectful to Re. She wanted to drink the blood of mankind, but Re got her drunk instead with drugged beer, and she forgot her destructive plans. Every New Year, in celebration of the appeasement of Sekhmet, the ancient Egyptians drank beer.

We do know what sort of magical accoutrements the magician-priests used, for in 1896 a magician's tomb was discovered. In that year J.E. Quibell was excavating the Ramesseum at Thebes, built by Ramses II. It was his mortuary temple, where offerings could be made to sustain his soul until it reached the next world. Egyptian temples were not quiet, solemn places, as we today might expect a temple to be. This particular one had, just outside the temple, mud-brick residences for priests who made the daily offerings. There were also mud-brick storehouses, where supplies of offerings and food for the priests were kept. The entire temple complex had been built on top of some tombs dating from the Middle Kingdom.

When Quibell cleared away the storehouses, he found the entrance to a tomb of the Twelfth Dynasty. The entrance, a shaft going thirteen feet down, was clogged with rubble. Buried in the debris were two types of shawabtis, or magical servant statues: one of green faience, the other of unbaked clay painted yellow. The two different kinds of shawabtis might have indicated a dual burial, perhaps of husband and wife. However, also within the rubble were small wax figures of the four sons of Horus. Figures of these gods are quite common in tombs, as these are the deities which supposedly protect the internal organs of the mummy. But it is rare for them to be of wax. Wax was essential for the magician because from it he fashioned his magical images. The wax sons of Horus were the first clue that this was a magician's tomb.

When the shaft was cleared, two small chambers were found. Unfortunately, they were empty. However, Quibell found in a small pile of rubble in the shaft a wooden box measuring about 18″ x 12″ x 12″ inches. The box was covered with white plaster and on the top, drawn in black ink, was a picture of a jackal. Inside the box were a number of small papyrus rolls, but they were in such a delicate condition that Quibell was unable to unroll them. Instead, he sent them to England, hoping that F. L. Griffith, the great translator, would attempt the job of unrolling and translating the papyri. But Griffith did not have the time and sent the box of papyri to the library of University College of London, where they remained for several years until Flinders Petrie and P.E. Newberry undertook the task.

One of Petrie's great talents as an excavator was his ingenuity, an especially valuable asset when working with these delicate papyri. Once, when he was excavating at Illahun, he discovered some intact tombs where the mummies were covered in beautiful bead-network shrouds. These shrouds were decorated with the face of the deceased and with various protective deities woven in beads. The problem was that they were strung on what by then was three-thousand-year-old thread that crumbled when touched. In his *Ten Years' Digging in Egypt* Petrie describes his technique for preserving the bead pieces.

> . . . When we entered a tomb, I opened the coffins in the gentlest way, drawing or cutting out the pegs which fastened them; and then a glance inside showed if any bead-work existed. If there were bead patterns, the next step was to fetch a petroleum stove down into the chamber, melt a batch of beeswax, and then when it was on the point of chilling, ladle it out, and dash it over the bead-work. If the wax is too hot it sinks in, and soaks all the mummy wrappings into a solid mass; if poured on, it runs off the body in a narrow stream. When all the beads were covered, and the wax set, I then lifted up the sheet of wax with the bead-work sticking to it, flattened it out on a board, and it was ready for fixing in a tray permanently, with the lower side turned out.[3]

Petrie used a similar technique on the papyri from the magician's tomb. He smeared a thin layer of beeswax on glass plates. Then he unrolled the papyri directly onto the wax so that, even though they fragmented as they were unrolled, most of the fragments remained in place. Petrie and Newberry unrolled two papyri in this manner. One was a medical treatise, the other a literary text called "Discourses of Sisobek."

The remaining papyri were sent to Berlin to be unrolled by the legendary Hugo Ibscher. Ibscher's reputation as a miracle worker in the field of papyrus conservation is well known to Egyptologists. The papyri on which he worked were so fragile that he wore a surgical mask for fear that his breath might blow away the surface of the scrolls.

For more than a quarter of a century Ibscher intermittently worked on unrolling these papyri. When the task was completed, it became clear that several of them were magical or medico-magical works. However, because of their extremely poor condition, they present a formidable challenge to any translator. Even now, seventy-five years after their discovery, several of the magical texts remain untranslated. They do establish that the box almost certainly did belong to a magician, perhaps a medical magician. For this reason, the other objects in the box are of extreme interest because they give us a clue as to what equipment magicians used in their trade.

The box itself is important. In ancient Egypt short stories involving magicians were quite common. In these stories it is often mentioned that "the magician called for his box," or "the magician reached into his box." So it seems traditional that magicians kept the tools of their trade in a box. This was not to keep hidden the fact that they were magicians, but rather to keep their equipment out of sight. This added an additional element of mystery to their trade. The fact that the box in the magician's tomb had a jackal on it is curious. Anubis, the jackal-headed god, was the god of embalming and had no particular association with magic. A more likely candidate to be painted on a magician's box would be Isis, the goddess of magic.

The box was only about one-third full of papyri, leaving ample room for other objects. There were remains of four ivory magical wands with mythical animals carved on them (Figure 9). The wand was an important tool for the magician and goes very far back in Egyptian history. The remains of a gold-covered wooden wand was found in the unfinished step pyramid of the pharaoh Horus-Sekhem-Khet of the Third Dynasty (see Chapter 6, "The Pyramids"). The most common material for these wands seems to have been ivory. They were frequently used for drawing magic circles on the ground. For example, the spell to assure that one will not be bitten by a scorpion while sleeping involves saying a certain incantation and drawing a protective circle around the bed. A wand might be used for the purpose.

Also inside the box were three dolls, each made of different material. One was an extremely crude figure of painted wood, which had no arms or head, very much like the sexless paddle dolls of ancient Egyptian children. Another of the dolls was of limestone and the third was of wood; both of these were females and both

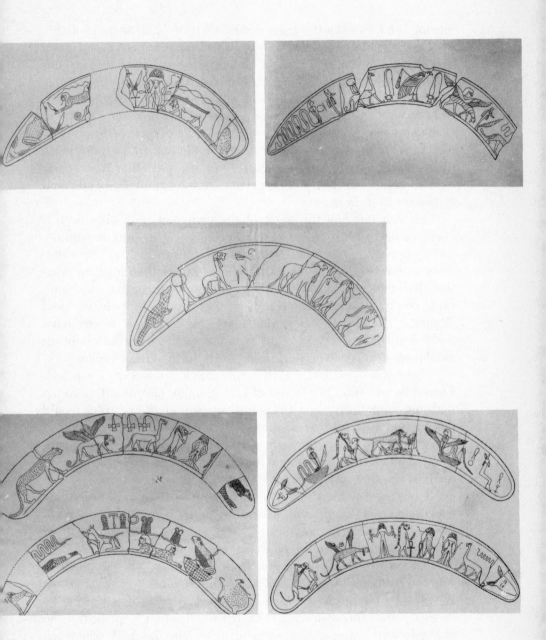

FIGURE 9. The creatures depicted in this assortment of magical wands were called upon to protect their owners. The Metropolitan Museum of Art

missing the legs from the knee down. All three dolls were probably used as magical images. There was also a bronze uraeus tangled in a ball of hair. The uraeus was, of course, the symbol of royalty, but why this one was tangled in a ball of hair is a mystery.

There were several additional objects in the box: some seeds from the dom palm; a statue of a masked girl holding a snake in each hand, very suggestive of magic; a bundle of reed pens, possibly used to write the magical papyri found in the box, or, perhaps more likely, used to write incantations for clients; and other items common to any Twelfth Dynasty person's tomb—amulets, beads, and fragments of utensils.

One can imagine the work of the owner of such objects. If a client came to him with a specific problem, if he was not immediately certain of the solution, he might consult his papyri, which were probably copied from earlier works rather than his own creation. Judging from the medical papyri found in the box, a significant percentage of his customers were people with physical ailments. Depending upon the case, the magician might have molded an image of wax, written out a spell, given the client an amulet to wear, or even performed a rite in the client's home.

There is a good chance that this magician was also a priest. Even if he was from the House of Life, though, he was still in touch with his community. The system of rotation at the temples would permit him to spend three-fourths of his time outside. Undoubtedly, while he was living with his family in town, he would continue to function as a magician for whomever needed his services in medical or other day-to-day problems.

It is probable that magicians augmented their reputations by trickery, or sleight of hand, as well as by their scholarship. While this is likely, given human nature, there is some evidence that there were standard illusions which these men could perform.

One possible example comes from the Bible. When Moses and Aaron went before the pharaoh to ask him to let the Israelites leave Egypt, they intended to impress the pharaoh with their power. To do this, Aaron threw down a staff. It turned into a serpent, but the pharaoh was unimpressed, evidently because he had seen such tricks before. He called upon his magicians to do the same, and their rods, too, turned into serpents. It is possible that the trick of turning a staff into a serpent was a standard effect used by magicians in the ancient Near East.

There is another situation that might give the impression that magicians used deception to gain status. In the story of "Khufu and the Magicians," the old magician had the reputation for being able to restore a severed head to its body. When he was called before the pharaoh to perform, the king said that he would have a prisoner brought from jail, so that his punishment could serve a dual purpose. The magician refused to do the miracle on the prisoner, claiming that he would prefer to do it on an animal. A goose was brought, the head cut off, and the magician successfully restored the head to the body. This sounds very much as if the magician knew a sleight of hand that could be done with animals only, which is why he refused to do it on a human. If he really could do such a miraculous thing as restore severed heads, then it would not kill the prisoner to perform the trick on him.

One magician who could never be accused of trickery was the pharaoh. By virtue of his position he was the most powerful of all magicians. It was he who caused the waters of the Nile to rise and fall and who brought fertility to the land. It was the pharaoh who was responsible for maintaining *maat*—the divine order—throughout Egypt. Descended from the gods, the pharaoh had the greatest of magical powers.

Tradition says that Nectanebo, the last native king of Egypt, was the greatest magician of all pharaohs. Nectanebo supposedly could read the stars, interpret omens, and most important, control other kings by magic. If Egypt were being invaded by the sea, Nectanebo would go to a special room he used for his magic. There he would fashion out of wax figures of the enemy's ships and soldiers as well as figures of his own fleet and men. These he would place in a basin filled with water. Then he would put on a magic cape and say magic words over the miniature battle scene. These words would cause winds. Eventually, the enemy ships would sink and the miniature Egyptian fleet would triumph. As it happened in miniature, so it always happened in the actual battle.

Nectanebo was the last Egyptian to rule Egypt, and according to the Greek tradition, magic had something to do with Nectanebo's decline. One day a scout came to the pharaoh and informed him that the combined forces of several countries were about to invade Egypt. Nectanebo was not perturbed. He went to his secret room, where, as usual, he fashioned the images, placed them in the basin, and said his incantation. This time the winds turned against him and sank his own fleet. Nectanebo realized that the powers which had always helped him had turned against him. He shaved his head and beard, put on clothes of a commoner, and fled Egypt for Macedonia.

Arab tradition tells of a queen who protected Egypt by magic. The historian Mas'Ûdî records that at the time of the Exodus, when pharaoh's army was drowned in the sea, the people feared that they might be attacked by foreign countries. They selected as their ruler a woman skilled in magic, so that she could use her skills to protect them. She built a wall around Egypt and placed sentries outside it. She also had statues made of crocodiles and other fierce animals which magically protected the country.

She built many temples in Egypt and in them collected all the writings on magic. In this way she learned the magical properties of plants, animals, and minerals. She also learned how to control the powers of nature. If she heard that a hostile country was going to invade Egypt, she made wax figures of them and buried them in the earth, causing the enemy forces to disappear into the ground. Through such means she protected Egypt for the thirty years of her reign.

Another Arab tradition, through Abu-Shâker, the thirteenth-century writer, says that part of the reason Alexander the Great triumphed over Egypt was that he used magic wax-figures. This tradition holds that Aristotle, Alexander's teacher, gave him a box of wax images and told Alexander never to relinquish possession of the box. The figures were detailed miniatures of the armies Alexander might encounter. Some had broken bow strings, others bent swords—the idea being that the miniature would mirror full-scale battles. In this way Alexander conquered Egypt.

These Arab and Greek traditions are supported by ancient Egyptian sources. The pharaoh's duties included numerous magical rites. One ceremony was essential not primarily for the country, but for the pharaoh himself. This is the *heb-sed* festival (Figure 10). This festival goes back to the oldest historical period of Egypt, and while there are many representations of it, the *heb-sed* festival is not fully understood.

The representations usually show the pharaoh striding or running with a flail in his hand. Many Egyptologists believe that this is a rejuvenation festival for the king. As we have seen, in ancient

FIGURE 10. A faience plaque shows Tuthmose III engaged in his *heb-sed* celebration. His crown and the plants behind him indicate that he is performing the rites for southern Egypt. Over his shoulder and trailing behind is his flail. Photograph by Russell Rudzwick

times the rulers often were not only the political heads of their countries, but also the military leaders. So it was crucial for the king to be fit to lead the army in battle. If the pharaoh became old and senile, then the country could become weak. This situation may be the cause of the *heb-sed* festival. Periodically, the pharaohs would demonstrate their vigor by running a course. Later the ceremony became not so much one of demonstration of vigor, as rejuvenation of vigor. Often the ritual was celebrated thirty years after the pharaoh's ascent to the throne, but many pharaohs held it at shorter intervals.

While the rite almost certainly was one of rejuvenation for the pharaoh, it was probably much more, involving his powers as the arch-magician of Egypt. There are temple reliefs that show the pharaoh striding as in the *heb-sed*, but instead of holding the flail, he holds an object that looks like this: ⟨symbol⟩ . This sign is the hieroglyph for "Hap," which designated the Apis bull. "Apis" is the ancient Egyptian name, "Hap," with the Greek, "is," ending. In reliefs showing the pharaoh holding this sign the hieroglyphs read: "Bringing Hap to Amun-Re, Lord of the Heavens." Since the Apis bull was a symbol of fertility, this may be a representation of the king as the magician who brings fertility to the land. Fertility in Egypt was brought by the Nile overflowing its banks and depositing new topsoil. That the ancient Nile god was named Hapi, meaning "The One of Hap," indicates the strong association between the Apis bull and the renewing waters of the river.

This connection is supported most strongly by a relief in which the pharaoh is shown striding with the Apis bull and carrying two water vases. The text reads, "Presenting the water to Amun that he may give life eternally." This may be a depiction of a magical ceremony in which the king causes the Nile to rise, bringing the waters of inundation to the land. The association of the *heb-sed* festival with the Apis bull may help to explain the name, *heb-sed*. *Heb* means "festival," but *sed* means "tail." The Festival of the Tail may refer to the tail of the Apis bull. Indeed, the object represented by the ⟨symbol⟩ sign is not known, but it is remotely possible that it represents the tail of the Apis bull.

From earliest times the *heb-sed* festival may have been connected with later festivals in which the pharaoh was the magician in a rite responsible for causing the waters of the Nile to rise and bring fertility to the land. We do know that the *heb-sed* was traditionally held on the first day of the month Tybi. Tybi was the first month of the season of Emergence. Hence the ceremony was held on the day when the waters of the Nile were supposed to recede and the fertile land emerge.° That the most crucial of all ceremonies was performed by the most powerful of magicians indicates how important magicians were to the ancient Egyptians.

The pharaoh was called upon for only the most important rituals, but equally essential was the entire cadre of priest-magicians forming the hierarchy beneath him. The magical rites performed by the pharaoh had national consequences; those performed by magicians affected towns and individuals, and every Egyptian relied upon magicians to help him obtain food, health, love, and wealth.

° While the date—the first day of Emergence—would suggest that on this day the Nile began to recede, actually it did not. Because the Egyptian calendar was not based on a three-hundred-and-sixty-five-and-a-quarter-day year, the first day of Emergence very rarely would fall on the actual day when the land began to emerge.

Beginning the secret of the Physician;
Knowledge of the heart's movement and
knowledge of the heart. —There are vessels
from it to every limb. As to this, when any
physician, any Sekhmet priest, or any exor-
cist applies his hands or his fingers to the
head, to the back of the head, to the hands
. . . then he examines the heart because all
of his limbs possess its vessels, that is, it
speaks out of the vessels of every limb.

—Papyrus Ebers

4. Medicine

ONE RELATIVELY WELL-DOCUMENTED aspect of ancient Egyptian life
is medicine. Although several extensive medical papyri have been
found, they give somewhat conflicting pictures of what the Egyptians called "the necessary art." Some papyri, such as the Edwin
Smith Surgical Papyrus, are extremely precise and clinical in their
description and treatment of injuries, while others, such as the
London-Leiden Papyrus, give an almost totally magical treatment
of medicine. Obviously both approaches were used.

Some evidence exists that the kind of illness determined the
method of treatment. If the cause was known, as in the case of
broken bones and such perils as crocodile bites, then the treatment
tended to be nonmagical. For instance, for a crocodile bite, a practical suggestion was to sew the wound closed and place raw meat
on it. If, however, the illness was something such as a fever, where
the cause would be unknown to the Egyptians, then it might be
attributed to demons or malicious magic, and consequently the
treatment might be magical. There was even a title for a specialist
trained in "unknown diseases," who probably dealt with illnesses of
no known cause. It is also possible that some physicians preferred a
more clinical approach, while others chose a magical orientation.

The highest ranking physicians were priests. Since Sekhmet was
probably the most important god associated with the medical arts,
it was from the priests of Sekhmet that the doctors came. It is
somewhat surprising that the lioness-headed goddess should be a
patron deity of medicine, since throughout Egyptian history she
was feared for her temper, and at one time, as mentioned earlier,
she considered destroying mankind. The priests of Sekhmet often
had several titles, one medical. Nedjemou was "Chief of the Priests

of Sekhmet" and "Chief of the Physicians," while Heryshefnakht was "Chief of Magicians," "High-priest of Sekhmet," and physician to the pharaoh.

Isis, Horus, and Toth were gods also associated with the healing arts. Isis was connected with medicine for two reasons. She reassembled her deceased husband, Osiris, who had been hacked to pieces by his evil brother Seth. Quite a medical feat! Also, she was known as the goddess of magic, and these powers could be called upon to heal the injured.

Toth, who was usually depicted as an ibis-headed god (but sometimes as a baboon), was the traditional inventor of writing and was usually shown carrying the scribe's palette. The Greeks attributed a series of forty-two books to him comprising an important body of knowledge. According to Clement of Alexandria, thirty-six of these books dealt with philosophy and general knowledge, while the remaining six concerned medicine. There was a volume for each of the following medical topics: anatomy, diseases, surgery, remedies, diseases of the eye, and diseases of women. Toth was identified with Hermes by the Greeks; thus these works became known as the Hermetic Books. It was also Toth who restored Horus' damaged eye after the battle with Seth. Because of his association with the healing of eyes, Horus became the patron of the oculists in ancient Egypt.

Since physicians were priests, sick people normally came to the temples for healing. There, they were treated with a combination of medicine, theology, and magic. Several temples obtained great reputations as places of miraculous cures, and to these came a constant procession of the suffering. One such place of healing was the Temple of Dendera, which seems to have provided two different methods of treatment. One used magical water to bring about cures. There was a long corridor lined with statues which had healing incantations inscribed on them. Water was poured over these statues and drained from channels into cubicles of various sizes and depths. In this way the water became empowered by the spells; the diseased could bathe in it and be cured.

In addition to receiving the water treatment, patients could sleep at Dendera in the hope of inducing a therapeutic dream. It must have been quite an experience to spend a night at the temple. Patients slept in small crypts that were totally dark at night. Special lamps were used to bring about the desired dreams. The patient must have been in a state close to hypnosis. Then when he finally did fall asleep he was expecting to be able to converse with the gods to determine his cure.

Another temple where miraculous cures were said to take place was the mortuary temple of Queen Hatshepsut at Deir el Bahari. One of the most colorful figures in Egyptian history, Hatshepsut refused to rule as queen and had herself crowned king. She was closely involved with a commoner, Senmut, who was given numerous titles by the queen/king, including Royal Architect, Royal Tutor, and Steward of Amun. This last put him in charge of the vast fortune controlled by the temples of Amun during the Eighteenth Dynasty. Because he rose so quickly to power, some have asserted that he was Hatshepsut's lover, though there is no evidence to support this.

As Royal Architect, he designed her mortuary temple, where he left more than just his signature. Behind each of the doors to the various rooms in which the priests would store their robes and other paraphernalia necessary to make the daily offerings for the well-being of Hatshepsut's soul, he placed his portrait! This was unheard of, but he did it in such a clever way that he apparently got away with it, for some of them still remain. They were placed so that whenever anyone opened the door to enter the cubicle, the door would hide the portrait.

The walls of Deir el Bahari are covered with descriptions of Hatshepsut's reign, or at least her version of it. She describes three major events. The first is her divine birth, which was propaganda intended to establish her claim to the throne. She claimed that the god Amun slept with her mother and so was her true father. The second event she commemorated was the quarrying and transporting from Aswan of two huge obelisks she had erected at the Temple of Karnak. The third event she had inscribed on her temple walls was a trading expedition to the land of Punt. The reliefs on the temple show the Egyptians obtaining myrrh, frankincense, giraffes, monkeys, and other desirable exotic commodities.

Long after Hatshepsut had been forgotten by the Egyptians, medical miracles took place on the upper terrace of her temple. (Figure 11). Under the reign of Ptolemy II, the upper level of Deir el Bahari was dedicated to two famous Egyptians, Imhotep and

FIGURE 11. The funerary temple of Hatshepsut at Deir el Bahari was the site of miraculous cures, said to have been performed on the upper terrace. Photograph by Barbara Benton

Amenhotep, son of Hapu. They were both physicians and wise men. Imhotep, the architect of the step pyramid at Saqqara, was deified by the Greeks as Asclepius, the god of healing. On the terrace a small room was built where the infirm could come to be cured. The walls are covered with graffiti of the sick who prayed to the gods for cures. One reads: "Andromachos, a Macedonian, a worker for hire, came to the good god Amenathen: he was sick, and the god succoured him on that very day. Farewell." [1]

In addition to the priest-physicians, the *wabu,* there were the *sunu,* who were the lay-physicians. Since the medical profession was carefully regulated with severe penalties for improper practice, these men were almost certainly trained in medicine, although they were not associated with any particular temple, nor were they devoted to a particular god. Thus their practice was probably more eclectic than the priest-physicians', as they could draw from all available sources.

While both the priest-physicians and the lay-physicians used a combination of sound clinical medicine and magic, there was a third kind of physician, the magician, who was not trained in medical practice but used only incantations, amulets, and other magic to cure his patients. Most of the medical papyri that have survived undoubtedly come from this third class of medical men, for they are lists of spells and potions with little evidence of scientific knowledge or careful observation.

The one exception to this rule is the Edwin Smith Surgical Papyrus, which dates from approximately 1700 B.C. It is a copy of a papyrus of the Old Kingdom, now lost. The treatments written in it are thus more than four thousand years old, dating from the pyramid age. This is especially interesting because it has led some Egyptologists to speculate that the author of the original document was Imhotep. What makes this somewhat plausible is that the Smith Surgical Papyrus deals mainly with injuries such as fractures and broken bones, and the physician writing it clearly had extensive firsthand knowledge of such injuries. Imhotep, as architect of the step pyramid, would have had opportunity to accumulate such knowledge because undoubtedly many bones were broken in accidents during the building of the pyramids.

It may be precisely because the papyrus deals with *injuries* rather than *diseases* that it is primarily scientific and not magical in its approach. The causes were apparent and not attributable to demons and malicious gods. Even when this is taken into account, the document is still amazing for its clinical precision.

There are forty-eight specific cases discussed. Each case is preceded by a title, such as "Instructions Concerning a Wound on the Top of His Eyebrow," which is followed by "The Examination." Here the surgeon is told how to probe and examine. Then there is a "Diagnosis." Here the physician is told to state the injury and then whether or not he can treat it. Actually, there were three things he could say: (1) "An ailment which I will treat"; (2) "An ailment with which I will contend"; (3) "An ailment not to be treated."

It is interesting that the surgeon divided his cases into those he could cure, those he might cure, and those he could not cure. The last category offers a clear contrast to the magician-physicians, who would make up a spell for anything. If the illness was one which could be treated or contended with, the treatment followed. Directions here involved the bandages, splints, plaster, tape, sutures, and other stock-in-trade still in use today. Indeed, in the entire papyrus there is only one case in which magic plays a part. In the ninth case, a crushed frontal bone, the treatment involved sympathetic magic. A poultice of grease and ostrich egg was to be applied to the wound, probably because the shell of the ostrich egg somewhat resembles the frontal bone and the desire was for the bone to knit and resemble the shell. Over the poultice a spell was to be recited:

> Repelled is the enemy that is in the wound!
> Cast out the [evil] that is in the blood,
> The adversary of Horus, [on every] side of the mouth
>   of Isis.
> This temple does not fall down;
> There is no enemy of the vessel therein.
> I am under the protection of Isis;
> My rescue is the son of Osiris.[2]

It is difficult to believe that the surgeon who so clinically describes forty-seven surgical cases should include one purely magical treatment. It is almost easier to accept that whoever was copying the original had this treatment inserted from one of the many recipe books available at the time. This single magical spell in the papyrus supplies us with an interesting literary first. The scribe was copying the manuscript and omitted a word. Seventeen centuries before Christ, he inserted a small red "X" between two words and above the line inked in the missing word. This is the first caret in history.

While the original author of the Smith Surgical Papyrus had a rather scientific approach to medicine, the ancient owner of the copy we have today may not have. On the reverse of the papyrus he had copied a work on medicine that is almost purely magical in approach. One of the strangest aspects of this brief medical work is that, while it is indeed magical and contains exorcisms of demons, incantations to gods, and so forth, it seems to contain something like the germ theory of how disease is spread. The first eight incantations are all concerned with "The Pest of the Year," an epidemic which apparently afflicted the Egyptians annually. From these spells, it appears as if they believed the disease came on "the plague-bearing wind," could also be carried by flies, was lodged in food and beds or bed linens, and entered the body through the mouth and throat. The text of course does not talk about germs, but rather malicious gods and demons, especially Sekhmet, as the cause, but the Egyptians do seem to have made some observations about how diseases spread. The title of one spell calls the disease causers "the demons of disease, the malignant spirits, messengers of Sekhmet." The spell suggests that they come on the wind:

> Withdraw, ye disease demons. The wind shall not reach me, that those who pass by may pass by to work disaster against me. I am Horus who passes by the diseased ones of Sekhmet, [even] Horus, Horus, healthy despite Sekhmet. I am the unique one, son of Bastet. I die not through thee.[3]

This spell was to be spoken by a man who had a stick of *des*-wood in his hand. He was to hold the stick, walk around his house and say the spell. In this way he would be drawing a circle of protection around his house. The stick seemed to serve as the wand that was so common to Egyptian magicians. These same words could also be said as one drew a circle on the dirt floor around a bed to protect the sleeper from the bite of a scorpion. The *des*-wood stick prevented the winds from entering.

The spell for a man who has swallowed a fly is unique. It asserts that the mouth of the man who has swallowed the insect is as clean as the mouth of a newborn calf who has never eaten, and that the fly will pass out of the man in his excrement without injuring his stomach. It would seem as if the Egyptians recognized flies as disease-bearing creatures since the cure involved ridding the body of the fly.

There was a general spell for cleaning everything, including beds. This collection of eight spells against "The Pest of the Year" makes the "disease demons" spoken of sound very much like our modern bacteria. These spells are followed by a hodgepodge of several spells on such diverse topics as what to do for a woman whose menstrual flow has stopped or how to treat hemorrhoids, but by far the most intriguing is entitled, "How to Transform an Old Man into a Youth." This formula must be the forerunner of the medieval alchemist's elixir of life. The Egyptian version is merely a wrinkle cream for smoothing the skin. It was made of a fruit called *hemayet* by the Egyptians. The name is still untranslatable. This fruit was crushed, husked, and winnowed like grain. It was then placed in a new jar filled with water and boiled. The residue, which has the consistency of clay, was put in a *hin*-jar. Then after it had thickened a bit, it was put on top of a linen cover of the *hin*-jar, perhaps to drain. Then the mass was to be kept in a vase of costly stone.

This cream was to be placed on the face. The spell promises that it removes wrinkles, blemishes, all signs of age on the flesh and has been shown to be effective millions of times. There was a second method for preparing the cream, but since we do not know what the *hemayet*-fruit was, one should be more than adequate.

The surgical portion of the Smith Surgical Papyrus is unique in its clinical treatment of medical problems and in its orderly procession of ailment, starting from the top of the head and working downward. More typical of the several medical papyri which have survived the centuries is the Papyrus Ebers, which is an unorganized collection of primarily magical concoctions and spells designed to alleviate suffering. Sometime during the American Civil War the papyrus was found in a tomb in Thebes, and while it is not certain, there is a tradition that it was found with the Edwin Smith Surgical Papyrus. This sixty-eight-foot papyrus undoubtedly does not have a single source but contains remedies copied from numerous sources. In all, more than eight hundred medical situations are dealt with, from how to stop a baby from crying (make a potion with opium as an ingredient) to how to speed up a woman in labor (apply peppermint to her bare posterior).

If a single theme prevails, it is the belief in the magic of similars. For any substance or object believed essential to health, a substance or object similar in color, or texture, or shape might be substituted. Since blood was a life-giving fluid, then drinking a potion made from a red plant or saying a spell over an amulet of carnelian might be the solution. An interesting example of such a medico-magical belief was discovered by Dr. G. Elliot Smith, a physician interested in ancient Egyptian medical practices. He found the grave of several small children who had died more than five thousand years ago. An analysis of their stomachs showed that just prior to death they had eaten skinned mice. The mouse to the ancient Egyptian was a sign of life because each year when the Nile receded after depositing the rich topsoil, the sun would dry the mud and cracks would form. From these cracks mice would be seen emerging, and the Egyptians believed that these mice were formed from the mud of the life-giving Nile. Thus the mice were associated with life and administered to the critically ill children in a desperate effort to sustain their lives.

Because of the principle of similars, ancient Egyptian remedies often had rather unusual ingredients, such as testicles-of-a-black-ass, milk-of-woman-who-has-borne-a-son, vulva-of-a-bitch, cat's dung, etc. Often the Papyrus Ebers gives specific spells to be spoken over the ingredients while they are being prepared to enhance their magical potency.

For a burning anus, tail-of-a-mouse was mixed with onion meal, honey, and water. This mess was then strained and drunk for four days by the sufferer. (Apparently, the Egyptians thought a mouse never had a burning anus!)

An interesting connection between modern folk-nutrition and ancient medicine is provided by a remedy for headaches. Today we have the expression that fish is "brain food." The principal ingredient in the ointment to be smeared on the sufferer's head was fish. Redfish, skull-of-crayfish, and bone-of-swordfish were mixed with onions, fruit of the *am*-tree, honey, and other ingredients to make the salve. Apparently, external applications were considered best for headaches.

For cataracts a spell was said over brain-of-tortoise mixed with honey. This was then applied to the eyes. If the eyes were discharging matter, then a ground-up statue would be mixed with honey and leaves from the castor tree and applied, the principle being that a statue was inert, and this was what was desired of the running eyes.

For blindness, two eyes of a pig were used. The instructions dictated that the water be removed from them, but it was not clear how this was done. The pig's eyes were mixed with collyrium, red lead, and wild honey. This paste was injected into the ear of the patient while the physician said, "I have brought this thing and put it in its place. The crocodile is weak and powerless." This seemingly inappropriate spell was to be repeated two times and the patient would be cured instantly of his blindness. Blindness was often viewed as a punishment of the gods. There are numerous prayers to a god who it was believed made the patient "see darkness during the day."

For a disease of the nose known today as coryza, a plug made of fragrant bread and milk-of-a-woman-who-has-borne-a-son was inserted in the nostrils. While the plug was being prepared the magician had to repeat four times that foulness was rising from the earth. As the spell would cause foulness to come out of the earth so the foulness would leave the nose.

The Egyptians never explained the potent aspect of the ingredients they used, so it is not clear what is special about the milk of a woman who has had a son. It may have been that the Egyptians believed that the milk of such a mother was actually different from the milk of a woman who has had a daughter, and that difference was the active ingredient in the remedy. Aristotle, in his *Healing of Animals,* Book VII, Chapter 4, says that women who give birth to sons are stronger than mothers of daughters. This may give some explanation for the ingredient.

More likely, however, is the belief that a woman who has borne a son, by sympathetic magic, might have the powers of Isis, who was the mother of Horus. Her milk would be like the milk of Isis, who nursed Horus. Indeed, such milk was stored in a special vessel shaped like a woman with a child on her lap. First the milk was

placed in a vessel depicting the child as frail, then after an incantation, the milk was transferred to a similar vessel depicting the child
as robust. The milk was then ready to be used in healing the sick.

The principle of magical similarity was a guiding force in the
use of ingredients. A worm, which was hairless, when ground up
and applied to the head, could cause baldness; or urine from a
pregnant woman would make crops prosper. This Egyptian magical principle continued during the Greek occupation of Egypt and
even after. The London-Leiden Papyrus amply illustrates the continuation of the belief in portions of animals being able to transmit
properties of the entire animal.

This papyrus, dating from the third century A.D., is called the
London-Leiden Papyrus because half is in the British Museum and
half is in the Leiden Museum. No one knows exactly how the papyrus came to be torn in half. It was purchased in the early part of
the nineteenth century by Anastasi, the Swedish consul at Alexandria, who was collecting Egyptian manuscripts. He probably
bought both halves separately and was most likely not even aware
that they belonged together. When his estate was sold, the two
parts were sold separately, going to different museums.

Written in demotic, the main subject of the papyrus is magic
and medicine. Because it dates from after the Greek occupation of
Egypt, the spells are a mixture of Egyptian and Greek mythology.
One spell which clearly demonstrates the principle of magical similarities is for curing the foot of a man with gout. The magical
words—Ὁεμβαρα θεμ, ουρεμβρενονζιπε, αιοχθον, σεμμαραθεμμου,
and ναιοου—are written on tin or silver and bound by a deerskin to
the foot of the man, who is called δέρμα ελάθιον. Here the skin of
the fleet deer will render the lame foot well. A late-period addition
to the Egyptian magical medical paraphernalia is the stipulation
that this is to be done when the moon is in the constellation of Leo.
This astrological specification is purely Greek, as the Egyptians did
not practice astrology.

To make a woman amorous, the papyrus suggests that you place
stallion saliva on your phallus and sleep with her. It would seem
that if you got far enough along to try out the stallion's saliva, you
wouldn't need the spell!

Other ingredients in medical recipes were used, not because
they transferred properties of the animals from which they came,

but because they were considered repulsive and might frighten away the evil spirits causing a disease. This is why there is a surprising number of concoctions using donkey's dung, snake's urine, excrement, and other unsavory ingredients.

Many plants were selected because they resembled parts of the body or had other significant shapes. For example, the mandrake was an aphrodisiac and also was believed to promote fertility because some of its species are shaped like male genitals. Indeed, one of the Arabic names for the plant is "devil's testicles." Paul Ghalioungui, one of the great authorities on ancient Egyptian magic, gives an interesting account of how the mandrake was picked in antiquity.

> Mandrakes could be picked only on certain nights, by moonlight, or with the morning dew. The picker stopped his ears with wax, tied the plant to a dog, and ran away; the dog running after its master uprooted it and then dropped dead, for the mandrake was said to utter out when torn away such a horrible cry that anyone who heard it or touched it ran mad or died on the spot.[4]

As part of his pharmacopoeia the Egyptian physician used a great variety of minerals, plants, and parts of animals. Some of the ingredients seem logical to us, such as castor oil for indigestion or opium (!) to quiet a crying child. While the vast remainder of ingredients seem arbitrary, this was not the case; they were chosen in accord with established magical principles. Sometimes it might be the color of the mineral that was important, another time the shape of the plant, and still another time it might be some attribute of the unfortunate animal who was ground into the physician's remedy. Should such magical treatments fail, one could always call on the gods for help.

5. *Mummification*

ASK THE CURATOR of any large Egyptian collection which exhibit
draws the most interest year after year, and he will tell you it is the
mummy collection. There is something awesome about mummies.
It certainly is not their beauty, for few mummies are attractive to
look at. Perhaps it is their mystery, but more probably it is their
age. There before the onlooker is the remains of a person who lived
perhaps three thousand years ago and is still recognizable as a person. In some sense, he did achieve his goal of immortality (Figure
12).

There is a popular misconception that mummification is a lost

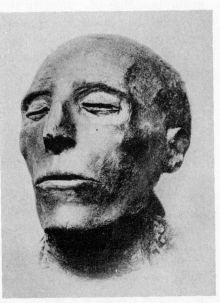

FIGURE 12. After more than 3,000 years, the
features of this mummy are still recognizable
as those of Seti I.

67

art, that the method used by the ancient Egyptians is no longer known. This simply is not true. Egyptologists have a fairly complete knowledge of how bodies were mummified, lacking only a few minor details. But there were *two* aspects to the preparation of a body for eternity—the physical and the magical. At the same time various physical stages of preparation were being completed, magical rites were enacted. Only a prescribed combination of the two could preserve the body for eternity.

To fully understand the rites of mummification, one must know the Egyptian myth of the god Osiris, who is the archetype of all mummies: Osiris and Isis were brother and sister and husband and wife. They had another brother, Seth, and another sister, Nephthys, who were also brother and sister, husband and wife. Osiris brought civilization to Egypt by introducing farming and cattle raising and so freed the early inhabitants of the Nile Valley from misery. He set out to do the same for neighboring countries. Seth, his evil brother, plotted while Osiris was gone. By trickery, he obtained Osiris' exact body measurements and constructed a wooden chest that would precisely fit Osiris. At a banquet, Seth tricked Osiris into getting into the chest and immediately sealed it shut, poured molten lead over it, and threw it into the Nile. There was a violent storm, and the chest washed up on the island of Byblos, where it came to rest in the branches of a tree. In time the tree grew to extraordinary size, and the trunk encompassed the chest with the dead Osiris in it. The king of Byblos was building a palace and needed such a tree for one of the pillars. The tree was cut down and incorporated into the palace.

Isis learned what had happened to her husband and set out to recover his body. Enlisting the aid of the queen of Byblos, she recovered the body of Osiris and brought it back to Egypt for proper burial. Seth discovered the body, hacked it into fourteen pieces, and scattered them throughout Egypt. Isis recovered all the pieces but one, the phallus, which had been thrown into the river and eaten by the fish. She reassembled her deceased husband, fashioning an artificial phallus for him. In the form of a bird, she hovered over Osiris' body and brought him back to life by saying magical words.

From this myth came the practice of mummification. The Egyptians were preoccupied with the dead body and with the notion that it must be intact and have a proper burial for resurrection. Even the practice of burying the dead in anthropoid coffins may have come from the part of the myth about the chest constructed to Osiris' measurement. Osiris, who achieved immortality, became the god of the dead, and all Egyptians wished to join him. This is why in the *Book of the Dead* and in other magical spells dealing with the dead the deceased is often called Osiris or his name is joined with that of Osiris (for example, Osiris-Ani). This is so that the deceased, too, will resurrect.

We probably will never know exactly when and how mummification originated. It was not practiced in prehistoric times when the dead were buried in desert pits. Bodies mummified naturally by the dry, hot sand still were recognizable as individuals a thousand years later. Sometime toward the end of the prehistoric period, just before the dynastic period, the Egyptians started burying their dead in chambers cut into moist bedrock beneath the sand. This may have been done to protect the bodies from robbers or from being uncovered by the shifting desert sands, but, ironically, it led to the destruction of the bodies. Without contact with the dehydrating hot sands, they were subject to decay. This probably gave the Egyptians impetus to invent mummification.

We were not able to learn the details of the ancient process of mummification by deciphering Egyptian texts. No complete embalmer's manual has been found, and the Egyptians left few writings on their unique art. However, it has been possible to learn how it was done by modern analyses of ancient mummies.

The Paleopathology Association, an organization that studies the diseases of ancient man, periodically performs autopsies on mummies. With modern techniques and equipment, they can type and study the blood from the inside of a three-thousand-year-old artery or tell if a pharaoh died of poisoning. In the course of such autopsies much has been learned about the process of mummification.

The precursor to modern autopsies on mummies and societies such as the Paleopathology Association was Dr. Thomas Pettigrew, one of the most interesting characters in the history of Egyptology. Pettigrew, a physician, became interested in Egyptology in 1820 when he met Giovanni Belzoni. Belzoni was a six-foot-six Italian circus strongman who traveled to Egypt to discover and remove antiquities for collectors. He was an extraordinary adventurer and an even better storyteller. Many of his stories revolved around his adventures in the mummy trade. One of the best is of his finding a tomb stacked high with mummies.

> But what a place to rest! surrounded by bodies, by heaps of mummies in all directions . . . the blackness of the wall, the faint light given by candles or torches for want of air, the different objects that surrounded me, seeming to converse with each other, and the Arabs with the candles or torches in their hands, naked and covered with dust, themselves resembling living mummies, absolutely formed a scene that cannot be described. . . . [I] sought a resting place, found one, and contrived to sit; but when my weight bore on the body of an Egyptian, it crushed like a band-box. I naturally had recourse to my hands to sustain my weight, but they found no better support; so that I sunk altogether among the broken mummies, with a crash of bones, rags, and wooden cases, which raised such a dust as kept me motionless for a quarter for an hour, waiting till it subsided again.[1]

Stories such as this one probably aroused Pettigrew's interest. Soon after meeting Belzoni, he bought a mummy and unwrapped it in his home. It was more than ten years later—when Henry Salt's collection of antiquities, including several mummies, was auctioned at Sotheby's—that he had the chance at another. He then bought one for £23, and Thomas Saunders, a friend, purchased another for £36.15. They decided to unwrap both at the same time. This was done on Saturday, April 6, 1833, before a distinguished audience in the lecture theater of Charing Cross Hospital. The event was such a success that soon Pettigrew was being invited by English gentlemen who owned mummies to unwrap them before audiences.

At one time in his career as mummy-unwrapper *par excellence,* Pettigrew gave a course on Egyptian antiquities and concluded it dramatically by unwrapping a mummy. One such performance, on the island of Jersey in 1837, was covered by the press and seems to have excited observers considerably.

> Mr. Pettigrew's last lecture, combined as it was with the unrolling of the Mummy, which has served as a nucleous [*sic*] and ornament of our infant Museum, attracted, as might have been expected, on Saturday last a greater concourse of spectators than on any previous occasion: the room was literally crowded with the first families of the island, and all who had any pretensions to fashion, science or

literature attended on this interesting occasion. The learned lecturer assumed with an air of modest triumph his station at the table on which the Mummy was placed: behind him were ranged its several cases, and the wall was covered with sheets of paper on which were delineated accurate copies of the Hieroglyphical inscriptions referring to the subject of the day's lecture, now about to be divested of the bandages which had enveloped it untouched for many centuries. Extreme attention was apparent throughout the numerous audience, and eager curiosity was visible on every countenance as Mr. Pettigrew commenced his lecture, of which we offer the public the following very inadequate sketch.

[Here follows a long report of the lecture.]

The learned lecturer now commenced unrolling the mummy, which bore, he said, a striking resemblance to the one opened at Leeds some years ago. On the body was laid a garland of lotus and other flowers: the leathern strap contains emblems indicating a king, and is probably a description of Amenoph. When the flowers and fillets were removed the whole body appeared covered with a sheet that was laced at the back, in a manner, said Mr. P., which might give a lesson to our modern stay-makers (laughter). The sheet was tied in a knot at the back of the head, and when it was renounced [*sic*] the multitudinous rolls of bandages came into view . . . as the unrolling went on, the room became filled with a strong but not very disagreeable odour, arising probably from the resinous materials used in the process of embalming . . . The operator now came to a layer of bandages entirely covered with asphaltum which could not be unrolled: it was therefore picked off, and was composed of a common kind of cloth. After removing this a layer of bandages appeared with a coloured border in accordance with specimens Mr. Pettigrew had exhibited to the audience (applause) . . . The lecturer now exclaimed "Here at length is something to repay one's caution (applause): in a preceding lecture I mentioned the scarabeus as an ornament found frequently between the bandages: I will now lift this portion of the covering and you will see a very fine one." Here the mummy was carried round, and every one rose to see the ornament on the breast, which was a fine scarabeus formed of greenish porcelain. The work of unrolling now again proceeded until the joyful announcement was made that something new was discovered which had never before been found on a mummy. Mr. P. now exercised his scissors very freely, and soon released the scarabeus which was found to be fixed above a plate of metal . . . found to be fashioned in the form of a hawk . . . The wings of the hawk were expanded, and he held in his talons the emblem of eternal life; it was handed round for inspection and excited much applause and admiration. A new description of the bandage now appeared, and the arms and legs were shown to be separately bandaged. . . . At length the left foot was displayed to sight, and though black and shrivelled, it excited much applause. . . .[2]

All did not always go so well as in this incident. For example, once when Pettigrew was unwrapping a mummy before a large audience, he encountered a layer of resin which had so severely hardened that his chisels and picks could not penetrate it. The disappointed audience had to be sent away, promised that the completely unwrapped mummy would be exhibited at a later date.

Perhaps the high point of Pettigrew's career came not in unwrapping a mummy, but in creating one. When Alexander, the tenth Duke of Hamilton, died, he left instructions that his body be mummified in the Egyptian manner. Years previous to his death, on August 18, 1852, the duke had bought a basalt sarcophagus and had it brought to Hamilton Palace to hold his remains. He also had constructed on the grounds of the estate a mausoleum which the London *Times* of September 7, 1852, described as ". . . the most costly and magnificent temple for the reception of the dead in the world—always excepting the Pyramids." Pettigrew embalmed the duke's body and also served as high-priest at his funeral.

Despite the theatrics, Pettigrew was a careful observer, and his demonstrations yielded much important information on the embalming process. His major work on the subject, *History of Egyptian Mummies,* published in 1834, was the first English work on Egyptian archaeology.

The best ancient source of information on the details of embalming is Herodotus, who visited Egypt as a tourist around 500 B.C. He appears to have been fascinated with mummies and left a lengthy account of mummification in *The History,* II, 86–89:

> There are a set of men in Egypt who practice the art of embalming, and make it their proper business. These persons, when a body is brought to them, show the bearers various models of corpses, made of wood, and painted so as to resemble nature. The most perfect is said to be after the manner of him whom I do not think it religious to name in connection with such a matter; the second sort is inferior to the first, and less costly; the third is the cheapest of all. All this the

embalmers explain, and then ask in which way it is wished that the corpse should be prepared. The bearers tell them, and having concluded their bargain, take their departure, while the embalmers, left to themselves, proceed to their task. The mode of embalming, according to the most perfect process, is the following: —They take first a crooked piece of iron, and with it draw out the brain through the nostrils, thus getting rid of a portion, while the skull is cleared of the rest by rinsing with drugs; next they make a cut along the flank with a sharp Ethiopian stone, and take out the whole contents of the abdomen, which they then cleanse, washing it thoroughly with palm wine, and again frequently with an infusion of pounded aromatics. After this they fill the cavity with the purest bruised myrrh, with cassia, and every other sort of spicery except frankincense, and sew up the opening. Then the body is placed in natrum for seventy days, and covered entirely over. After the expiration of that space of time, which must not be exceeded, the body is washed, and wrapped round, from head to foot, with bandages of fine linen cloth, smeared over with gum, which is used generally by the Egyptians in the place of glue, and in this state it is given back to the relations, who enclose it in a wooden case which they have had made for the purpose, shaped into the figure of a man. Then fastening the case, they place it in a sepulchral chamber, upright against the wall. Such is the most costly way of embalming the dead.

If persons wish to avoid expense, and choose the second process, the following is the method pursued: —Syringes are filled with oil made from the cedar-tree, which is then, without any incision or disemboweling, injected into the abdomen. The passage by which it might be likely to return is stopped, and the body laid in natrum the prescribed number of days. At the end of the time the cedar-oil is allowed to make its escape; and such is its power that it brings with it the whole stomach and intestines in a liquid state. The natrum meanwhile has dissolved the flesh, and so nothing is left of the dead body but the skin and the bones. It is returned in this condition to the relatives, without any further trouble being bestowed it.

The third method of embalming, which is practiced in the case of the poorer classes, is to clear out the intestines with a clyster, and let the body lie in natrum the seventy days, after which it is at once given to those who come to fetch it away.

Herodotus' account has been confirmed as basically accurate by modern analyses of Egyptian mummies. The most elaborate of the three processes he describes is really the culmination of two thousand years of the embalmer's art. Mummification varied considerably from its beginning in the Old Kingdom to the time of Herodotus.

The earliest mummies were merely tightly bandaged bodies in wooden coffins. Because they were placed in moist rock tombs, the bodies decomposed to only bones and bandages. The crucial lacking element was dehydration: As long as the body retained moisture, tissue-destroying bacteria would invade it. In the Third Dynasty two successful solutions to the problem were found. The first was to remove the internal organs through an incision in the abdomen, eliminating a great deal of moisture and a major source of decay. The second was to use natron to dehydrate the tissues. Natron is composed of sodium bicarbonate and sodium chloride (salt), which is found in several places in Egypt. Not far from Cairo is the Wadi el Natrun, a dried riverbed where natron is plentiful and where the ancient embalmers probably went for their supply. The earliest evidence of natron used in embalming is from the unique tomb of Queen Hetepheres. She was the mother of Khufu, the builder of the Great Pyramid.

Hetepheres was buried twice, or at least part of her was buried twice. Her first tomb at Dashur, known for thousands of years, was robbed in antiquity. Her second remained undisturbed for more than four thousand years and was finally discovered by accident. A photographer with the Boston Museum of Fine Arts and Harvard University joint expedition to Giza had set up his tripod to photograph one of the pyramids when one of the legs of the tripod sank into the ground. He looked down and saw that the tripod leg rested not on bedrock, but on plaster. The sand was quickly cleared away from the area and the team discovered that the plaster covered a shaft going one hundred feet down into the rock. At the bottom of the shaft was the burial chamber of Queen Hetepheres, still sealed and intact. Why did she have two burials? Probably, when it was discovered that her first tomb had been plundered, her son Khufu had a second, secret tomb prepared and his mother's body, funerary furniture, and jewels moved to the safer resting place.

In the queen's burial chamber was her alabaster sarcophagus, still sealed. Imagine the disappointment of everyone present at the opening when it was found to be empty, except for the queen's bracelets. In a small chest nearby were four small jars containing Hetepheres' internal organs. Why was the body missing? No one knows for certain, but the theory is that, when the overseers of her first tomb discovered that the tomb had been broken into, they also found that the body had been taken or severely damaged by thieves looking for jewels. Afraid to tell the pharaoh that his mother's body had been destroyed, they resealed the alabaster sarcophagus and told Khufu that it was untouched. Then when everything was re-buried, the empty alabaster sarcophagus went along with the chest containing the internal organs and the funerary furniture. Thus, only part of the queen, her internal organs, was buried twice.

An analysis of the internal organs showed that although they had been soaked in a 3-percent solution of natron—the earliest known use of the substance—they were not extremely well pre-served. Sometime after the Old Kingdom a much more efficient way of dehydrating the body was discovered—covering it with *dry* natron. Dry natron absorbed the body's moisture much more quickly.

This question of whether Egyptian embalmers used dry natron or a solution has been the subject of some controversy and has an interesting history going back as far as Herodotus. When Herodotus described the use of natron in embalming, he used an ambiguous verb. The word really means "to preserve," in a manner similar to preserving fish. The Greeks normally packed fish in dry salt, but sometimes immersed them in brine. In the edition of Herodotus that Pettigrew read, Herodotus' verb was translated as "to steep," and Pettigrew assumed that a bath was used. Following in this tradition, Warren R. Dawson, one of the greatest experts on Egyptian mummies, states that embalmers "immerse the corpse in the salt bath." [3] Later the assumption was challenged by A. Lucas, a specialist in ancient Egyptian technology, who experimented by mummifying pigeons with a natron bath and with dry natron.[4] He found that while both methods preserved the unfortunate birds, the dry natron was by far superior and probably was the one used by the ancient Egyptian embalmers. Interestingly, Herodotus did not realize that natron dehydrated the body. He believed that it dis-solved the tissue, leaving only skin and bones.

Aside from its desiccating effects, natron may have been believed to have magical purifying properties. One of the spells (Spell 26) carved on the walls of the pyramid of Unas instructs the following to be recited four times:

> Thou purified thyself with natron,
> Together with the followers of Horus.

During the Old Kingdom, embalmers left the brain in the skull. Later they developed the technique described by Herodotus. A long, thin, sharp instrument was inserted through the nostril to break through the ethmoid bone and into the brain cavity. Then a long thin tool with a spoonlike end was used to remove the brain in small pieces. The brain was one of the few parts of the body the embalmers threw away. Apparently they thought it had no important function and thus did not have to be preserved. The ancient Egyptians believed that a person thought with his heart, not his brain. In excitement it is the heart that beats quickly, not the brain. In some papyri the word for heart, $\stackrel{\triangledown}{\shortmid}$, can also be translated as *mind*. (Paradoxically, some medical texts recognize the importance of the brain and the effects of brain damage.)

With the brain and internal organs removed, the body would then be dehydrated with natron. Because the body is approximately 75 percent water and is a fairly large object, this part of the process took a long time. The seventy days mentioned by Herodotus has been noted also by other Greek writers and may be close to accurate. Undoubtedly some embalmings took more, and others less, time than this. The Bible mentions forty days. When Joseph and the physicians embalmed his father, Israel, it took forty days to complete, and there was a seventy-day mourning period (Genesis 50:2–3).

For most procedures, the body was placed on an embalming table, elevated so that the embalmers did not have constantly to bend over. The table slanted slightly and had a groove at the lower end so that the various fluids could run off. Probably embalming did not take place in a permanent building. Anubis, the jackal-headed god of embalming, is often referred to as "in his tent." This probably refers to the embalmer's tent, which was called "the pure place of the Good House." A tent would allow for better ventilation and could be taken down after each embalming.

When the body was completely dehydrated, the stomach and

chest cavities were washed with palm oil and aromatic spices, and the abdomen was packed with linen or linen soaked in resin so that the body would retain its original shape. Sometimes sawdust and onions placed in small linen bags were used as packing material. The incision through which the viscera were removed would be drawn closed and a metal or wax plate inscribed with an Eye-of-Horus placed over it. The face was also padded with linen in the cheeks and under the eyelids. (There is even one instance of onions being placed in the eye sockets.) The body was then covered with a mixture of cedar oil and spices. Finally, a protective coating of resin was poured over all to keep out moisture.

This use of resin led to the mummy trade that prospered for centuries and even gave rise to our word *mummy*. Since the Middle Ages bitumen, a mineral formed of hardened pitch, was viewed as a cure-all by physicians. The major source of bitumen was a mountain in Persia where the substance was called *mummia*. When early travelers to Egypt first saw mummies with blackened, solidified resin, they thought it was bitumen. Soon the embalmed bodies from which the pseudo-*mummia* was extracted were called *mummies*. Eventually, in addition to the resinous part of the mummy, the flesh and bones were also desired. Ground mummy became a popular fifteenth-century prescription and a standard item in apothecary shops. Paracelsus, the German physician-alchemist, included *mummia* in the ingredients of the life-prolonging elixir he administered to his patients. Eventually, the supplies of authentic mummies were nearly exhausted, and this led to the manufacture of fake mummies. At these modern mummy factories, the bodies of prisoners and slaves were bandaged, placed in the sun to dry, and then ground up and fed to ailing patients.

Once the body was coated with resin, it was almost ready for bandaging, but first the following incantation was recited by a priest, who probably wore a mask of Anubis:

> The perfume of Arabia hath been brought to thee to make perfect thy smell through the scent of the god. Here are brought to thee liquids which have come from Ra to make perfect . . . thy smell in the Hall [of Judgment]. O sweet-smelling soul of the great god, thou dost contain such a sweet odour that thy face shall neither change

nor perish . . . Thy members shall become young in Arabia, and thy soul shall appear over thy body in Ta-neter [the "divine land"].[5]

Then the embalmer anointed the body twice from head to toe with oil mixed with spices and perfumes, being especially careful to cover the head thoroughly with the magical unguent. Then the incantation continued:

> Osiris [the deceased], thou hast received the perfume which shall make thy members perfect. Thou receivest the source [of life] and thou takest the form of the great Disk [Aten], which uniteth itself unto thee to give enduring form to thy members; thou shalt unite with Osiris in the great Hall. The unguent cometh unto thee to fashion thy members and to gladden thy heart, and thou shalt appear in the form of Ra; it shall make thee to be sound when thou settest in the sky at eventide, and it shall spread abroad the smell of thee in the nomes of Aqert. . . . Thou receivest the oil of the cedar in Amentet, and the cedar which came forth from Osiris cometh unto thee; it delivereth thee from thy enemies, and it protecteth thee in the nomes. Thy soul alighteth upon the venerable sycamores. Thou criest to Isis, and Osiris heareth thy voice, and Anubis cometh unto thee to invoke thee. Thou receivest the oil of the country of Manu which hath come from the East, and Ra riseth upon thee at the gates of the horizon, at the holy doors of Nieth. Thou goest therein, thy soul is in the upper heaven, and thy body in the lower heaven . . . O Osiris, may the Eye of Horus cause that which floweth forth from it to come to thee, and to thy heart for ever! [6]

The magical unguents used in embalming were the same lotions used in daily life. There was a traditional group known as the Seven Sacred Oils (Figure 13), and cosmetic kits frequently had seven little pots to hold them. The Metropolitan Museum of Art in New York has an alabaster tablet with seven holes for unguents. Above each hole is the name of the unguent: Festival Perfume, *Hekenu* Oil, Syrian Balsam, *Nechenem* Salve, Anointing Oil, Best Cedar Oil, and Best Libyan Oil. These seven formed the basis for all the magical oils used in embalming. As far back as the Old Kingdom, they were considered an essential part of the funerary ritual. Several of the magical spells of the Pyramid Texts mention them:

> O ointment, O ointment, arise, hurry!
> [Thou who art] on the brow of Horus, arise!
> *First quality cedar oil.*

Hurry! [Thou who art] on Horus,
thou art placed on the brow of this Unas,
so that he may feel sweet under thee,
that thou makest him a spirit under thee.
Thou grantest him to have power over his body,
thou grantest that his terror be in the eyes
of all the spirits when they look at him,
and of everyone who hears his name.

Osiris Unas, I bring thee the Eye of Horus
   which he takes, which is on thy brow,
First quality Libyan oil.

—Spells 52–54

With this ritual of the unguents completed, the bandaging could
begin.

On another table near the embalming table were the hundreds
of yards of bandages needed to wrap the mummy. In a newspaper
account of one of Pettigrew's unwrappings (*Morning Chronicle,*
May 30, 1836, p. 5, col. 5), Pettigrew is quoted as having told the
audience that one mummy he unwrapped had more than two thou-

FIGURE 13. These alabaster jars were for storing the Seven Sacred Oils used for embalming
and other purposes. The Metropolitan Museum of Art

sand yards of linen. Approximately sixty yards were taken from the nostrils alone, having been forced up into the cranium. These bandages were made from the bedding of the deceased or from other discarded linens. They were made ready for use by the embalmers, who tore them into strips about four inches wide and as long as fifteen feet. They were then rolled up, prior to use, just like modern bandages. However, the bandages of pharaohs were probably woven just for the purpose of mummification. Many of Tutankhamen's bandages had edges finished on both sides, indicating that they were not torn from larger pieces of linen, but were specially made in that width.

At this point the internal organs, which had been removed from the body and dehydrated, were wrapped and placed in the four jars made especially for the purpose. These jars, often highly ornamented, were associated with the four sons of Horus (Figure 14). Each contained a different organ. The lid of each was carved in the shape of one of the sons: Mesti, the human-headed son; Duamutef, the jackal; Hapi, the baboon; Qebesenef, the hawk. The jars were made of various materials, most commonly limestone, but also alabaster and faience. These jars were called "canopic jars" from the Greek legend of Canopus, the pilot of Menelaus, who was buried in Egypt. He was said to have been worshiped in the form of a jar with feet.

Once the wrapped internal organs were placed in the canopic jars, a fluid called the "liquid of the children of Horus" was poured in and the jars sealed. The four jars were then placed in a small chest (Figure 15) with four compartments, one for each jar. At this point a magical spell was recited to invoke the protection of the sons of Horus.

> Mesti says: 'I am Mesti, thy son Osiris. I come so that I may protect thee. I cause thy house to prosper, to be firm, by the command of Ptah, by the command of Re himself.'

> Hapi says: 'I am Hapi, thy son Osiris. I come so that I may protect thee. I bandage for thee thy head and thy limbs, killing for thee thy enemies under thee. I give to thee thy head, for ever.'

> Duamutef says: 'I am thy son Horus, loving thee. I come to avenge my father, Osiris. I do not permit his destruction to thee. I place it under thy feet for ever and ever.'

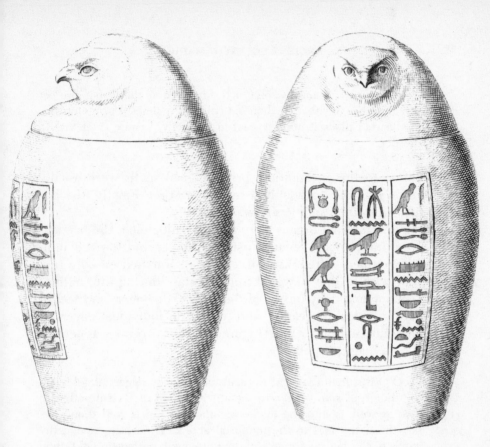

FIGURE 14. An eighteenth-century drawing of a canopic jar illustrates the head of Qebesenef, the falcon-headed son of Horus.

FIGURE 15. This wooden chest housed the canopic jars containing the internal organs of Khonsu, a nobleman of the Nineteenth Dynasty. The gods painted on the sides protect the remains for eternity. The Metropolitan Museum of Art

Qebesenef says: 'I am thy son Osiris. I have come that I may protect thee. I gather together thy bones, I collect thy limbs, I bring for thee thy heart. I place it upon its seat in thy body. I cause thy house to prosper.' [7]

In addition to this incantation, brief magical spells were usually written on each jar to doubly assure protection. Finally, the jars were placed in the canopic shrine.

After the internal organs were ritually embalmed, the bandaging of the intact body began. First each finger and toe was individually wrapped. Often, as well, each nail was tied on by a tiny thread or wire so that it would remain intact during the preliminary cleaning and dehydration of the body. The fingers and toes of pharaohs and wealthy people were placed in individual covers of gold for additional protection (Figure 16). This process was accompanied by a magical spell:

O Osiris, thou receivest thy nails of gold, thy fingers of gold, and thy thumb of *smu* [or *uasm*] metal; the liquid of Ra entereth into thee as well as into the divine members of Osiris, and thou journeyeth on thy legs to the immortal abode. Thou hast carried thy hands to the house of eternity, thou art made perfect in gold, thou dost shine brightly in *smu* metal, and thy fingers shine in the dwelling of Osiris, in the sanctuary of Horus himself. O Osiris, the gold of the mountains cometh to thee; it is a holy talisman of the gods in their abodes, and it lighteneth thy face in the lower heaven. Thou breathest in gold, thou appearest in *smu* metal, and the dwellers in Re-stau receive thee; thou who art in the funeral chest rejoice because thou hast transformed thyself into a hawk of gold by means of thy amulets. . . .[8]

The head was done next, bound very tightly to show the contours of the face. Head bandages had names and were applied in a very specific manner: Bandages of the god Nekheb were placed on the forehead; Hathor, on the face; Toth over the ears; Nebt-hotep, on the neck; and Sekhmet, on the top of the head. The number of linen strips was also prescribed: four on the forehead, two on top of the head, two around the mouth, four on the neck, until there were twenty-two pieces on each side of the face. When the face was entirely bandaged, the Lady of the West was implored:

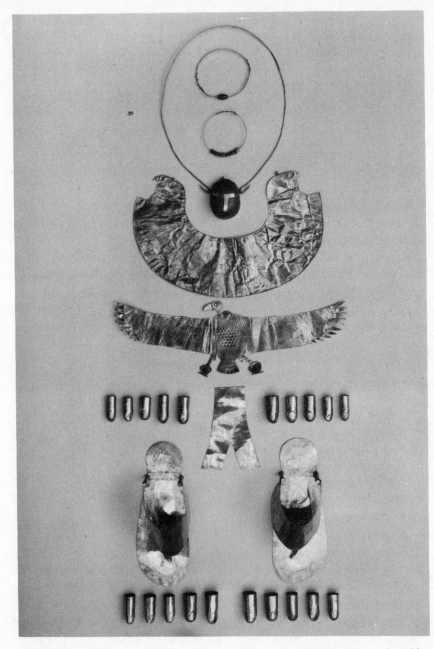

FIGURE 16. Among the trappings from the mummy of a wife of Tuthmose III are the golden sandals and toe and finger stalls intended to protect the extremities from decay. The golden pectorals and scarab torque were for magical protection. The Metropolitan Museum of Art, Fletcher Fund, 1926

Grant thou that breathing may take place in the head of the deceased in the underworld, and that he may see with his eyes, and that he may hear with his two ears; and that he may breathe through his nose; and that he may be able to utter sounds with his mouth; and that he may be able to speak with his tongue in the under-world. . . .[9]

This spell was crucial because in the next world the deceased would have to convince the various gods of his worthiness to be admitted into their company.

Arms and legs were bandaged next. First a ring was passed over the fingers of the left hand. Minute quantities of the thirty-six substances used in embalming were placed in the hand. Then the hand was wrapped in linen folded six times. On the bandages of the left hand were drawn figures of Isis and Hapi; on the right, Re and Min. Similarly, after wrapping and anointment with magical ointments, the leg bandages were drawn with figures of jackals. Within the wrappings, priests secured flowers of the *ankh-imy* plant to protect the limbs. Finally, while priests recited appropriate incantations, the torso itself was wrapped and magical amulets of turquoise and carnelian were tucked in the bandages. Many of the bandages had protective magical spells written on them (Figures 17, 18).

Of all the rituals performed during mummification, by far the most important was the opening-of-the-mouth ceremony. This was performed in front of the tomb on the day of burial. It must have been more like a mystery play than a religious ritual, as more than a dozen participants were required for the performance: the officiating priest, who held a papyrus describing how things should proceed; actresses, often members of the family of the deceased, who portrayed Isis and her sister Nephthys; a character called "The-Son-Who-Loves-Him"; a small group of people representing the guards of Horus; and various priests with specific functions. The ceremony was lengthy and detailed.

First the area in which the play was to be performed was purified with water from four different vases, each representing one of the corners of the earth. Then incense from four burners was lit, and various gods were invoked. A ritual slaughter was performed, commemorating the battle in which Horus avenged Osiris' death.

FIGURE 17. A magical spell written in hieratic is still visible on this segment of a mummy bandage. Photograph by Russell Rudzwick

FIGURE 18. Elaborate bandaging, as in this mummy of Pasheryenhor, sometimes concealed negligent embalming. Reproduced by courtesy of the Trustees of the British Museum

In the myth, Seth's conspirators, in dismembering Osiris' corpse, attempted to escape Horus by changing into various animals, but Horus caught them and cut off their heads. Therefore, at the opening-of-the-mouth ceremony various animals were ritually killed, including two bulls (one for the south and one for the north), gazelles, and ducks. When the bull of the south was slaughtered, one of the legs was cut off and, along with the heart, offered to the mummy.

This was sympathetic magic in which the deceased was associated with Osiris: The sacrificial killing of the animals, representing the conspirators who attempted to destroy the body of Osiris, assured that the body of the deceased would be safe from such an attack. Another purpose of slaughtering animals was to provide food for the deceased. Indications are that the practice of providing this special food was cruel. Numerous tomb reliefs and paintings show that one offering of food for the deceased was the foreleg of a calf, amputated while the animal was still alive. Exactly why it was

crucial to perform a live amputation we do not know, but perhaps the ancient Egyptians insisted on an almost-live offering so that the deceased would be nourished by the living.

There is no doubt that the animal was alive at the time of the offering. A common scene shows the shaven-headed priest-butcher cutting off the leg while the animal is standing with its mother behind it in obvious distress. Other scenes show the unfortunate animal standing on three legs. Such representations also appear in vignettes of the various copies of the *Book of the Dead* as well as on tomb walls.

In the ceremony, the high-priest touched the mouth of the mummy with the leg of the bull, and then an assistant brought forward an implement shaped like an adz (Figure 19). (Actually, two of these tools were used.) Touching the mouth of the mummy with the implement, the priest said:

> Thy mouth was closed, but I have set in order for thee thy mouth and thy teeth. I open for thee thy mouth, I open for thee thy two eyes. I have opened thy mouth with the instrument of Anubis, with the iron implement with which the mouths of the gods were opened. Horus, open the mouth! Horus, open the mouth! Horus hath opened the mouth of the dead, as he in times of old opened the mouth of Osiris, with the iron which came forth from Set, with the iron instrument with which he opened the mouths of the gods. He hath opened thy mouth with it. The deceased shall walk and speak, and his body shall be with the great company of the gods in the Great House of the Aged One in Annu, and he shall receive the ureret crown from Horus, the lord of mankind.[10]

FIGURE 19. Models of the miniature adz used in the opening-of-the-mouth ceremony and other wooden carvings representing magical knots were found in the foundation of Hatshepsut's funerary temple at Deir el Bahari. The Metropolitan Museum of Art

Then, with a wooden ram-headed scepter called "Great of Magical Spells," the priest touched the mouth and eyes of the mummy four times and proclaimed that the deceased had all the powers needed in the next world. The Son-Who-Loves-Him stepped forward and, with a metal chisel, touched the mummy's mouth and eyes. The high-priest again touched the mouth and eyes, this time with his little finger. Then, the priest touched the mouth and eyes with a small bag of carnelian chips, perhaps to restore color to the corpse. The Son-Who-Loves-Him took up implements called the "Iron-of-the-South" and the "Iron-of-the-North" and placed them on the mouth and eyes, while another priest recited yet another spell to assure their use in the next world. Finally, the high-priest touched the mouth of the deceased with a forked implement and said, "O Osiris, I have established for thee thy two jaw-bones in thy face, and they are now separated." It is clear that, of all the parts of the body, the mouth received the most attention. This was because, while the Book of the Dead provided the words of power, the deceased had to be able to say them properly or they would have no effect.

The opening-of-the-mouth ceremony described above, while complex, is actually a somewhat abbreviated form of what took place. Many papyri and tomb paintings describe the ritual part. In an attempt to reconstruct the complete ceremony, T.J.C. Baly combined the various versions and came up with a composite ritual involving seventeen different steps.[11] Interestingly, the ceremony did not have to be performed on the mummy itself, but could just as well be performed on a lifelike statue of the deceased, which may have been more common.

The embalming and burial with the accompanying magical rites were not considered sufficient to send the deceased on his way through "millions of years." There was still one last ceremony to be performed before the tomb was sealed: the funerary meal.

The exact significance of the ritual last meal is not known for certain. It may have been a sort of farewell to the deceased, a symbolic nourishment of the deceased. Whatever its purpose, it was a common and expected part of every burial. The meal was attended by close relatives of the deceased and often took place in an antechamber of the tomb, the burial chamber being left open until it was over. There was a variety of foods, often including a leg of a bull, bread, beer, and wine. All evidence indicates that it was a festive rather than a solemn event. Frequently, the guests wore specially prepared pectorals made of flower petals and faience beads sewn in colorful designs onto papyrus backing. When the meal was over, the remaining food was carefully placed in the burial chamber and the tomb sealed.

Not every last meal, however, was buried with the deceased. One that was not was the one eaten by the relatives of Tutankhamen on the day he was buried. The story of the finding of the remains of this meal is one of the most curious in the history of Egyptology, and it suggests a close connection between the funeral meal and the embalming ritual.

Theodore M. Davis, the man who discovered the remains of this meal, was a wealthy American businessman who, in 1908, had the concession to the Valley of the Kings. This was at a time when it was relatively easy to get a concession—exclusive permission to excavate a particular area—from the Egyptian government. All one needed was the money to finance the digging and a few well-placed friends. Davis excavated in the Valley of the Kings for several years and made a number of important finds. Unfortunately, he was not a trained archaeologist and his techniques and judgments were somewhat deficient. His discovery of the remains of the last meal is an example.

In January of 1908 Davis discovered a small pit dug into the bedrock about a hundred yards away from the tomb of Tutankhamen, which of course had not yet been discovered. The pit was about six feet long, four feet wide, and four feet deep. In it were about a dozen large storage pots which had been sealed with mud. The jars contained a curious admixture. Most of the contents were the remains of an embalming: yards and yards of linen and small packets of natron tied into the center of a square piece of linen. Some of the linen was marked with Tutankhamen's name and "linen of year 6." This meant the linen was new in the sixth year of his reign, about three years before he died. There were also several seals with the king's name. It would have been obvious to almost any scholar that this was the embalming cache of Tutankhamen, but Davis did not realize it. Earlier, not far from this spot, he had found a small faience cup with Tutankhamen's name on it. Somehow Davis associated the cup (which probably had been stolen by the thieves who broke into the tomb in ancient times) with the pit cache and assumed that he had found the only remains of Tutankhamen's tomb.

Perhaps one reason for Davis' assumption is that, in addition to the embalming equipment buried in the pit, there were a small mummy mask and the remains of a last ritual meal: numerous cups and plates, bones of various animals, and wine jugs. Also found were the remains of the funerary pectorals worn by the participants at the last meal (Figure 20). The smaller cups and dishes were intact, but all the larger pieces of pottery had been broken, probably intentionally, to make them fit through the mouths of the storage jars. There were also two brooms. From these remains it is possible to reconstruct what the last meal might have been like.

From the dishes and cups we can guess that there were eight participants. Unfortunately, we shall never know who they were, but almost certainly there was Ankhesenamen, Tutankhamen's young widow, and quite possibly Aye, his successor and the future husband of Ankhesenamen. The participants wore brightly colored pectorals made of flowers and beads. We cannot be sure how many

FIGURE 20. This floral pectoral was worn by one of the participants in the ritual last meal of Tutankhamen. The Metropolitan Museum of Art, Gift of Theodore Davis, 1909

collars there were, as Davis ripped up some of them to impress visitors with just how strong papyrus remained after three thousand years! The participants dined on sheep or goat, four different kinds of duck, three different kinds of geese, and probably bread. They washed the meal down with considerable quantities of wine (Figure 21). When they were finished the servants broke the dishes and placed the fragments. along with the bones of the meat and fowl, inside the storage jars. They then swept the area with the brooms and placed the brooms in the jars. The jars were then sealed and carried to the pit where they were buried

While it is almost certain that what Theodore Davis found was a burial of both the funerary meal and leftover embalming paraphernalia, the question is, How did the two come together? It is

FIGURE 21. Wine from this jar (now repaired) was drunk at the ritual last meal for Tutankhamen. The Metropolitan Museum of Art, Gift of Theodore Davis, 1909

highly unlikely that the ritual meal was consumed in the embalmer's tent. Perhaps they were separate events, even taking place on different days. The equipment from the actual embalming—the natron, the linen, etc.—would surely have been cleaned up prior to the day of entombment, when the meal was eaten. It would be helpful if we knew what was in each jar, so that we could determine if embalming material and ritual meal remains were intermingled in the same jar. This would suggest a very close proximity between the two events. But here again we will probably never know, as Davis did not record what was in each jar and even threw some material out before he gave the pit material to the Metropolitan Museum of Art in New York. Still another question remains: Why were the remnants of the funerary meal not sealed in the tomb, as was traditional? Perhaps for some reason the tomb was sealed prior to the meal so that the remains had to be buried separately. In any event, we do know that Tutankhamen was provided with the ritual meal necessary for his journey to the next world.

Humans were not the only creatures mummified. Various sacred animals also were preserved for eternity. The most famous animal cemetery is the Serapium at Saqqara, where the mummies of the Apis bulls were entombed.

The word "Serapium" is a Greek corruption of the names of two gods who became closely associated. The original Egyptian name for Osiris was *Osir;* Apis was *Ap.* When the Greek endings were added, *Osir-Ap* became "Serapium," the place of Osiris and Apis.

The Serapium was discovered in 1851 by the famous French Egyptologist, August Mariette, under rather unusual circumstances. Mariette had been sent to Egypt by the government of France to purchase Coptic manuscripts from the monasteries. During numerous bureaucratic delays, Mariette visited the sites of Cairo. While at Saqqara he came across an avenue of sphinxes protruding from the sand and remembered the geographer Strabo had reported that the temple of Serapis was at the end of such an avenue. Mariette completely forgot about his mission to buy the manuscripts, hired a team of thirty workmen, and began excavating. After discovering 134 sphinxes, various tombs, statues, and other antiquities, he finally reached the burial place of the sacred

FIGURE 22. This highly romanticized nineteenth-century drawing depicts the feeding of the sacred ibises in the Hypostyle Hall at the Temple of Karnak.

Apis bulls. They were elaborately wrapped and inside huge granite sarcophagi.

Not all animal mummies were afforded such careful treatment. Since there probably was only one Apis bull alive at any one time, and since the Apis was associated with the fertility of Egypt, it was an especially important animal. Less revered animals mummified in great numbers included cats, jackals, falcons, fish, ibises, and even scarabs (Figure 22). These were not really embalmed; often they were merely wrapped intact and buried in the sand or in niches cut in rock tombs (Figure 23).

Mummification, which is so closely identified with ancient Egypt, is often taken as evidence that the Egyptians were preoccupied with death. The truth is quite the opposite. The Egyptians loved life so much that they developed elaborate embalming rituals and techniques in order to prolong it. The goal of mummification was not to preserve a dead body, but to prepare it for an eternal life.

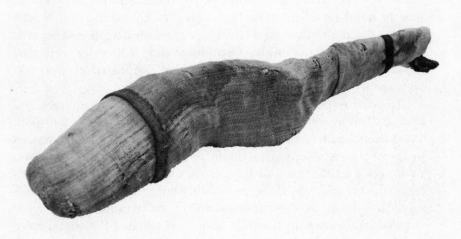

FIGURE 23. The sacred fish *Bagrus bayad*, here mummified, may have been worshiped because of its electrical properties. Photograph by Barbara Benton

6. The Pyramids

THE MODERN VOGUE of "pyramid power" began in 1970 with the publication of *Psychic Discoveries Behind the Iron Curtain*, by Sheila Ostrander and Lynn Schroeder. This massive book is the journal of two reporters who traveled throughout Russia and the satellite countries, trying to find out what the communists were doing in parapsychology research. One chapter, "Pyramid Power and the Riddle of the Razor Blades," tells of the writers' visit to Czechoslovakia, where they were told that the shape of the pyra-mid has the power to generate energy. Indeed, Czech patent 91304, for the "Cheops Pyramid Razor-Blade Sharpener," was is-sued to Karel Drval in 1959. Drval claimed that dull razor blades become sharp and that food is preserved when placed inside card-board miniature pyramids. Ostrander and Schroeder reported Drval's claims verbatim, and their book popularized pyramid power.

Today it is possible to purchase pyramids of various sizes and materials either direct from specialty stores or through the mail. One hears of people using them to store everything from tomatoes to razor blades, sleeping in them, meditating in them, and even wearing them. The ancient Egyptians, obsessed as they were with magical rites and practices, probably would have thought all this silly. All indications are that the shape of the pyramid had *no great magical significance* to them. It almost seems as if the shape were accidental, or perhaps even an afterthought.

The first pyramid was the "step" pyramid of King Zoser, the founder of the Third Dynasty, and evidently it was not originally intended to be a pyramid. Prior to Zoser, pharaohs and nobility were buried in low, mud-brick tombs resembling benches. They are thus called *mastabas,* the Arabic word for "bench." Zoser originally intended to be buried in a mastaba and had one constructed of stone, the first major use of stone in Egyptian building. He had the mastaba built in Saqqara, the "city of the dead" for the Old Kingdom, just across the river from Memphis, which was then the capital. Saqqara is vast, stretching over thirty miles on a plateau along the Nile just south of Cairo. Its name comes from Sokar, the god of the dead for Memphis. The original mastaba for Zoser was roughly square, constructed so that the four sides were oriented to the cardinal points—obviously for religious or magical reasons. After this mastaba was completed, Zoser's architect had five additional mastabas built onto it, each on top of the other, until there were six distinct layers, giving the mastaba a stepped effect (Figure 24).

We know very little about this architect of the first pyramid, yet he is one of the most intriguing figures in all of ancient Egyptian history. On the base of a statue found near the pyramid was an inscription bearing the name Imhotep. This Imhotep had many

FIGURE 24. The step pyramid of Zoser was the first pyramid and the first major building of stone. Photograph by Barbara Benton

titles, among them Vizier, Physician, Chief Builder for the Pharaoh
Zoser, and High Priest of Heliopolis. While this is practically all we
know of him, we do know that Egyptians of later dynasties revered
him as a sage, and the Greeks deified him as Asclepius, the god of
healing. The late Walter B. Emery, an eminent Egyptologist, spent
years looking for Imhotep's tomb, but died without finding it.

Given the way the step pyramid evolved, it is doubtful that its
shape had any great significance for the ancient Egyptians, especially since, after several smaller stepped-pyramids were constructed, the shape was abandoned. Other buildings in Zoser's
funerary complex certainly did have magical import.

One of the most important structures in the complex was the
heb-sed courtyard. Every pharaoh was to perform a magical ceremony of rejuvenation every thirty years (or often less). So he could
remain young forever, Zoser needed the facilities for this magical
ceremony in his pyramid complex. Part of the ceremony involved a
reenactment of the pharaoh's coronation, symbolizing a new beginning. There was a procession from chapel to chapel, where the king
obtained permission to be crowned from the various gods. Then he
proceeded to one shrine where he would be given the white crown
of Upper Egypt, next to a second shrine where he would be given
the red crown of Lower Egypt, thus rejoining the two lands. Then,
to demonstrate his vigor and agility, the king would run around a
fixed course. Zoser's *heb-sed* courtyard was designed to enable him
to perform the ceremony for eternity. It is a large rectangular yard
surrounded by a series of shrines and temples. In the pavilion the
soul of the dead pharaoh could obtain permission from the gods, be
crowned again and be rejuvenated.

If there is a single magical theme to Zoser's pyramid complex it
is this rejuvenation through performance of the *heb-sed*. Inside the
pyramid itself are the burial chamber and numerous smaller chambers to store the provisions he would need on his journey to the
next world. Some of these chambers have wall paintings showing
the pharaoh performing the running portion of the ceremony.
Other chambers contain thousands of alabaster jars to symbolically
contain the magical unguents for the ceremonies the king would
perform. Some of these chambers have still not been excavated, but
vases and jars can be seen piled from floor to ceiling. (It is interesting that one of Imhotep's titles was "Maker of Stone Vessels.")

The interior of the step pyramid was robbed in antiquity, and few remains of Zoser have been found by modern archaeologists. The remains of a child in an alabaster sarcophagus and a mummified foot, possibly Zoser's, were found in the burial chamber. The foot had had all the flesh and skin removed, and the bones had been bandaged. Other fragments indicate that Zoser was in fact buried in the step pyramid. If this is true, what was the function of the mysterious mastaba in the complex?

About two hundred yards south of the pyramid is a mastaba called "The Southern Burial." Beneath the superstructure are galleries and a small burial chamber. Almost everything points to the fact that Zoser was buried here, but clearly this cannot have been the case. The rooms, though smaller, are almost identical to those beneath the pyramid. In some of the rooms the walls are inlaid with blue-green faience tiles made to imitate bundled papyrus, which was used in the construction of Zoser's earthly palace.

One possible use of this "southern burial" was as a dwelling place for the *ka* (the spirit) of the pharaoh. This would not be without precedent, for many of Zoser's predecessors, the kings of the First and Second dynasties, had two burials performed. The cenotaph, or unused one, was at Abydos, the mythological burial place of Osiris. It was hoped that while the king's physical body was buried in the north, the soul would make a pilgrimage to Abydos in Upper Egypt and thus reap the benefits of association with Osiris. Thus Zoser, within the same complex, may have had a northern and southern burial in keeping with tradition, the southern one being for purely magical purposes.

Another purpose for the southern burial has been suggested by Jean-Philippe Lauer, the chief excavator and restorer of the step-pyramid complex: that it may have been used for the burial of the canopic jars containing the internal organs of Zoser. While the burial chamber is too small to have housed a sarcophagus, the remains were found of what may have been a canopy for the canopic chest.

On the north side of the pyramid was a mortuary temple which has almost completely disappeared. In this temple, offerings for the well-being of the soul of Zoser would have been made daily by priests. Next to the mortuary temple was a small chamber called the *serdab,* housing a life-size statue of Zoser seated on his throne.

Like almost every other aspect of the complex, it too was associated with the *heb-sed*, for Zoser wears the white cloak of the jubilee. Indeed, the whole point of the funerary complex of Zoser is a magical one summed up on an incantation written on one of the vessels found inside the pyramid: "May the King celebrate one million *sed* festivals."

The entire complex was surrounded by a rectangular wall thirty feet high, more than a quarter of a mile long, and eight hundred feet wide. It resembles the fortified walls of an ancient town, and indeed it was a city for Zoser. The wall was encased in polished white limestone and contained fourteen false doors. The only true door (Figure 25), at the southern corner, led to an entrance colonnade (Figure 26).

The entire structure must have seemed magical to the ancient Egyptians. Up until the time of Zoser no building of any size had been constructed of stone. This was a virtual city, duplicating details of the pharaoh's palace, temples, and shrines, so that he would have a suitable dwelling place for eternity.

If the two burial places for Zoser raise a question, the pyramid of his probable successor, Horus-Sekhem-Khet, raises an even more difficult one. Little is known about this pharaoh whose pyramid was discovered in 1951. Only a short walk from Zoser's complex, Horus-Sekhem-Khet's pyramid seems to have been constructed along a similar design. It is even possible that Imhotep was the architect of this structure, too. Quite possibly he outlived Zoser, and if so, he almost certainly would have been the chief architect for the new king. To support this notion are some graffiti on the wall surrounding Horus-Sekhem-Khet's pyramid. One reads 𓏢𓃀𓏤 , "Imhotep," and could refer to the same man.

The pyramid of Horus-Sekhem-Khet was never finished. Unlike Zoser's, which had six steps, it was apparently intended to have seven. As it was almost totally covered in sand, its excavation took several years. During the 1953–54 season, the entrance was found on the north side. The doorway was still sealed, indicating that, even though the pyramid was unfinished, the pharaoh evidently had been buried inside. It appeared as if an intact royal tomb of the Old Kingdom had been found. When they opened the door, the excavators found a descending corridor framed by an arch—possibly the earliest known arch. At the bottom of the corridor huge lime-

FIGURE 25. This, the only true entrance in the wall surrounding Zoser's pyramid complex, was intended for the passage of priests. Zoser's soul could pass through any one of the numerous false doors. Photograph by Barbara Benton

FIGURE 26. To reach Zoser's *heb-sed* courtyard, one passes through a stone colonnade carved to resemble tied bundles of papyrus. Photograph by Barbara Benton

stone blocks and debris blocked the entrance to the burial chamber. When they removed the debris they found gold jewelry on the corridor floor: 21 gold bracelets, 388 hollow gold beads, 420 gold-plated faience beads, and the remains of a wooden magic wand covered in gold (the wood had decayed, leaving only the gold). Perhaps the jewels—the oldest known royal gold objects—were left there to appease tomb robbers in the hope that, after clearing the corridor, they would find the jewelry and be satisfied to leave the burial chamber in peace. Perhaps the idea was that, if that strategy did not work, the magic wand would protect the pharaoh's resting place. Neither of these strategies was needed, because for some reason thieves never entered the pyramid. The door to the burial chamber was intact when archaeologists reached it.

The burial chamber, a large room, did not contain the usual grave goods, only a translucent alabaster sarcophagus. On the lid were plant remains, which could have been used as incense in some rite. The sarcophagus was sealed and obviously had not been touched since it was placed in the pyramid more than four thousand years before. Opened, it was found to be completely empty, and careful inspection of the interior showed that it had never been used. The empty sarcophagus raises two obvious questions: Where was Horus-Sekhem-Khet buried? What was the purpose of this pyramid? Maybe the pyramid was merely a decoy, intended to throw thieves off the track of the pharaoh's true burial. If this is correct, it may explain why the pyramid was never plundered. Robbers frequently got inside information from tomb workers. If they did in this case, they would have known that the unfinished step pyramid of Horus-Sekhem-Khet was a decoy.

Horus-Sekhem-Khet's immediate successors built on a much smaller scale, probably fearing that, like Sekhem-Khet, they might die and leave their pyramids unfinished. As a result, about half a dozen small step-pyramids were built by kings of the late Third Dynasty. One of these, at El-Kula, has a strange deviation from all the other pyramids in ancient Egypt: Its corners, rather than its sides are oriented to the four cardinal points.

The Third Dynasty left the legacy of the step pyramid; the Fourth Dynasty completed the transition to the true pyramid. At present tremendous argument exists about how this occurred, centering on the pyramid at Meidum. The Meidum pyramid is one of the most imposing structures in all of Egypt, yet little is known about it. That it looks more like a tower built on a hill than a pyramid built on a plain (Figure 27) is the source of much of the controversy. Until recently, most Egyptologists agreed that the reason for the ruinous state of the pyramid was that the local villagers used it as a quarry for building stone, stripping off its fine white limestone casing. Recently, however, Kurt Mendelssohn, an Oxford physicist, challenged this explanation asserting that, because the angle of inclination was too steep, the walls of the pyramid collapsed during construction. That very little stone has been used in village buildings supports Mendelssohn's thesis. The "hill" upon which the pyramid seems to rest is the remains of the upper levels of the collapsed pyramid.

The pyramid of Meidum in many ways is the model for later pyramids of the Fourth Dynasty. To the east is a temple, usually

FIGURE 27. An early nineteenth-century representation of the Meidum pyramid shows the mysterious and still unexcavated mound of sand at its base.

called the "valley temple" because it is situated in the valley. Connecting the temple with the pyramid was a roofed causeway constructed of white limestone. Mummification of the king's body and the opening-of-the-mouth ceremony probably were performed in the temple. Then by solemn procession the body was carried by shaven-headed priests along the causeway to the pyramid. The body then was placed in the burial chamber and the pyramid sealed. Afterward, in the mortuary chapel on the east face of the pyramid, the priests made daily offerings for the pharaoh's soul.

But who was this pharaoh who built the Meidum pyramid? And if Mendelssohn is correct, and it collapsed while under construction, where was the pharaoh buried? It appears that the owner of the pyramid was Sneferu, a powerful pharaoh who was the first king of the Fourth Dynasty. The walls of the mortuary temple are covered with numerous graffiti left by New Kingdom visitors. One of these visitors, the scribe Aakheperkare-seneb, said he found the temple of Sneferu to be beautiful. Thus we know that, at least in ancient times, the pyramid was believed to have been Sneferu's. If this is true, the question becomes, If the pyramid collapsed before it was completed, where was Sneferu buried? The answer to this question is at Dashur, about fifty miles north of Meidum.

There are two huge pyramids at Dashur, known as the Bent Pyramid and the Red Pyramid. The Bent is so called because about two thirds up its face the angle of inclination changes, giving the pyramid its distinctive shape: △ . The Red derives its name from the color of the sunlit stones. Dashur has a long history of association with magic. The medieval Arab magicians who hunted for buried treasure frequently mention the site:

> Let the pyramids [of Dashur] behind you and walk half a mile towards the west where you will find a white pyramid built of stone, and near it, at the eastern side, you will find an important necropolis known by the name of Atwaq [necklaces]. Over the tombs are put stones which resemble the frogs: go and search in whatever tomb among them, you will find a dead person and near him all what he owned, and around his neck a necklace of gold. This is all.[1]

In the same work there is reference to the tomb of a princess which contains three magical rings:

> Remove the body, and you will find under her head a box which contains three rings; if you press hard on the stone of any of them,

the spirit of the ring will appear to you and follow your instructions. Put the body into its place and make the tomb in order [before you leave it].[2]

We know for certain that the owner of the two pyramids at Dashur is Sneferu. Now the question becomes, Why did one pharaoh have *three* pyramids? It has been known since ancient times that Sneferu had *two* pyramids because records refer to the "northern" and "southern" pyramids of Sneferu. It was always assumed that the southern one was at Meidum, but recent excavations have fairly conclusively proven that both the Bent Pyramid and the Red Pyramid belonged to Sneferu. Possibly the Red and the Bent were the northern and southern pyramids, one representing the king as ruler of Upper Egypt and the other as ruler of Lower Egypt. He could have been buried only in one, so the other may have been for his *ka*. If the theory of the collapse of the Meidum pyramid is correct, the Red Pyramid is the first true pyramid, evolving out of about a half dozen step pyramids, the unsuccessful Meidum pyramid, and finally the Bent Pyramid. This makes it somewhat unlikely that the pyramid shape had any great magical significance to the Egyptians. Rather, it was the result of gradual architectural changes.

One of Sneferu's seven sons, Khufu, was the builder of the Great Pyramid, the one most associated with magic. Although the hieroglyphs for his name were pronounced "Khufu," when the Greeks conquered Egypt they corrupted the name to "Cheops," so that it is by this name that he is often known. Among many claims about the Great Pyramid are: that it was built primarily as a storehouse of the ancient Egyptian's advanced knowledge of geography and astronomy, and that this knowledge is coded into the measurements of its sides, edges, height, and so forth; that it was constructed as a granary during the time of Joseph's sojourn in Egypt; and that it contains coded into the proportions of the internal chambers a corroboration of the Bible. Most of these theories were started in the seventeenth or eighteenth centuries, and some persist to this day. The simple truth is that the Great Pyramid—an architectural wonder constructed with astounding precision—is not magical. Its Old Kingdom name—"Cheops is one belonging to the horizon"—clearly indicates its funerary purpose. It means that the pharaoh, when placed in the pyramid, was considered to have "gone west."

The Great Pyramid was the high point of pyramid building

FIGURE 28. An early nineteenth-century engraving shows the Great Pyramid *(left)* and the pyramid of Kephren *(right)* at the time of Napoleon's campaign through Egypt.

(Figure 28). When complete (the capstone and top courses are gone), it was more than 480 feet high. The base covers more than thirteen acres, its corners are almost perfect right angles, and the sides are oriented to the four cardinal points. It is composed of more than two million limestone blocks averaging two and one-half tons each. It was once covered with fine white Tura limestone, quarried nearby. Most amazing is the precision of its construction. From corner to corner, no two sides differ by more than eight inches, and the elevation at the base never varies by more than one inch. While externally the Great Pyramid complex is similar to the Meidum Pyramid, having a valley temple, causeway, and mortuary temple, the interior is unique and not fully understood.

The entrance to the pyramid is on the north side. Once concealed by the limestone casing, this entrance is now exposed. It opens onto a small passageway—only about four feet high and three and one-half feet wide—that goes down through the pyramid and into the bedrock a total distance of about 350 feet. Called the

Descending Passageway, it ends in a small unfinished chamber. This probably was originally intended to be the burial chamber but was left unfinished. It is called the Queen's Chamber because of its vaulted ceiling; modern Arabs bury their women in tombs with such roofs. Another passage, the Ascending Passageway, tunnels upward from this chamber. At its top is a horizontal corridor leading to the middle of the pyramid and ending in a small chamber with a pointed ceiling. This room, too, was abandoned before it was completed, and at the point where the Ascending Passageway becomes horizontal, a new upward sloping passage begins. This type of passage is unprecedented, and no one is certain of its purpose. Called the Grand Gallery, it is 128 feet high and 153 feet long (Figure 29). Why the fantastic height was needed, no one can guess. At its termination is a low short passage to the King's Chamber. This room is seventeen feet high and approximately seventeen by thirty-four feet. The only object found there in modern times is an unmarked stone sarcophagus, slightly larger than the entrance. It must have been brought in prior to completion of the upper causeway of the pyramid.

Of all the aspects of the Great Pyramid's construction, the Descending Passageway is the most precise. Its angle is 26° 17', a measurement possibly chosen for religious or magical reasons. When Sir Flinders Petrie surveyed the passage, he found that the height never varied by more than one tenth of an inch and the width by more than one fourth of an inch. The reason for this precision is that it aligns exactly with the celestial north pole. This point in the sky may have been of special significance to the Egyptians, since it alone appears permanent, with all other stars revolving around it. These revolving stars were called "indestructibles," and one pyramid text says that the dead king ascends to heaven to join the "indestructible stars." Therefore, the king in his burial chamber must have had some relationship with the celestial north pole. Another reason the Descending Passageway may have been so precisely aligned with celestial north is that this point could have been used as a bearing to survey the accuracy of the pyramid as it was being built.

One of the Great Pyramid's most famous visitors, who apparently believed in its magical properties, was Napoleon. On August 12, 1797, Napoleon entered the Great Pyramid and asked to be left

FIGURE 29. A nineteenth-century engraving shows the vaulted construction of the Grand Gallery in the Great Pyramid.

alone in the burial chamber. When he came out, an aide, noticing that his emperor was pale, jokingly asked if he had had a mystical experience. Napoleon replied that he had no comment and, further, that he never wanted the incident mentioned again. Later, on St. Helena, he is reported to have been on the verge of divulging his experience inside the pyramid, but apparently having second thoughts, he said, "No. What's the use. You'd never believe me."

Near the Great Pyramid are several deep pits that once held boats the pharaoh would need for his journey to the next world. These have been empty since antiquity, undoubtedly robbed for the wood, a valuable commodity in tree-barren Egypt. However, in 1954 an intact boat-pit was discovered, containing a complete, dismantled 143-foot boat in a perfect state of preservation. This may have been the very boat that ferried the body of the king across the Nile to the valley temple, or it may have been buried so that Khufu would have transportation to the next world. If the boat was intended to have this latter magical purpose, it is difficult to imagine exactly what the Egyptians believed would happen. Would the boat actually leave the pit and journey through the sky? Perhaps it was the model of a spiritual double of the boat that would make the journey unseen. When the intact boat-pit was discovered a second one also was found nearby. It seems to contain a similar boat, but has been left sealed for future generations to excavate when preservation techniques are more advanced.

Khufu's successor, his son Re-Djedef, chose to build his pyramid at Abu Rawwash about five miles north of Giza. Re-Djedef did not reign for very long and was succeeded by Khaef-Re (whom the Greeks called "Chephren"), his brother who built the second of the three large pyramids at Giza. It is curious that, in an era when each pharaoh attempted to outdo his predecessor, Khaef-Re built his pyramid smaller than Khufu's. Possibly, he did this out of respect for his father. There is some evidence that his brother Re-Djedef did not esteem their father and for that reason chose to build his pyramid away from Giza.

The most unique aspect of Khaef-Re's pyramid complex is the Sphinx, a huge, recumbent lion with the head of Khaef-Re. The statue is more than sixty-five feet high and 240 feet long and has been the subject of considerable speculation. Its inclusion in the complex seems to have been more of an afterthought than part of the plan. When Khufu's workmen were quarrying the stones for the inside of Khufu's pyramid, they left behind a huge outcropping of rock in the nearby quarry. Later, Khaef-Re's workmen, encountering the rock in the midst of their building site, carved it into the Sphinx.

Occultists attribute the Sphinx with great mystical significance:

> . . . the Sphinx's ambivalent form was a device invented by the priests of the Old Kingdom as a secret sign, understood only by the initiates, to symbolise the priesthood itself and its guardianship of the cosmic mysteries enshrined in the Pyramid to which they alone possessed the secret clues.[3]

The Greeks, certainly, believed the Sphinx to be a symbol of occult wisdom. Also, the medieval Arab writer, Abd-al Latif, says that the Sphinx is rarely discussed because it inspires terror. To this day, Egyptians living in the village nearby, call it *Abu Khawl,* "father of terror." There is an entire line of Freudian interpretation based on the mistaken belief that the Sphinx is the figure of a woman. In spite of all these magical and occult interpretations of the meaning and origin of the Sphinx, the simple truth is that it ultimately was the result of the workmen's decision to carve the huge rock rather than move it. So surrounded is the Sphinx by even factual error that one of the best modern guidebooks on Egypt, *Nagel's Encyclopedia Guide: Egypt,* is not without fallacy: ". . . the nose is now in the British Museum." [4] No one knows where the nose is. It probably was worn away by erosion.

As Abd-al Latif points out, during long stretches of history the Sphinx is not mentioned. Herodotus, describing his visit to the pyramids, never mentions the Sphinx. Probably he never saw it. Periodically, the Sphinx has been covered over with sand. In fact, as recently as 1925, the Service of Antiquities has had to dig it out (Figures 30, 31).

Khaef-Re's successor, Men-Kau-Re (whom the Greeks called Mycerinus) built a much smaller pyramid (Figure 32) which was obviously unfinished at the time of his death. Herodotus offers an explanation as to the pharaoh's premature death.

FIGURE 30. After centuries of burial, the lower quarters of the Great Sphinx were freed from the sand by the Service of Antiquities in 1925.

FIGURE 31. The alabaster sphinx of Memphis, buried in the sand for centuries, is now eroded on one side. Photograph by Barbara Benton

FIGURE 32. Early drawings of the Giza pyramids almost always represented them too small and too steep. In this eighteenth-century engraving, they are also too numerous.

An oracle reached him from the town of Buto, which said, 'Six years only shalt thou live upon this earth, and in the seventh thou shalt end thy days.' Mycerinus, indignant, sent an angry message to the oracle, reproaching the god with his injustice—'My father and uncle,' he said, 'though they shut up the temples, took no thought of the gods, and destroyed multitudes of men, nevertheless enjoyed a long life; I, who am pious, am to die so soon!' There came in reply a second message from the oracle—'For this very reason is thy life brought so quickly to a close—thou hast not done as it behooved thee. Egypt was fated to suffer affliction one hundred and fifty years—the two kings who preceded thee upon the throne understood this—thou has not understood it.' Mycerinus, when this answer reached him, perceiving that his doom was fixed, had lamps prepared, which he lighted every day at eventime, and feasted and enjoyed himself unceasingly both day and night, moving about in the marsh-country and the woods, and visiting all the places that he heard were agreeable sojourns. His wish was to prove the oracle false, by turning the nights into days, and so living twelve years in the space of six.[5]

Men-Kau-Re's successor, Shepseskaf, the last king of the Fourth Dynasty, departed from tradition and was not buried in a pyramid, but in a *mastaba* shaped like a sarcophagus. One reason has been suggested for this change: The three successors of Khufu—Re-Djedef, Khaef-Re, and Men-Kau-Re—all had their names compounded with that of Re, the sun god. It is striking that, not only did Shepseskaf not build a pyramid, he also did not compound his name with Re. This name change which publicly announced a religious break may have signified deep differences. Therefore, it resulted in the cessation of pyramid building.

The founder of the Fifth Dynasty, Sabu-Re, returned to building pyramids, but on a much smaller scale than those of the Fourth Dynasty. His complex had a unique feature which may have been magical. The roofed portions of the complex were decorated with stone spouts in the shape of lions' heads. Rain falling on the roofs would run into these spouts and out the lions' mouths. One expert suggests: "This type of gargoyle may have been chosen because rain was sometimes regarded as a manifestation of Seth and other hostile gods who were thus consumed and expectorated, after being rendered harmless, by the lion, the protector of sacred places." [6]

The last king of the Fifth Dynasty, Unas, began a very important and truly magical pyramid tradition. Located at Saqqara, his pyramid is, on the outside, quite like those of the other kings of the Fifth Dynasty. On the inside, however, the walls are covered with hundreds of magical inscriptions. The hieroglyphs are colored blue so that they stand out clearly against the white limestone. There are long vertical lines from ceiling to floor separating each column of hieroglyphs, each column forming a separate unit called "an utterance" by the Egyptians. These inscriptions are called the "Pyramid Texts." They are spells that deal primarily with three stages in a king's resurrection: (1) his awakening in the pyramid; (2) his ascending through the sky to the netherworld; and (3) his admittance into the company of the gods. There is no clear logical order to the spells, so Egyptologists disagree about the order in which they should be read. Most believe that the spells are intended to be read from the antechamber inward, concluding with the burial chamber. This order is logical if the spells were to be recited by the priests at the time that the body of the pharaoh was carried into the burial chamber. In any case, the magical principle behind all the texts is the same: The word is the deed. Saying something, or having it inscribed on the pyramid wall, made it so. So important is magic in these texts that in Unas' pyramid one of the first spells on the entrance to the antechamber states, "Unas does not give you his magical power." [7]

The spells state that in the second stage of the king's resurrection, he ascends to heaven in a variety of ways (a type of overstatement on the theory that, if one does not work, another will). He flies:

> The Opener of the Ways has let Unas fly towards heaven amongst his brothers, the gods. Unas has moved his arms as a *smn*-goose, he has beaten with his wings like a kite. He flies up, he who flies up, ye men. Unas [also flies up] away from you.[8]

He rises on incense:

> The earth is beaten into steps for him towards heaven, that he may mount on it towards heaven, and he rises on the smoke of the great fumigation.[9]

He ascends by a ladder, helped by Re and Horus:

> The ladder is tied together by Re before Osiris. The ladder is tied together by Horus before his father Osiris when he goes to his spirit. One of them is on this side, one of them is on that side, while Unas is between them.[10]

If Unas' wings tire, the ladder breaks, and the incense does not reach to heaven, then he can ride there, ferried across by the ferrymen who transport the gods:

> Awake in peace, Thou-Whose-Face-Is-Behind, in peace, Thou-Who-Lookest-Behind, in peace, Ferryman of the Sky, in peace, Ferryman of Nut, in peace, Ferryman of the Gods, in peace.
> Unas comes to thee, that thou mayest ferry him in that ferryboat in which thou ferried the gods.[11]

Once Unas has made it to the next world, there are spells to assure that he is welcomed into the company of the gods:

> Thou standest [there as a king], ruling over them [the gods] as Geb rules over his Ennead. They come in, they strike down evil [with magical spells]; they come out, their faces are lifted up. They see thee as Min, who rules over the two shrines. He stands, who stands

behind thee; thy brother stands behind thee; thy relative stands behind thee; thou goest not under, thou wilt not be annihilated, thy
name remains with men, thy name comes into being with the gods.[12]

Outside Unas' pyramid was a mortuary temple where priests were
supposed to make offerings of food for the sustenance of the dead
pharaoh's soul. Part of the prayer these priests had to recite each
day is on one of the walls of the burial chamber. In case the priests
do not do their jobs, the written word will be an adequate substitute:

> O Unas, stand up, sit down to the thousand loaves of bread, the
> thousand jars of beer. The roast of thy double rib is from the slaugh-
> ter house, thy *retch*-bread is from the Wide Hall. As a god is supplied
> with the offering meal, Unas is supplied with this his bread.[13]

This offering text was considered crucial throughout Egyptian history. The ancient Egyptians knew by the experiences of previous
generations that the priests were fallible. Setting up a fund to pay
the priests to make the offerings did not guarantee that they would
do it. Often an Egyptian would have the offering prayer inscribed
on the outside of his tomb so a passerby could see it. Also inscribed
would be a plea to the passerby to recite the prayer and so assure
that the deceased would have food.

The pyramid of Unas was named "Beautiful are the places of
Unas." While it is not nearly so large as many of the other pyramids, the interior, with its thousands of beautifully carved hieroglyphs, far surpasses the interior of any other pyramid. Visitors to
the Great Pyramid often remark that it is amazing that such a
structure was built in one lifetime; it is equally amazing that the
pyramid of Unas was built in one lifetime.

Unas' successors, the royalty of the Sixth Dynasty, continued
the practice of building relatively small pyramids with magical
texts inscribed on the interiors. These pharaohs added to the Pyramid Texts whatever new spells their priests determined were essential.

The consecration text of Pepi I makes clear the purpose of the
pyramids for the Egyptians:

> I consecrate this pyramid and this temple to Pepi and his Ka. What
> this pyramid and this temple contain is for Pepi and for his Ka. Pure
> is the Eye of Horus.[14]

So it was that the pyramid was to house the body of the dead king and his *Ka*. The name of Pepi's pyramid suggests that this house for eternity was an important step in the pharaoh's resurrection: "Pepi is established and beautiful." The name of Pepi II's pyramid suggests an even more crucial function: "Pepi is established and alive." The name of his pyramid, by magic, assures that the king is alive.

While the most plausible explanation for the pyramid shape is that it was an architectural development devoid of any initial magical significance, some pyramid scholars still attempt to explain the shape in terms of deep magico-religious meanings.

James Henry Breasted believed that the pyramid was an imitation of the *benben*, the sun-god symbol kept in the holy of holies at Heliopolis. But this stone was probably somewhat more conical than pyramidical, and to view the pyramid as a similar shape seems a bit far-fetched, especially when one remembers that the first pyramids were stepped rather than true pyramids. If, indeed, there was any magical significance given to the pyramid shape it was done after the fact. The Pyramid Texts probably give the best indication of what this significance was.

The step pyramid may have represented the stairs by which the pharaoh would ascend to heaven. Spell 267 of the Pyramid Texts says that a staircase to heaven is constructed for the king so that he may go up to the heavens. In support of this, it has been pointed out by I.E.S. Edwards that the word for "ascend" is determined by the sign ⌂ , which has usually been assumed to represent a double stairway, but which might just as well be a step pyramid.

Other spells of the Pyramid Texts suggest a similar magical significance for the true pyramid. They mention the rays of the sun as being a ramp to the heavens. Here the pyramid may be associated, by magic, with the sun's rays. As anyone who has spent some time in Cairo will affirm, it is not unusual to see on a cloudy day the sun's rays bent at almost the precise angle of the sides of the pyramids, forming a natural pyramid in the sky.

The end of the Old Kingdom marked the end of the pyramid era—nothing like them would ever be built again in Egypt. Middle Kingdom pharaohs returned to pyramids, but these were mud-brick buildings cased with limestone. They have not withstood the centuries, and today, from a short distance, they look much like natural hills. One pyramid of the Middle Kingdom is worth discussing, however, for two reasons. It illustrates several magical practices of the Middle Kingdom, and it is the only royal pyramid ever found with the burial chamber body intact. (The burial chamber of the king Horus-Sekhem-Khet was found intact, but without the body.)

The pyramid of the princess Neferuptah, daughter of Amenemhet III, was discovered in 1955. Most of the limestone casing had been quarried, and the mud-brick interior had collapsed. In the middle of the pyramid, at ground level, were seven large limestone blocks, each fifteen feet long, which covered the underground burial chamber. When, in April of 1956, the limestone blocks were removed, the burial chamber was found to be half full of water. It is a rectangular room, about eight feet high, five feet wide, and fifteen feet long. It had been hewn out of the bedrock, then lined with limestone. About two feet from the north wall was a limestone partition, a foot thick, five feet long, and seven feet high. On one side of the partition was a huge red granite sarcophagus with the princess' name inscribed on the side.

There were an offering table and pottery vases. The offering table, in the shape of the *hotep* hieroglyph, ▵ , represents an offering on a table. An inscription along the side of the table is intended to assure that the offerings will be made by the king to the gods so that Neferuptah will be treated well:

> May the king grant a wish to Anubis, Toth, Osiris, the great and small Enneads of the sanctuary of Upper and Lower Egypt. [May the offering be] thousands of loaves of bread, jars of beer, oxen, *r*-geese, *tcherp*-geese, *zeb*-geese, *ser*-geese, *menweb*-geese, alabaster jars, clothing, incense, and ointments, and all good things upon which a god lives for the *ka* of the king's daughter, Neferuptah, true of voice, lady of veneration.

The vases were of the kind used in a purification ceremony in tombs. They would have been used to pour Nile water on the earth under the offering table, on the hands of a kneeling priest, and then probably on the offering table as well.

The sarcophagus was more than nine feet long, cut from one piece of stone, as was the lid. It was almost entirely full of water. After the water was siphoned off, it was discovered that all the remains at the bottom of the sarcophagus were only three inches high. In addition to some small jars, there were beads of faience and carnelian, pieces of silver, and other ornaments—undoubtedly the funerary jewelry of the princess—but her body had almost totally dissolved in the water in which it had been immersed for thousands of years. The jewelry has been reconstructed. It appears that the princess wore a broad collar, a necklace, a bead girdle, bracelets, and anklets. It is interesting that the hieroglyphs for "bracelets" and "anklets" are 〔 symbols 〕 , and 〔 symbols 〕 (*irt ewy* and *irt idwy*, which mean "to protect the arms" and "to protect the legs"). Originally, they probably were intended more to protect the princess by magic than to adorn her body.

Originally, there were gold bands with hieroglyphic inscriptions around the sarcophagus. The animal hieroglyphs are mutilated—such as birds with no legs and reptiles with no tails. This was a Middle Kingdom practice instituted out of the fear that, by magic, the animal hieroglyphs might come to life, run away, and spoil the text! For similar reasons, when a man was buried in his tomb with bows and arrows, they were frequently broken for fear that they would turn on their owner.

After the pyramids of the Middle Kingdom, there was yet a further degeneration of the pyramid form. Around 700 B.C. the Nubian kings of the Twenty-fifth Dynasty renewed the practice, constructing numerous pyramids in the Sudan for themselves and for their queens. These pyramids are quite small, some no more than thirty feet square at the base, with extremely steep sides. Today they all stand with their tops truncated. In the early part of the eighteenth century a traveler discovered gold hidden at the top of one of them and proceeded to decapitate all the others in an unsuccessful search for more treasure. These pyramids are the end of more than two thousand years of pyramid building.

7. The Coffin Texts

UNDOUBTEDLY ANY EGYPTIAN, royal or not, would want assurance of a safe journey to the next world, but the Pyramid Texts were for royalty only. Since they were carved inside the sealed pyramid, they were not accessible to the commoner. During the Old Kingdom there was little comparison between the spells carved inside the pyramids and carvings on the walls of the tombs of the nobility, which may suggest that the magical spells were a carefully guarded secret of the priests.

With the collapse of the Old Kingdom and the period of lawlessness that followed—the First Intermediate Period—the pyramids were opened by robbers. Perhaps it was at this point that the Pyramid Texts became known to more than just the priests. The First Intermediate Period lasted for about fifty years (2180–2134 B.C.). Little remains from this time. When Egypt reestablished stability in the Eleventh Dynasty, a new custom arose. The nobility began placing magical spells on their coffins. Because these spells are so similar to the Pyramid Texts, it has been suggested that the impetus for the new custom was the opening of the pyramids.

In the Old Kingdom, sarcophagi and coffins were viewed primarily as houses for the deceased. They were usually rectangular, and false doors were often painted on the outside to imitate the facade of a palace. The lids were so heavy that they had to be raised and lowered into position with ropes. Often holes were drilled in them for that purpose.

Usually, the sarcophagus and lid were sealed by a thin layer of cement along the edges. These sarcophagi were sparsely decorated, merely imitating the earthly house of the deceased. The difference between a sarcophagus and a coffin is mainly the material of which each is made. One fits inside the other. The inner is made of wood, the outer of stone. The Egyptian name for the outer stone coffin was *neb-ankh,* or "lord of life," since its function was to protect the inner coffin.

Ironically, the Greeks called such a container a *sarcophagus,* or "flesh-eater," because those sarcophagi made of limestone reacted chemically with the body and ate away at it. An interesting example of this kind of sarcophagus is in the Metropolitan Museum of Art in New York City. It belonged to an Eleventh Dynasty priestess named Henhenet. The sarcophagus is unusual in that it is made up of six limestone slabs which fit together (Figure 33). It is sparsely decorated. The inscription in the illustration asks that a boon be granted by the king to the god Anubis so that Henhenet will be provided for.

An example of an elaborate New Kingdom sarcophagus is that of the Pharaoh Seti I. Discovered in 1815 and taken to London, this sarcophagus is almost ten feet long and is inscribed with texts on

FIGURE 33. The limestone sarcophagus of the priestess Henhenet is constructed, like a jigsaw puzzle, out of six interlocking limestone slabs. The Metropolitan Museum of Art

both the inside and outside surfaces describing the journey of the sun god through the twelve hours of the night. In the Middle Kingdom, by far the most popular coffin was the wooden rectangular one. At times these coffins were highly decorated, both inside and out. Frequently, the interiors were painted much like a tomb wall, with representations of the deceased seated in front of rows of offerings. These coffins are important for historical reasons, as often they show jewelry, jars, food, and other objects in realistic detail, and so provide us with knowledge of daily life in ancient Egypt.

One feature common to most Middle Kingdom coffins was the double *udjat*-eye (Figure 34). Two *Eyes-of-Horus* were painted on the outside of the coffin so that the deceased could look out. Interestingly, the eyes usually were painted on the panel of the coffin facing east, not west as might be expected. Because the world of the dead was west, this shows that the Egyptians were not totally oriented toward death, but wanted to maintain contact with the land of the living.

The gods of the Egyptians were called upon to protect the coffin and its contents. Each had his or her specified place on the coffin dictated by religious ritual. The lid of the coffin was called

FIGURE 34. The House Mistress Senebtisy was able to look out of her coffin through two painted Eyes-of-Horus. The Metropolitan Museum of Art, Museum Excavations 1906–1907; Rogers Fund, 1908

the *sky*, so it is not surprising that Nut, the goddess of the sky, the "Coverer-of-Heaven," is called upon to protect the deceased. Nut swallows and protects the sun each night and gives birth to him again in the morning. Metaphorically, she was expected to give the same protection and rebirth to the deceased. Frequently, the inside of the coffin would have a picture of her stretching her arms out as she does in the heavens. The corners of the rectangular coffin were guarded by the four sons of Horus. Amset and Hapi were by the shoulders, while Qebesenef and Duamutef were by the feet. The side panels might be protected by Osiris, "Foremost-of-the-Westerners," on one side and Anubis, "He-who-is-before-the-divine-embalming-tent," on the other. If these gods were not enough, across the head and foot panels of the coffin invocations might be written to Isis, wife of Osiris, and Nephthys, her sister.

Perhaps the most important feature of these coffins of the Eleventh and Twelfth dynasties was the magical spells written on them. These spells, which have become known as the "Coffin Texts," are really a link between the Pyramid Texts and the *Book of the Dead*. Many Coffin Texts are obvious variants of the Pyramid Texts. Their concern is basically the same, the well-being of the deceased. Eventually, these texts would become so numerous and complex that they would not fit on a coffin. This led to their being written on papyrus, which became known as the *Book of the Dead*. There was, then, a rather orderly literary progression from Pyramid Texts to Coffin Texts to the *Book of the Dead*.

Like the Pyramid Texts which preceded them and the *Book of the Dead* which followed, the Coffin Texts have no real structure. They are merely a collection of diverse spells designed to bring about specific effects. Because the spells were written on the limited space of coffin panels (Figure 35), frequently words or entire sentences were omitted, making them rather difficult to translate. The late Egyptologist, Adriaan De Buck, devoted more than thirty years to collecting all known Coffin Texts. They were published, untranslated, in seven huge volumes by the Oriental Institute of the University of Chicago. The layman may wonder what was the purpose of publishing only a hieroglyphic transcription of the texts, but this was a great service. It made available to Egyptologists around the world texts which would have taken them a lifetime to amass. Recently, using De Buck's transcriptions, R.O. Faulkner

FIGURE 35. Coffin Texts line the interior of the coffin of Gua, a high official of the Middle Kingdom. Reproduced by courtesy of the Trustees of the British Museum

translated the entire body of Coffin Texts, making these unique spells available to everyone.

There are more than a thousand coffin spells, but many are repetitious. One theme that emerges from them is magic. Magic or the magician's power is mentioned specifically in more than one hundred of the spells, and it is clear that to survive in the next world magic had to be used effectively. There are two aspects to the role of magic in the Coffin Texts, one negative, one positive. One intention of the spells is to assure that the deceased will not be harmed by those who might work malicious magic on him. This is why the spells frequently contain the phrase: "I will not listen to magic," [1] or,

> ". . . my soul shall not be seized by magic . . . I have caused their dignities to pass away, I have destroyed their magic, I have cut off their powers." [2]

Aside from evil magic being worked on the deceased, there was also the fear that the deceased's magical powers would be taken from him by a god in the guise of a crocodile. To combat this evil, there is a spell entitled: "Driving off a Crocodile which Draws Near in Order to Take Away a Man's Magic from Him." The spell involved first a certain protective incantation and then a dialogue with the crocodile. The deceased is given the last word:

> Get back! Go away! Get back you dangerous one! Do not come upon me, do not live by magic! May I not have to tell this name of yours to the great god who let you come: "Messenger" is the name of one and *Bedjet* is the name of one.

> *The crocodile speaks:* Your face is towards righteousness. The sky encloses the stars, magic encloses its settlements, and this mouth of mine encloses the magic which is in it. My teeth are flint, my tusks are the Cerastes Mountain.
> *The deceased replies:* O you with a spine who would work your mouth against this magic of mine, do not take it away, O crocodile which lives by magic.[3]

Not all references to magic in the Coffin Texts are negative. Many are intended to assert the deceased's magical abilities. The phrase most frequently used in connection with the deceased having magical powers is, ". . . I have filled my belly with magic. . . ." [4]

Indeed, the dominant metaphor for having magic seems to involve eating. In one spell the deceased says, "I am a soul who eats his navel-string. . . ." [5] Perhaps it was believed that the umbilical cord contained magical powers. Eating it gave the eater powers and kept the power from others who might devour it. It may be that the Egyptians believed certain plants (drugs) gave them magical powers. One coffin text says, ". . . and I will eat magic in the Barks of Assembly." [6] One spell has the deceased say that he eats the magic and powers of other magicians, a kind of supernatural cannibalism:

> And there are no potentates who shall act by des-
> troying
> My favourite place in the whole of the Two Lands.
> I eat of their magic,
> I gulp down their powers,
> My strength in me is more than theirs.
> Their powers are within me,
> Their souls are with me,
> Their shades are with their lords,
> Their magic is in my belly. . . .[7]

Obtaining and keeping magical powers was crucial to the deceased. It was by these powers that he could fend off opponents in the next world, open sealed passages that hindered his entrance to the West, and appear as a worthy comrade to the gods. The power of magic is summed up in one of the names of the possessor of magical abilities: "If-he-wishes-he-does." The deceased who has that title is told to say:

> I have come to take possession of my throne and that I may receive my dignity, for to me belonged all before you had come into being, you gods; go down and come upon the hinder parts, for I am a magician.[8]

Just being a magician, without using the power, will enable the deceased to pass by the various guardians to the netherworld. At various points in the crossing he will be asked, "Who are you?" The answer that will admit him is, "I am a magician."

Aside from eating other magicians' powers, there are other ways the deceased will obtain magical ability. It will be brought to him by mysterious characters known as the "porters of Horus."

These porters, who brought Horus his magic, are commanded to do the same for the deceased. Interestingly, while they bring (magical) knowledge, they also have the power to make one forget things it is better to forget:

> O you porters of Horus who bring the magic of Horus to him as his great protection, bring the magic of Horus to him as his great protection, and bring this magic of mine to me wherever I may be; tell me what I should know and what I should forget. . . .[9]

It is knowledge of magic that protects the deceased from all enemies:

> Mighty is the fear of you, great is the awe of you, mighty is your striking-power, great is your magic in the bodies of your foes, and the hostile ones have fallen on their faces because of you. . . .[10]

It is knowledge of magic which creates passageways to the next world:

> . . . beware, O you who guard the ways in the northern sky; prepare a path for me so that I may pass on it, for I am your head-man. My magic spells are on my mouth, and I have power over my foes who are in the Island of Fire, so that I pass unharmed.[11]

Because of the crucial role of magic, the Egyptians wanted to be sure that once they had power they would not lose it. It is thus typical of the Egyptians, in their encyclopaedic listing of things desired, that they included a spell to ensure that magic not be stolen (". . . magic power is in my body and it will not be stolen." [12]) and that it will not be forgotten (". . . I have called to mind all the magic which is in my belly." [13]).

For some of the spells in the Coffin Texts, the words alone were not adequate for the desired effect and instructions were provided as to *how* the incantation was to be spoken. While relatively rare, these instructions do give us a fuller picture of the way the Egyptians believed magic worked.

Several of the Coffin Texts were designed to help the deceased overcome his foes. Spell 37 ends with the phrase, "May you break and overthrow your foes and set them under your sandals." Instructions written at the end of the spell specify that the words were to be spoken over a wax figure of the enemy and that his name was to be incised on the heart with the bone of a synodontis fish. This is a clear case of sympathetic magic; what happens to the figure will happen to the foe, as the last line of the spell suggests.

The use of figures was quite common in Egypt. Many spells specify that the figure is to be made of wax. Wax was specified not because it was a magically potent substance, but merely because it was easily fashioned into whatever shape was desired. At times the effigies used for magical spells were rather elaborate. One which the author recently unwrapped (Figure 36) was made of two sticks tied together to form a cross. These sticks were padded with coarse cloth to give them the general shape of a person, and then three small tunics of three different kinds of cloth were tied on the figure. The purpose of using three different cloths is not known, but undoubtedly there was some magical reason.

At times the spells were to be recited over images of the gods. Spell 81 states that it was to be recited over the figures of the eight primordial gods, who were in the waters of chaos, and that it was to be written on the hands of the images with yellow pigment and Nubian ochre. This was to be washed off the figures early in the morning. Perhaps the strangest instruction of all the spells is one requiring a man to intone the spell over a louse taken from his head. He was to place it on his knee and spit until a fly came and snatched the louse! [14]

One of the most curious facts about the Coffin Texts is that, while many gods were named and invoked, Osiris, the god of the

FIGURE 36. Effigies were constructed of sticks, cloth, and twine. This figure was wrapped with three kinds of cloth. Photograph by Russell Rudzwick

dead, whom one would expect to be the most important, was not the most prominent of the gods mentioned. Shu, the air god, seems to be the most important in the texts.

According to one Egyptian version of creation, in the beginning there was a watery chaos in which eight gods lived. These gods that lived in the primordial waters called Nu were not typical Egyptian gods in that they had negative attributes indicative of the chaos. They were the gods of darkness, hiddenness, formlessness, etc. Out of the waters arose a self-created god, Atum. By masturbation he created two gods, Shu and Tefnet. Shu, the male, was air while Tefnet, the female, was moisture. In some sense Shu had a claim to being the first god on earth, since before him there were only the eight of the watery abyss and Atum, the self-created one. But this primacy would not explain why Shu should feature so prominently in the Coffin Texts. The explanation for this is probably his role as air. The Egyptians believed that to reach the netherworld one had to travel through the sky. For this reason, Shu would be crucial. One very short spell states, "I have gone up in Shu, I have climbed on the sunbeams." [15] The instruction after this spell states that it was to be recited when the deceased went forth: ". . . so that his heart may endure in every shape in which one wishes to go forth, and that he may ejaculate his seed safely on earth, his heir existing forever. His soul shall not be seized, nor shall his shade be snared. A matter a million times true."

Shu was not viewed merely as the medium by which the deceased ascended to the next world. Because he supported the sky, he was also a symbol of strength. This is why the deceased also wanted to be identified with Shu: "I am strong as Shu is strong, I am hale as Shu is hale, I am beneath the sky, I strengthen its light, I command the bulls to forget the cows." [16]

The focusing of the Coffin Texts on Shu, rather than on Osiris, illustrates a peculiarity of the spells. They are more concerned with the journey than with the arrival. Surprisingly little in the Coffin Texts deals with the next world. It is almost as if the Egyptians were merely concerned with avoiding the perils that might end the journey or reduce their powers; once they arrived in the West they would be safe.

During the period of the Coffin Texts, the Middle Kingdom, mummies were often covered with a mask intended to protect the

face of the deceased. By the New Kingdom this mask developed
into the anthropoid coffin, shaped realistically like the human body
and serving as an envelope for the corpse. These coffins, while
stylized, were often of extraordinary beauty. Frequently, the goddess Isis and her sister Nephthys are on the lid of the coffin, spread-
ing their wings in protection of the deceased as they did for Osiris.
On such coffins the deceased is almost always represented as wearing a beaded collar or pectoral with terminals in the shape of
Horus, the falcon. (During the later periods actual collars and
shrouds of beads covered the mummy. Figure 37.) Some of the most
beautiful of these New Kingdom coffins were made not of wood,
but of cartonage, which is linen dipped in plaster which was
molded, then painted. This medium gave the artists even more
flexibility than wood. Such coffins were costly and would have been
made primarily for royalty and nobility. For the commoner there
was the less expensive alternative of clay coffins which were always
available from the potter.

Just as there were changes in the shape of the coffin from the
Middle to the New Kingdom, there were changes in the text which
accompanied it. The Coffin Texts were a relatively short-lived phenomenon, being in vogue primarily during the Middle Kingdom.
With the advent of the New Kingdom, they were replaced by
something far more elaborate, the *Book of the Dead*.

FIGURE 37. Shrouds woven entirely of thousands of tiny disk-beads were draped over
the mummy for magical protection.

8. The Book of the Dead

OF ALL THE MAGICAL OBJECTS an ancient Egyptian would want, perhaps the most important was the *Book of the Dead*. The *Book of the Dead* is not really an accurate title. It was not a single work but rolls of papyrus recording roughly similar material, of which hundreds of versions have been found. Collectively, they are known under the title the *Book of the Dead*. These papyrus rolls were not books in the sense of coherent works having a central theme steadily developed. Rather, they contained a collection of spells, incantations, prayers, hymns, and rituals. The various papyri contain in all about two hundred different spells that have been given standard chapter numbers so that, for example, any spell dealing with the heart not opposing the deceased would be called Chapter 30.

The *Book of the Dead* is an outgrowth and logical development from two earlier practices—Pyramid Texts and Coffin Texts. While the Pyramid Texts were magical spells for the pharaohs only, the Coffin Texts were for anyone who could afford a coffin with magical inscriptions. The problem with placing the spells on the coffins was that space was limited, and eventually there were so many different spells intended to protect the deceased that they could not all fit. Thus, in the New Kingdom, the *Book of the Dead* came into existence, enabling the deceased to have copies of those texts which would not fit on his coffin.

Scribes prepared for eager customers papyrus rolls having spells for protection, instruction on how to behave when being judged in the next world, how to avoid working in the next world, how to get your body working again, and so forth. In general, the *Book of the Dead* dealt with several different phases of the deceased's existence. The important stages were: 1) the protection of the body in the tomb; 2) the journey to the netherworld; 3) the judgment by the gods; 4) existence in the next world, once accepted by the gods.

The *Book of the Dead* was a major industry in Egypt and as in all industries, quality varied considerably. Some of the books were as long as ninety feet and had beautiful colored paintings illustrating the different spells. Others were rather brief and had no illustrations at all. Frequently, the books would be written before there was an intended customer, with places for the deceased's name left blank. These are the first "forms" in history. After the purchase the proper name would be filled in by a scribe. Because these papyri were drawn up before the owner was known, sometimes the language is general: "Ask the local god of your town for protection."

Often, apparently, the scribes did not fully understand what they were writing or were extremely careless: Sometimes the same spell or chapter is repeated twice in the same papyrus. Perhaps two scribes were simultaneously working on the same *Book of the Dead* and, unknown to each other, they copied the same chapter. Later, when the various sections of the papyrus were joined, the errors were not noticed.

Another common problem was that at times the artist was called in first to do the illustrations on the top of the papyrus sheets (Figure 38) and then the scribes would write in the appropriate text. Frequently, the artist did not leave enough space for the scribe to enter the entire spell, so the books often contain chapters that are severely abbreviated or condensed, sometimes to the point of being unintelligible. In spite of all these difficulties with translating and understanding the *Book of the Dead,* these papyri reveal a great deal about the magical beliefs of the ancient Egyptians, especially concerning life after death.

While about two hundred different spells or chapters appear in the various copies of the *Book of the Dead,* and there is no fixed order in which they appear, marked similarities have been found among the many discovered copies. From these similarities it is possible to determine several geographical areas where differing versions were produced. The most important version is what is known as the Theban Recension of the *Book of the Dead.* During the Eighteenth Dynasty the nobility of Thebes were buried with

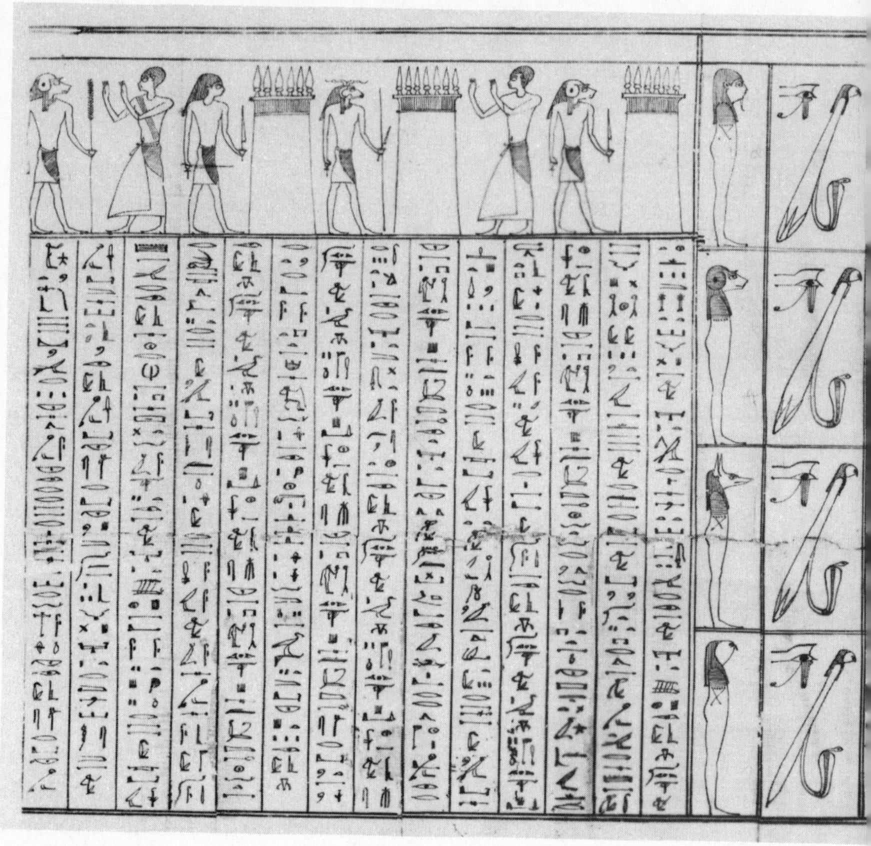

FIGURE 38. In this section of the *Book of the Dead* of the priest Nes-Min, the artist who drew the vignettes, as was often the case, did not work closely with the scribe who copied the text;

the *Book of the Dead*—usually found between the legs of the mummy. These papyrus rolls were almost always written in black hieroglyphs running from top to bottom, with the lines of the text separated from each other by thin black lines. Across the top of the papyrus sheets were drawings illustrating how the deceased wanted to be treated in the next world.

The actual title of these books was 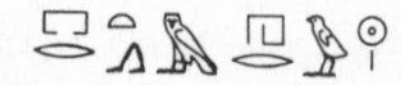, which means "The Going Forth by Day." The exact meaning of this is not clear. One possibility is that it refers to the going forth to the netherworld. The Egyptians were fearful of the night, and it would have been considered an advantage to make the journey during the day. One of the best modern translators of the *Book of the Dead*,

consequently, the illustrations have little relevance to the accompanying hieroglyphs. Photo by Terrence McGinniss, Inc., courtesy of Phillips

Thomas Allen, believes that the title refers to the Egyptian's desire to return by day to this world from the next. No matter what the title actually means, it undoubtedly connoted something about death to the Egyptians. It is typical of the ancient Egyptians not to mention death directly. They had numerous euphemisms for death and the deceased. For example, because the west bank of the Nile was associated with death (the sun died there every day, and the dead were buried in cemeteries on the west side), if someone died, it was said of him that "he went west." The dead were called "Westerners" or "True of Voice."

Many of the Theban versions of the *Book of the Dead* contain a praise or hymn to the gods, especially Osiris, god of the dead. Aside from buttering up the gods, the hymn served as an introduction to Osiris. An abbreviated example of such a hymn, from the papyrus of Ani, a scribe of the Eighteenth Dynasty, goes as follows:

> Adoration of Re when he appears in the eastern horizon of the sky. Behold Osiris, the scribe of the divine offerings of all the gods, Ani. He says, praise to thee who has come as Kheperi, the god of existence who is the creator of the gods. . . . May he give pleasure and power as one who is dead. The living soul [of Ani] goes forth to see Horus of the two horizons, to the soul of Osiris, the scribe of Ani, true of voice before Osiris. . . . May a place be made for me in the boat of the day of the going forth of the god; may I be received in the presence of Osiris in the land of the true voice of the *ka* of Osiris-Ani.[1]

In this hymn in praise of Osiris, two important aspects of the deceased are mentioned—the *ba* which I have translated as "soul," and the *ka* which I have left untranslated, but which was a kind of spiritual double. The Egyptians perceived the deceased as being composed of several elements, the most important of which were the *ba*, the *ka*, the shadow, and the physical corpse. The *ba* is the most difficult to describe because, while it was a part of the deceased, sometimes the Egyptians viewed it as a complete mode of existence of the deceased. In some ways it was a part and in some ways it was the whole. The *ba* was represented as a bird with the head of the deceased. Because the Egyptians rarely spoke of the *ba* of someone who was alive, it seems as if it came into existence when the person died, or was the mode of existence of the deceased. The *ba* had physical needs and activities. Relatives of the deceased were supposed to leave food offerings in front of the tomb to sustain the *ba* until it reached the next world. Numerous representations show the *ba* flying around the tomb or outside of it. In some ways, the *ba* was the alter ego of the dead person. One amusing papyrus tells the seemingly impossible story of a man who, while alive, had an argument with his *ba*. The *ba* told him to shape up or he would desert him in the next world.

Because the *ba* was essential for the deceased's continued existence in the netherworld, a special chapter in the *Book of the Dead* was intended to assure that the *ba* would be reunited with the deceased. Chapter 89 is called "The Spell for Causing the Uniting of the *Ba* and Its Body in the Netherworld."

> . . . Oh great god, cause that my soul may come to me from any place where it is. If there is a problem, bring my soul to me from any place where it is. . . . If there is a problem, cause my soul to see my body. If you find me Oh Eye-of-Horus, support me like those in the Netherworld. . . . May the soul see the body and may it rest upon its mummy. May it never perish, may it not be separated from the body for ever.—Say this spell over an amulet of the *ba* made of gold and inlaid with stone which is placed on the deceased's neck.[2]

Next in importance to the *ba* was the *ka*. This entity was a kind of astral double, an abstract duplicate of the deceased which needed a place to dwell. The first choice of a dwelling place was the corpse, but in case the body was destroyed, often an Egyptian was buried with a *ka*-statue, a likeness of the deceased which the *ka* could recognize and in which it could live.

Because the Egyptians were resurrectionists, it was important that the body be intact. It is not surprising, then, that many of the spells in the *Book of the Dead* were concerned with preserving and reanimating the body. Of all the spells for reanimating the body, the opening-of-the-mouth ceremony was perhaps the most important. After mummification was completed a rite was performed by a high-priest using an implement shaped like: ⌐. This ceremony was so important that even in the tiny and hastily constructed tomb of Tutankhamen, one of the few scenes painted on the walls shows Aye, who was the new pharaoh, serving as the high-priest, wearing the leopard skin indicative of that office. He holds in his hand the ⌐ in front of the mummy of the king. The "Spell of the Opening of the Mouth" usually included in the *Book of the Dead* is probably what Aye recited.

> My mouth is opened by Ptah. (Say this twice.) The local god of my town unties the bandages which are over my mouth. Toth comes, fully equipped with magical charms (say this twice) with which to untie the bandages of Set which fetter my mouth. . . .[3]

The Egyptians were almost encyclopaedic in their concern with the various parts of the body. Often the *Book of the Dead* seems to have been written by a priest who sat down and tried to think of every part of the body that would be needed in the next world and who then wrote a spell for each. Among numerous chapters with titles such as "The Chapter of Not Permitting the Heart of a Man to Be Taken Away," are:

The Chapter of Not Permitting the Head of a Man to
Be Cut Off in the Next World

I am the great one, son of the great one. I am fire, son of fire, whose head was given to him after it was cut off. His head shall not be taken away from him. . . .[4]

The Chapter of Walking with Two Legs and Going Forth
from Earth

Words spoken by the deceased: Do what thou doest Sokar. (Say this twice.) Sokar who is in his dwelling place within my legs in the Netherworld. I shine above heaven; I go forth from heaven. I sit by the God's spirit. I am weak and feeble. (Say this twice.) I walk wearily and am motionless in the presence of those whose teeth gnash in the Netherworld.[5]

When it came to magical spells in the *Book of the Dead,* the Egyptians clearly believed in overkill. Even after all the various spells for the parts of the body were listed, there was a general summarizing spell for the entire corpse not to perish. The title alone seems more than enough:

Spell for not letting a man's corpse perish in the god's domain, to rescue him from the eater of souls who imprison [human beings] in the nether world, also for not letting his crimes upon earth be brought up against him, for keeping his flesh and his bones sound against worms and any God who may transgress in the god's domain, for letting him ascend or descend at will, and for doing whatever he desires without his being hindered.[6]

The deceased is then told to say that he has magical power to protect his corpse from "the Grim-faced One who gains control of hearts and seizes limbs."

Even if the body was protected, the difficulties for the deceased were not yet over. The Egyptians believed in a judgment; the test for admittance into the next world was crucial. Actually, there were two judgments, one impartial and objective, the other somewhat subjective and depending upon the theatrical and oratorial abilities of the deceased.

In the objective test the heart of the deceased is weighed against a feather. The ∫ hieroglyph designated the word "maat," or "truth." Thus the heart was being examined to see how truthful the individual was. The use of the balance scale is purely objective, the implication being that if this life has been unjust to you, the judgment in the next life will be the equalizer. To further assure fairness, Osiris is usually shown presiding over the judgment while the god of writing, Toth, in the form of a baboon, records the result.

If this test is passed, then the "True of Voice" goes on to a second judging. He will enter into the Hall of the Double Truth where he will be judged by forty-two different gods. He will have to "separate himself from his evil-doings," and he does this by making a negative plea. Before each god he denies having done a specific wrong. One of the important features of this chapter of the *Book of the Dead* is that it reveals the names of the forty-two gods, giving the deceased some power over them. The names are wonderfully mysterious. Some examples of the names and necessary denials follow:

> Hail Strider coming forth from Heliopolis, I have done no wrong.
>
> Hail Eater-of-Shadows coming forth from the caverns, I have not slain men. (Say this twice.)
>
> Hail He-Whose-Two-Eyes-Are-on-Fire, coming forth from Sais, I have not defiled the things of the gods.
>
> Hail Breaker-of-Bones, coming forth from darkness, I have not transgressed.
>
> Hail Eater-of-Intestines coming forth from the thirty-three, I have not desolated ploughed fields.
>
> Hail Doubly-Wicked coming forth from Ati, I have not defiled the wife of a man.
>
> Hail Disposer-of-Speech coming forth from Weryt, I have not inflamed myself with rage.
>
> Hail Provider-of-Mankind, coming forth from Sais, I have not cursed God.
>
> Hail White Teeth, coming forth from Ta-she. I have not slaughtered the divine cattle.[7]

After these denials of wrongdoing are made, the deceased is supposed to tell the gods of his magical powers. He relates the story that going north of some bushes past a town he saw a leg and a thigh. They gave him a flame and a crystal tablet which he buried along with "things of the night" near the Hall of the Double Truth. There, by the Hall of the Double Truth, he found a scepter of stone whose name was Causer-of-Winds. Then a magical spell was said over the buried flame and tablet, and the flame expired. Then the tablet was magically used to create a pool of water. (This may be by sympathetic magic, since the crystal might look like water.)

This story of the deceased's magical powers is told to impress the gods who then say, "Pass through the door to the Hall of the Double Truth, you know us." But there is yet another barrier to entrance. After obtaining permission from the forty-two deities to enter, admittance is prohibited by the very parts of the entrance way. The only way the deceased may pass is to demonstrate his magical power by reciting the names of the various parts of the entrance.

The first part to block the way is the bolt of the door. When the deceased tries to enter, the bolt says, "I will not let you enter unless you speak my name." The *Book of the Dead* supplies the name— "Weight-of-the-Place-of-Truth." The lintels to the left and right of the door also require the pass-names: "He-Who-Weighs-the-Works-of-Truth" and "Judge-of-Wine." The "Judge-of-Wine" is a rather curious one. It seems as if all kinds of judging and evaluations took place in the Hall of the Double Truth. (The Egyptian word for *wine* is funny. It was pronounced "irp," which was probably onomatopoeic, intended to sound like the results of drinking too much wine.)

The importance of doorways in connection with the *Book of the Dead* is illustrated by a curious practice found only in the tombs of the nobles at Thebes during the New Kingdom. Cones of baked clay were inserted into the limestone out of which the tombs were carved. These "funerary cones," as they are called, were placed with their rounded end facing out to form a lintel over the doorway of the tomb. On these cones were written magical formulae asserting that the deceased was venerated by Osiris and that he was judged "true of voice." (Figure 39).

All the parts of the doorway request their names. The bolt socket, the lock, the threshold, and other door parts, all require their names to be spoken. After the deceased properly gives all the

FIGURE 39. This funerary cone was found in the exterior construction of the tomb of Iahmose, the king's scribe. Photograph by Russell Rudzwick

names, the parts collectively say, "Thou knowest us, thus you may pass by us." It is interesting that knowing the names of the parts is the same as knowing the parts. This was a basic magical principle of the ancient Egyptians. Knowledge of the name of a thing is the same as knowledge of that thing; what is done to the name happens to the thing or person named. This is why the Egyptians believed that, if you erased the name of a pharaoh from all his monuments, that pharaoh ceased to exist.

After having passed so many tests and recited so many names, it must have come as quite a shock to the deceased to cross the threshold only to find that the floor requested its name too! But finally admittance was granted.

One of the puzzling sections in the *Book of the Dead* deals with magical transformation. This section consists of about a dozen magical spells that, if recited, will cause the deceased to change into various gods, animals, plants, or other animate things. All the spells have the same basic format. The deceased is told to say that he is the god, animal, or plant he desires to be, and then he lists the attributes he especially wishes to have. For example, if the deceased wants to be Sobek, the crocodile god, he says:

> I am the crocodile who is terrifying. I am the crocodile god. I bring destruction. I am the great fish in Qemay. I am the lord of homage in Sekhem; lord of homage in Sekhem.[8]

In all these spells, the basic principle is that the word is the deed. Saying it makes it so. What is curious in this particular group of spells is that the deceased should want to be all of these things. His prime concern is immortality. While being terrifying as a crocodile might help him survive the rigors of entering the netherworld, one of the spells is for transformation into a lotus flower, and how this could help is difficult to see. The only possible explanation lies in the property associated with being a lotus in the spell. Since the lotus was a sign of purity, perhaps this would help the deceased pass the test in the Hall of the Double Truth.

When the *Book of the Dead* first made its appearance in the New Kingdom it was considered to be essential to anyone desiring immortality. This belief continued well into the period of Greek occupation of Egypt. The texts themselves remained virtually unchanged for more than a thousand years. There can be no doubt that many of the purchasers of these texts could not read them, but this was of no great concern. *Having* the magical words was the important thing, not necessarily being able to read them.

9. Amulets

AN AMULET IS ANYTHING worn or carried by a person for magical
benefit. Of all the magical objects used by the Egyptians, the amulet was by far the most popular. Judging from the number of them
found in excavations, practically everyone in Egypt must have
worn them. Most amulets had small holes in them so they could be
mounted in necklaces, rings, bracelets, pectorals, and almost every
form of ornament the Egyptians wore.

One of the ancient Egyptian words for "amulets" was
𓏠𓏏𓏏 *(udjaou)*, which also meant "round" or "complete."
Sometimes the word 𓏠𓏏𓏏 *(mekt)* was used, which meant "protector." Both words suggest the function of amulets. Horapollo, a
Greek who wrote an almost totally incorrect book on hieroglyphs,
gives a wondrously inaccurate account of how the Egyptians wrote
the word "amulet." He says that:

> When they would denote an *amulet*, they portray two HUMAN
> HEADS, one of a male looking inwards, the other of a female look-
> ing outwards (for they say that no demon will interfere with any
> person thus guarded); for without inscriptions they protect them-
> selves with the two heads.
>
> Horapollo, Book I, XXIV

Amulets were made of almost every material available to the
ancient Egyptians. The finest were carved of stone: lapis lazuli,
carnelian, turquoise, feldspar, serpentine, and steatite. Metals were
used, too, gold being the most valuable, but copper, bronze, and
iron also were prized. Wood and bone were sometimes used. Of all
materials, however, the greatest number of amulets were made out

of faience. Faience is a paste made of ground quartz or of sand which has a high percentage of quartz. The paste was molded into whatever object was desired and then fired. When the object was baked, the glaze would migrate to the surface producing a smooth, glassy surface.

Faience amulets were produced by the thousands in factories throughout Egypt. The first step in mass production was to prepare the mold. A master amulet was made of some durable material, such as stone, and used to make an impression in a lump of soft clay. When baked, the clay became hard, like our modern bricks, and was the mold used to produce the amulets (Figure 40*a*). Any number of molds could be made from the master amulet and any number of amulets from the mold. (When Flinders Petrie excavated at Tel al Amarna, he found literally thousands of molds.) Usually a hole was made in the amulet for stringing. A small amount of quartzite paste was rolled around a string and pressed into the mold, string and all (Figure 40*b*). When the mold was fired, the paste hardened into faience and the string burned away, leaving the hole.

Amulets were designed according to strict traditions and their production probably was overseen by priests. The MacGregor Papyrus gives a list of seventy-five amulets, their names and uses. This papyrus, because it was part of a *Book of the Dead,* specifies that each amulet is to be made of gold. This is probably because gold does not tarnish and would be most appropriate for protecting the deceased for eternity. On the walls of the temple of Dendera (Figure 41) is another list of amulets which gives the materials they should be made of—lapis lazuli, feldspar, jasper, and so forth. Clearly, the ancient Egyptians believed that the material an amulet was made of was crucial for the magic to work. Perhaps just as crucial as the material was the color. If a person could not afford a carnelian amulet, then a faience amulet with a red glaze might do.

Magical amulets were believed to derive their powers by several closely related principles. Some amulets that were purely protective derived their power by invoking the gods. For instance, if you wore a small cat amulet around your neck, you carried with you the protection of the cat goddess, Bastet. Other protective amulets, not directly related to the gods, got their power by sympathetic magic. If you wore an amulet in the shape of an *ankh,* ♀ , you would continue to live because you wore the hieroglyph for

FIGURE 40*a*. Eyes-of-Horus amulets were most frequently made of faience.

FIGURE 40*b*. They were fired in clay molds such as this one, which retains a faint line on either side of the depression in the center. This was where a string burned away, leaving a hole in the amulet for stringing. Photographs by Russell Rudzwick

FIGURE 41. On the walls of the Temple of Dendera is a list of all the amulets and the materials of which they were to be made.

"life." There were also amulets especially for the deceased. They were placed on the mummy to assure that it remained intact and powerful in the next world. These funerary amulets were usually similar to those worn by the living.

By far, the most numerous of all amulets found in excavations is the Eye-of-Horus. This was the highly stylized eye of the falcon god Horus. According to myth, Horus fought his evil uncle Seth to avenge the death of his father Osiris. In the battle, Horus' eye was torn to pieces, but by magic, Toth, god of writing, assembled the pieces. Each element of the Eye-of-Horus represented a different fraction: the hieroglyph for ½ was ◁ , ¼ was ○ , and so on.

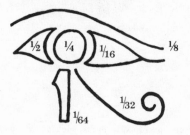

The total of the fractions is $^{63}\!/_{64}$ the missing $^{1}\!/_{64}$ supposedly supplied magically by Toth. The amulet was called *udjat,* or "sound eye." Because of its association with the regeneration of Horus' eye, it was worn to ensure good health. The sign of the modern pharmacist, Rx, is a corruption of three portions of the ancient Egyptian Eye-of-Horus: $^{1}\!/_{4}$, $^{1}\!/_{32}$, and $^{1}\!/_{64}$.

The Eye-of-Horus was also important as a funerary amulet. Chapter 140 of the *Book of the Dead* was to be recited on the last day of the second month of the second season over two Eyes-of-Horus. One was to be made of real lapis lazuli or of *hamaget*-stone set in gold; the other was to be of red jasper and worn on "any limb preferred." The reason for two Eyes-of-Horus of different colors possibly stems from a myth that states that one eye of Horus was the moon, the other the sun. Anyone who said the spell properly over the two eyes would be permitted to ride in the celestial bark of Re and enjoy the company of the gods. Also, when the "sound eye" (moon) was full, offerings were to be made on twelve altars: four for Re-Atum, four for the sound eye, and four to the other gods. On each of the altars were to be placed five loaves of white bread, five cakes of incense in the shape of white bread, five cakes of natron, one basket of fruit, and one basket of roast meat. This, too, was to assure that the crew of Re would row the deceased to the next world.

One ancient Egyptian amulet still popular today is the *ankh* (Figure 42). The word *ankh* meant both "life" and "hand mirror." Tutankhamen had a mirror in the shape of an *ankh,* a pun any Egyptian would have gotten. There are two curious aspects to the *ankh.* First, although it was a symbol frequently used in painting and sculpture, the objective evidence is that it was used as an amulet only rarely. Comparatively few have been found in excavations. Certainly scores of other amulets were far more popular. The second curiosity about the *ankh* is that, while it is often depicted, Egyptologists are not certain just what object it represented. Some believe that it represented sandal straps, but this is far from certain. The fact that there was no particular material from which *ankhs* were to be made indicates that the origins may have been lost even to the Egyptians.

Perhaps the reason the *ankh* was not more popular as an amulet was that there was another to serve the same function: the scarab.

FIGURE 42. On a column in the tomb of Amenhotep II, Anubis, the god of embalming, gives life in the form of an *ankh* to the pharaoh. Photograph by Barbara Benton

These are carved in the shape of a beetle, the *Scarabaeus sacer*, from which the modern word comes.

There are several reasons why the scarab became such an important amulet. The Egyptians were especially fond of puns, and the hieroglyphs for beetle 🪲 (pronounced *kheper*) also meant "to exist." So if you wore a scarab amulet, your continued existence was assumed. Another reason the scarab was held in special regard is that the ancient Egyptians believed that the beetle had offspring without the union of male and female. This false belief arose simply because the Egyptians never saw them copulating. Actually, after fertilization the female deposits her eggs in a piece of dung and rolls it into a ball, so that when they hatch, the newborn will be provided with food. Since this was the only part of the reproductive cycle the Egyptians saw, they assumed the beetle was somewhat like the god Atum who begot children without a female partner.

Horapollo gives a typical ancient account of how the scarab reproduces:

> To denote an *only begotten*, or *generation*, or a *father*, or the *world*, or a *man*, they delineate a SCARABAEUS. And they symbolise by this an *only begotten*, because the scarabacus is a creature self-produced, being unconceived by a female; for the propagation of it is unique after this manner: —when the male is desirous of procreating he takes dung of an ox, and shapes it into a spherical form like the world; he then rolls it from the hinder parts from east to west, looking himself towards the east, that he may impart to it the figure of the world (for that is borne from east to west): then, having dug a hole, the scarabaeus deposits this ball in the earth for the space of twenty-eight days (for in so many days the moon passes through the twelve signs of the zodiac). By thus remaining under the moon, the race of scarabaei is endued with life; and upon the nine and twentieth day after having opened the ball, it casts it into the water, for it is aware that upon that day the conjunction of the moon and sun takes place, as well as the generation of the world.
>
> Horapollo, Book I, X

Yet another reason the scarab was revered is that when the scarab fashions the dung ball it rolls it with its hind legs to a sunny place. To the ancient mind this in some way resembled the journey of the sun across the sky.

Scarab amulets were made from a variety of materials, faience and stone being the most common (Figure 43). Like other amulets, usually they were made with holes in them so that they could be strung. While the top was carved to resemble the beetle, the bottom was usually flat, with a carved inscription. Often the inscription was merely the owner's name, so that the amulet would bring him continued existence. Also, such scarabs could be used as seals to leave the impression of the owner's name. If he wanted to seal a jar of wine and be sure none of the servants sampled it, he could plaster the top of the jar and press the bottom of his scarab into the moist plaster. Then if the seal were broken, it could not be repaired undetected.

It was also common to wear scarabs bearing the name of a favorite pharaoh. The most numerous of these are scarabs with the name of Tuthmose III, *(men kheper Re)*. He was such a favorite

FIGURE 43. Scarabs often depict magical scenes. In this one of faience, a falcon hovers behind a pharaoh worshiping in front of an obelisk. Photograph by Russell Rudzwick

that scarabs with his name were being produced a thousand years after his death. It was also common to have scarabs with good wishes carved on the bottom. Many simply say, "good luck" or "Happy New Year." Some designs were purely decorative; some commemorated an event such as a hunt or festival. There are also numerous scarabs with gods carved on the bottom (Figures 44*a* and 44*b*).

Historically, the most interesting kind of scarab is the royal commemorative scarab. These were especially large, often as large as nine inches, and carved on the bottom with details of some event the pharaoh wanted to mark. These would be sent, much like a proclamation, to rulers of foreign countries and to high Egyptian court officials.

The most famous commemorative scarabs are those of Amenhotep III, who instituted the practice in the Eighteenth Dynasty. These memorialize five different events: a wild bull hunt which occurred in the second year of the king's reign; the lion hunting which took place in the first ten years of the king's reign; the arrival of a princess from Mitanni in the tenth year of his reign; the construction of a pleasure lake for Queen Tye (Figures 45*a* and 45*b*); and the marriage of Amenhotep III and Tye (giving the queen's parentage). The texts on these scarabs are definitely not magical.

FIGURE 44a. *Left:* The top scarab is a hedgehog, the middle is a small fish, and the bottom is a larger fish.

FIGURE 44b. *Below:* On the reverse sides, *from left to right,* the hedgehog has the jackal-headed Anubis, the large fish has a *djed-*pillar, and the smaller fish has a name in hieroglyphs. Photographs by Russell Rudzwick

FIGURE 45a. The cartouche on the top of this scarab identifies it as one issued by Amenhotep III.

FIGURE 45b. The bottom is inscribed with hieroglyphs commemorating the king's construction of a pleasure lake for Queen Tye. The Metropolitan Museum of Art, Rogers Fund, 1935

They commemorate a historical event which has happened rather than assist in the occurrence of a future event. However, the fact that Amenhotep III chose the scarab as the vehicle by which he would memorialize important events attests to the power ascribed to the scarab.

Scarab beetles were themselves mummified, so it is almost certain that they were sacred. Their magical powers can be assumed from several of their uses: Parts of the body and the wings were used to make an ointment for stiff joints; the wing cases were used in an unguent to facilitate child delivery; and evil spells were undone when a large beetle was beheaded, its wings removed, and the body burned.

Scarabs were an essential ingredient in various magical potions. One spell in the Leiden-London magical papyrus has an incredibly complex set of instructions involving a scarab and an incantation designed to make a woman fall in love with the magician. A special kind of scarab was needed, a small one with a "fish face" with horns. You must catch it while the sun is rising. While doing this you must have a magic cape on your back, palm fiber tied around your face, and a scarab painted on the front of your hand. While the sun is rising you must say:

> Thou art this scarab of real lapis-lazuli, I have taken thee out of the door of my temple; thou carriest [?] . . . of bronze to thy nose [?], that can eat [?] the herbage that is trampled [?], the field-plants [?] that are injured for the great images of the men of Egypt. I dispatch thee to N. born of N. to strike her from her heart to her belly, to her entrails, to her womb; for she it is hath wept [?] before the Sun in the morning, she saying to the Sun, 'Come not forth,' to the moon, 'Rise not,' to the water, 'Come not to the men of Egypt,' to the fields, 'Grow not green,' and to the great trees of the men of Egypt, 'Flourish not.' I dispatch thee to N. born of N. to injure her from her heart unto her belly, unto her entrails, unto her womb, and she shall put herself on the road [?] after N. born of N. at every time [?].[1]

This spell is recited seven times and then the scarab is drowned in the milk of a black cow. While doing this, you hold a branch from an olive tree. Leave the scarab in the milk until evening and recite the following spell:

Woe [?], great, woe [?] my [?] great, woe [?] his [?] Nun, woe [?] his [?] love. O scarab, thou art the eye of Phre, the heart [?] of Osiris, the open-hand [?] of Shu, thou approachest in this condition in which Osiris thy father went, on account of N. born of N. until fire is put to her heart and the flame to her flesh, until she shall follow [?] N. born of N., unto every place in which he is.[2]

Now take out the scarab and spread its bottom with sand and place a circular strip of cloth under it. Leave it for four days to dry. Burn frankincense in front of it. Cut it in half down its middle with a bronze knife. Take its right half and the nail parings of your right hand and foot and cook them in a new pot with vine-wood. The instructions stipulate that you pound all this with nine apple-pips combined with either your urine or your sweat. But be sure that your sweat is free from bath oil! While this brew is cooking in the pot you must say:

O my beautiful child, the youth of oil-eating [?], thou who didst cast semen and who dost cast semen among all the gods, whom he that is little [and?] he that is great found among the two great enneads in the East of Egypt, who cometh forth as a black scarab on a stem of papyrus-reed; I know thy name, I know thy. . . . 'the work of the two stars' is thy name, I cast forth fury upon thee to-day: Nephalam, Balla, Balkha [?], Iophphe; for every burning, every heat, every fire that thou makest to-day, thou shalt make them in the heart, the lungs, the viscera, the little viscera, the ribs, the flesh, the bones, in every limb, in the skin of N. born of N. until she follow [?] N. born of N. to every place in which he is.[3]

After this spell is recited and the potion cooked, all the ingredients are rolled into a ball and placed in wine. You then recite another spell seven times.

O scarab, thou art the scarab of real lapis-lazuli, thou art the eye of Phre, thou art the eye of Atum, the open-handed [?] of Shu, the heart [?] of Osiris, thou art that black bull, the first, that came forth from Nun, the beauty of Isis being with thee; thou art Raks, Rapa-raks, the blood of this wild boar [?] which they brought from the land of Syria unto Egypt . . . to the wine, I send thee; wilt thou go on my errand? Wilt thou do it? Thou sayest 'Send me to the thirsty, that his thirst may be quenched, and to the canal that it may be dried up, and to the sand of the *snyt* that it may be scattered without wind, and to the papyrus of Buto that the blade may be applied to it while Horus is saved for [?] Isis, catastrophes grow great for the Egyptians, so that not a man or woman is left in their midst.' I send thee; do like unto these; I send thee down to the heart of N. born of N. and do thou make fire in her body, flame in her entrails, put the madness to her heart, the fever [?] to her flesh; let her make pursuit of the 'Shoulder'—constellation after the 'Hippopotamus'—constellation; let her make the movements of the sunshine after the shadow, she following after N. born of N. to every place in which he is, she loving him, she being mad for him, she not knowing the place of the earth in which she is. Take away her sleep by night; give her lamentation and anxiety by day; let her not eat, let her not drink, let her not sleep, let her not sit under the shade of her house until she follow [?] him to every place in which he is, her heart forgetting, her eye flying, her glance turned [?], she not knowing the place of the earth in which she is, until she sees him, for her eye after his eye, her heart after his heart, her hand after his hand, she giving to him every. . . . Let fly [?] the tip of her feet after his heels in the street at all times without fail at any time. Quick, hasten.[4]

When you have said this spell seven times, you make the woman drink the wine. Then you take the other half of the scarab (remember?) and the nail parings of your left hand and foot and tie them in a strip of linen along with myrrh and saffron. Tie this to your left arm and sleep with the woman.

This spell shows not only the magical powers attributed to scarabs, but also the length to which an Egyptian would go to get his woman.

While the scarab was one of the most popular amulets, it was relatively late in use, not appearing until the Eleventh Dynasty of the Middle Kingdom. Although some extant ancient Egyptian scarabs are inscribed with the names of Old Kingdom pharaohs, almost certainly these were produced during the Middle Kingdom or later. No excavation of an intact Old Kingdom site has ever yielded a scarab; it seems unlikely that, if they were produced, they would not have been found.

Aside from its use as an amulet, a seal, and a commemoration, the scarab was also a crucial funerary object. Starting in the Middle Kingdom and continuing into the period of Greek occupation, scarabs were used to protect the heart of the mummy. These scarabs were almost always carved of stone, usually about four inches in length. On the bottom was carved a magical spell, designed not, as one might expect, to protect the heart and keep it intact, but to suppress the heart and keep it quiet! When the deceased entered the netherworld, he was judged and his heart weighed against the feather of truth. The fear was that the heart would betray its owner and testify against him! This is why part of the spell reads:

> Oh heart of my mother, Oh heart of my mother. Do not stand against me as witness. Do not outweigh me before the keeper of the balance.

Book of the Dead, Spell 30B

There are many versions of the spell, and various copies of the *Book of the Dead* give different instructions for preparations of the amulet. Some say it must be of lapis lazuli ringed with gold, others specify it should be of green jasper, still others require carnelian. In fact, all these materials were used.

An ancient Egyptian tradition says that one magical spell originated during the time of Men-Kau-Re in Hermopolis. Since no scarabs of the Old Kingdom have been found, the tradition was almost certainly wrong, but it shows that the Egyptians believed scarabs dated to the Old Kingdom. The tradition is preserved in a papyrus which reads:

> Words to be spoken over a scarab of green jasper bound with *wasmu*-metal, having a ring of silver. It is to be placed on the deceased by his throat. This spell was found in Hermopolis under the feet of his majesty, this god, [written] upon a slab of metal from the south with the writing of the god himself in the time of his majesty of the North and South Men-Kau-Re, true of voice, by the royal son Hordyef. He found it on his way to make inspection of the temples.[5]

One of the heart scarabs buried with the estate manager Wah at Thebes demonstrates a magical belief of the Middle Kingdom. Wah's heart scarab was solid silver and his name and titles on the top were inlaid in gold (Figure 46). On the bottom was an ♀ with a few other hieroglyphs. Before it was buried with Wah, the eyes and mouth were destroyed, so that if the scarab magically came to life it could not hurt the owner.

One amulet which seems to have been used only for funerary

FIGURE 46. An estate manager named Wah owned this silver scarab. The eyes and mouth were intentionally destroyed so that, if by magic it came to life, it would not injure Wah. The Metropolitan Museum of Art

purposes was the *djed*-amulet. This is supposed to represent the backbone of Osiris; its shape is consistent with this belief. The fact that it was not often worn by the living also suggests the connection with Osiris. It was used to assure stability for the deceased. Chapter 155 of the *Book of the Dead* is a spell to be said for the deceased who is to have a *djed* or pillar-amulet of gold on his throat. While the *Book of the Dead* specifies that the pillar is to be made of gold, most *djed* columns were not. Only a small minority of the ancient Egyptians could afford gold—or copies of the *Book of the Dead,* for that matter. A favorite substitute material was bone, for obvious reasons, associating the amulet with the bone from the body of Osiris (Figure 47). Also, while the *Book of the Dead* specifies that the pillar of gold was to be placed on the throat of the deceased, it was far more common for a string of about a dozen pillars to be placed across the belly of the mummy, just opposite the lower vertebrae.

A section for this spell from the *Book of the Dead* reads:

> . . . Thou hast thy backbone, Weary-hearted One; thou hast thy vertebrae, Weary-hearted One. Mayest thou put thyself on thy side, that I may supply thee with water. Behold, I have brought thee the pillar-amulet [of gold], that thou mayest rejoice forever.

FIGURE 47. *Djed*-columns, made of various materials, represented the backbone of Osiris. These two are carved of bone. Photograph by Ruṣsell Rudzwick

Instructions for how to recite the spell end with an ancient editorial comment on its efficiency:

> This spell is to be said over a pillar-amulet of gold strung on sycamore bast [moistened], with sap of the *ankh-imy* plant, and put at the throat of this blessed one. He enters through the gates [of the west] after speaking with the silent ones. He puts himself on his side (on [lunar] new year's day) like these Who Are in the Train of Osiris . . .
>
> A TRULY EXCELLENT SPELL (PROVED A MILLION TIMES)[6]

The following chapter of the *Book of the Dead,* Chapter 156 (Figure 48), describes one of the most curious of the funerary amulets, the *tet:* 𓋣 . While undeniably this amulet was associated with Isis, it is not clear precisely what it represented. Some scholars [7] believe it represented a primitive woman's girdle; others [8] believe it represented the stylized genital organs of Isis. In favor of the latter thesis is the fact that it is almost always carved out of a red stone, such as jasper or carnelian, or when not made of stone, the faience or glass versions of this amulet are red. The relevant chap-

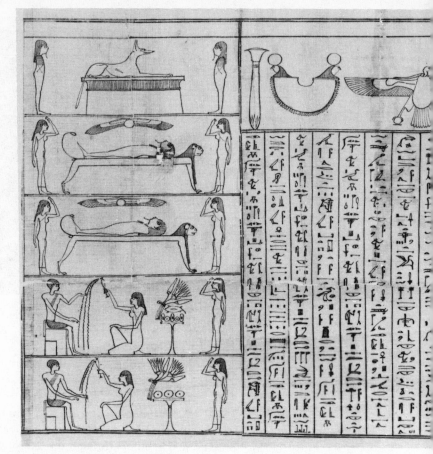

FIGURE 48. A vignette in the *Book of the Dead* of the priest Nes-Min designates the amulets to be placed on the mummy. In the top right panel, *from left to right*, they are: papyrus scepter, collar of Horus, vulture pectoral, knot of Isis, and *djed*-column. To the right of the

ter of the *Book of the Dead* gives its function, but does not state precisely what the *tet* is.

The *Book of the Dead* specifies that the *tet* is to be made of red jasper and is to be dipped in the sap of the *ankh-imy* plant. While this plant is not known to us, its name suggests some magical function having to do with overseeing life, since *ankh-imy* means "overseer of life." The *tet* was to be inlaid in sycamore wood and placed on the neck of the deceased. If this was done, he would have the power of Isis to protect him and no way would be blocked to him.

One group of purely funerary amulets considered absolutely essential for the mummy's protection was amulets of the four sons of Horus (Figure 49). Mesti is human-headed, Hapi is ape-headed,

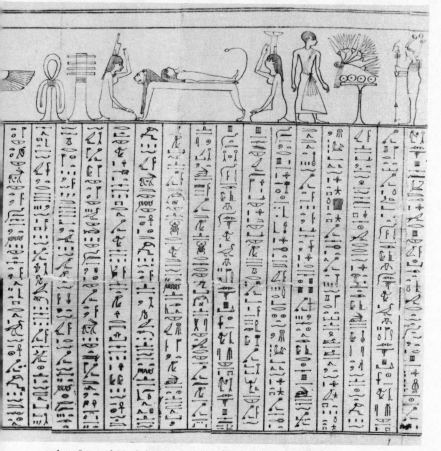

amulets, Isis and Nephthys kneel by the body of Nes-Min. Photo by Terrence McGinniss, Inc., courtesy of Phillips

Duamutef is jackal-headed, and Qebesenef is falcon-headed. Amulets of these four gods were usually made of blue faience and had several holes in them so they could be sewn onto the mummy wrappings. They were almost always placed across the chest of the mummy.

Judging from Tutankhamen's tomb, a very important amulet was a small model of a headrest which was placed under the mummy's head (Figure 50). Tutankhamen's headrest amulet was one of only three items in the tomb that were made of iron. It is one of the earliest known uses of that metal in Egypt. Normally, the amulet was made out of hard stone, such as hematite or diorite, or sometimes out of wood. The spell in the *Book of the Dead* which

FIGURE 49. These faience amulets of the four sons of Horus were made with holes so they could be sewn onto mummy wrappings. Photograph by Russell Rudzwick

FIGURE 50. A miniature headrest was put in the mummy wrappings to protect the head of the deceased and to help him arise in the next world. Photograph by Russell Rudzwick

was to be said when the headrest was placed under the neck of the mummy indicated its protective function. In the following translation *N.* refers to the space where the deceased's name would be.

> Awake! thy sufferings are allayed, N. Thou art awaked when thy head is above the horizon. Stand up, thou art triumphant by means of what has been done to thee. Ptah has struck down thine enemies. It has been ordered what should be done to thee. Thou art Horus, the son of Hathor, the flame born of a flame, to whom his head has been restored after it had been cut off. Thy head will never be taken from thee henceforth. Thy head will never be carried away.[9]

One of the rewards of carefully controlled excavation is the knowledge of the placement of amulets on mummies. (When plun-

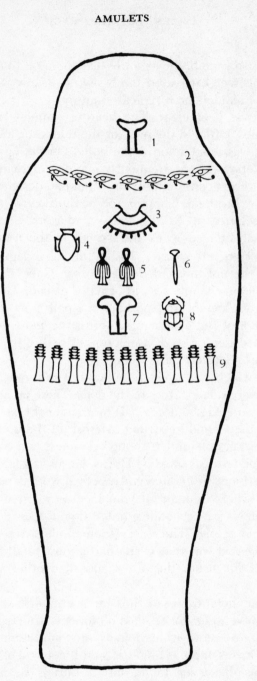

Placement of amulets on the mummy: (1) headrest amulet; (2) Eyes-of-Horus; (3) collar of sheet gold; (4) heart amulet; (5) *tets*, or knots of Isis; (6) papyrus scepter; (7) tool used at opening-of-the-mouth ceremony; (8) heart scarab; (9) string of *djed*-columns

derers discover a tomb, they simply tear them off to be sold.) From the numerous well-excavated tombs, we can now reconstruct the placement of amulets on a typical mummy.

The face was kept clear. The headrest amulet (1) was placed under the neck. Often in the neck or shoulder area a string of Eyes-of-Horus (2) was draped across the body. On the upper chest area was an amuletic pectoral, frequently made of extremely thin sheet-gold. These varied considerably but often had designs showing protective deities on them. Chapter 158 of the *Book of the Dead* indicates that the purpose of this collar was to assure that the deceased would be unbandaged when he arrived in the next world: "My father, my sisters, my mother, Isis! I am unbandaged; I see. I am one among the unbandaged ones who see Geb." Near the chest cavity a variety of amulets was normally placed. These always included a heart scarab, and perhaps a small stone amulet of the heart, the knot of Isis, or a scarab. Across the waist there often was a string of a dozen or so *djed*-columns. Usually, the area beneath the waist was relatively bare of amulets.

Amulets which were very popular—but infrequently placed on mummies—were small statues of the gods. These usually were made of faience, averaged about one half inch in height, and had loops in the back so they could be strung. Almost all the gods were represented in this kind of amulet, though the most numerous were Bastet the cat goddess, Isis suckling Horus, Horus as a falcon, and Ptah, the god of artisans. Just which god a person wore depended to some extent upon where he lived. If your local protective deity was Sobek, then you wore a crocodile amulet; if your local god was Bastet, you wore a cat amulet. The reason such amulets were rarely buried with the deceased was that Osiris had almost total dominion over the realm of the dead; the other gods had other spheres of influence.

All the amulets discussed thus far are models of recognizable objects. However, one entire class of amulets are rarely mentioned because no one knows what objects they represent or how they were used. One example is mud balls with magical objects in them. These curious objects are found only in burials, so they must have had some protective power for the deceased, but exactly what is not clear. The first of these balls found was in 1912 in an Old Kingdom mastaba at Abydos.[10] There were about forty of them, each the size of a golf ball. They were made of ordinary unbaked

Nile mud. Mixed with the mud were small bits of charcoal, pottery, and bone. On the surface of the balls a small grill pattern had been made:▦. After the grill pattern there were signs of some sort which resembled crude hieroglyphs but are undecipherable. The markings are consistent enough from ball to ball that it is definite that something was being indicated.

Three of these balls were cut open. Two contained fragments of a reed; in the third was a bit of linen. Similar balls containing human hair have been found in much later burials.[11] Clearly the purpose was magical, but precisely what is difficult to say.

An interesting amulet almost always depicted in tomb paintings as being carried, but rarely worn, is the *menyet* (Figure 51). This

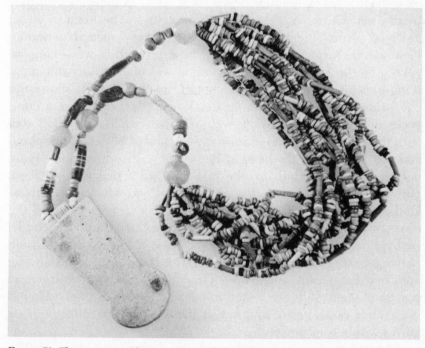

FIGURE 51. The *menyet*-necklace, not intended to be worn, was carried by Egyptian women as a sign of devotion to Hathor. Photograph by Russell Rudzwick

object was basically a necklace of beads with a counterpoise usually of this shape: ⛾ . Normally, Egyptian necklaces were so heavy with beads and amulets that they were counterbalanced by a counterpoise which hung down the back of the person wearing the necklace. While these *menyets* seem designed to be worn, they were normally held by ladies or priestesses as a sign of their devotion to Hathor. The bearer of a *menyet* would have the goddess' protection (Figure 52).

In the later stages of Egyptian history there was an innovative development. A new kind of protective amulet appeared which was more abstract than miniature representations of gods and objects—the written amulet. Apparently, for a while it was no longer believed that one needed a realistic representation of an object. The words of power were more important, and these could occasionally be accompanied by a drawing of a god. The Brooklyn Museum has a papyrus which is basically a magician's manual on how to use such amulets.

Although the papyrus is badly damaged, enough is left to make clear how written amulets were used. It is actually a two-part treatise on the use of two amuletic drawings. The magical ritual involved several elements, each having a very specific function. First was the drawing of the god whose protection was being invoked. To the Egyptian, to draw a god was almost the same as to bring him into being. The first vignette in the papyrus shows the god being invoked. He is fantastically complex, drawn as a composite of many elements (Figure 53). He is shown as a standing man with the head of Bes. (Bes, curiously, was god of both the household *and* war!) On top of the head of Bes are other heads in pairs facing outward. From bottom up, the first pair are a ram and a falcon, perhaps recalling Khnum, the ram-headed god who created mankind on a potter's wheel, and Horus, the falcon who avenged the death of Osiris. The second pair is a hippopotamus and a crocodile, perhaps Seth and Sobek. The third pair is a lion(ess) and a bull, perhaps Sekhmet and the Apis bull. The last pair is a cat and an ape, perhaps Bastet and Toth. Thus, the various attributes and powers of many gods are vested in one. Topping this stack of heads is a pair of ram's horns, and out of these spring six cobras and six knives, symbols of power.

The god has four arms and two pairs of outstretched wings. The wings may be indicative of the powers of Isis, goddess of magic.

FIGURE 52. In this tomb painting from Thebes, the Lady Thepu holds a *menyet*-necklace. The Brooklyn Museum, acc. no. 65.197, Charles Edwin Wilbour Collection

The arms grasp symbols of power: The arm on the extreme right holds a *was*-scepter with an *ankh* and *djed*-pillar on it, two harpoons with cobras at the top, and two knives. The arm on the extreme left holds identical symbols. The other right arm holds a single *was* scepter, while the other left arm holds an *ankh*. In case all this is not an adequate magical arsenal, the body of the god has various magical signs painted on it, and he is surrounded by a protective ring of eighteen flames. He stands on an oval containing several animals, undoubtedly representing foes to be overcome.

To the right is the god's name: Atum, lord of Heliopolis, lord of the two lands, Heliopolis. This name was crucial, for knowing it would enable the magician to call the god forth. On the extreme right of the vignette is a creature with the arms and legs of a man and the body and head of a serpent. In his hands he holds a circle, possibly the sun, with the child Harpocrates inside it. It seems as if he is presenting the disk and child to the god. Perhaps this represents the person who is in need of the god's help.

The second vignette (Figure 54) has the same format as the first, but the god with his composite representation is somewhat different. He has only two arms, but five sets of wings. In the right arm he has a flail, and in the left, a *was*-scepter. On his head are the heads of the falcon, lion, jackal, snake, and ram. Above the animals is the god Heh with the hieroglyph for "year" on top of his head. The feet of the gods are the heads of foxes. Like the god in the other vignette, his phallus is erect, perhaps suggesting the power of Min, the god of fertility.

The drawing was only the first step toward the completion of the magical ritual. The amuletic picture would probably be redrawn by the magician and placed around the neck of the client. The text of the papyrus tells the magician what to say for various situations. Because the papyrus is an instruction manual for the magician, the spells are in a general form. He might alter them according to the specific needs of the client. He first had to state the problem to be overcome. In the papyrus various enemies are mentioned. Some references are extremely general, such as "all things evil and harmful," and some are a bit more specific, such as "all thieves." It also seems that a problem of considerable concern was hostile actions by deceased enemies who returned to torment the living. There were also evil deities who had to be overcome.

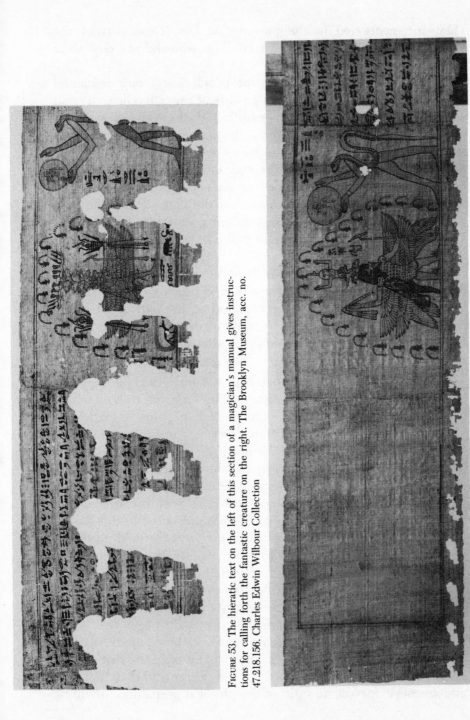

FIGURE 53. The hieratic text on the left of this section of a magician's manual gives instructions for calling forth the fantastic creature on the right. The Brooklyn Museum, acc. no. 47.218.156. Charles Edwin Wilbour Collection

FIGURE 54. In another section of the same papyrus, a magical creature surrounded by protective flames is called forth. The Brooklyn Museum, acc. no. 47.218.156, Charles Edwin Wilbour Collection

They are mentioned in the papyrus as the "Devourers of the West," who swallowed the heart of those who did not pass their judgment in the netherworld.

With the papyrus drawn and the problem stated, it remained for the magician to call forth the powers of the god. Once the god was invoked ("O Amun-Re, Come forth"), the next crucial step was to identify the client with the god: "His flesh is your flesh, his bones are your bones." The purpose of this was to direct the evil intentions of the adversary toward the god and not the man. This confrontation between the god and the enemy hopefully was not to take place, for the last step required of the magician was to convince the adversary that the confrontation would be fatal to him. This was usually done by reminding him of the awesome power of the god.

An interesting feature of this amuletic papyrus is that it shows that the magical spell was not considered infallible. Some skill in argumentation and cajoling was required on the part of the magician, first to convince the god to come forth and then to convince the adversary that he would lose the battle.

A special kind of amuletic papyrus was given to children, probably soon after birth. These papyri, usually long thin rolls on which a magical spell was written, were placed in either a leather or wooden container and worn around the neck to protect the child from any and all misfortunes. The magical spells were supposed to be the written word of a god or gods who promised to protect the child and then stated in considerable detail what dangers the amulet covered. These amulets do not deal at all with life after death, but are totally concerned with problems confronted in this world. Probably soon after the child's birth, the parents would go to the temple to purchase the amulet from the priests. Upon commission, the priests would draw up the amulet, mentioning the child by name, the parent(s), and the protection promised. The amulets are especially important because they draw a contemporary picture of what the ancient Egyptians feared.

Perhaps the greatest concern expressed in these papyri was over physical ailments. One typical amuletic papyrus in the British Museum first names the god who issued the decree and then launches into an encyclopaedic account of the physical protection provided:

Mont-Re-Harakhty, lord of Thebes, who is residing in (the Upper Egyptian) On, this great god, the eldest who was the first to come-into-existence, said: 'I shall keep safe Paditwerisheru called Djed-montefonekh, whose mother is Nespernut, son of Djedkhons [the] son of Hori, my servant. I shall keep him healthy [in] his flesh and his bone[s]. I shall keep healthy his head. I shall keep healthy every [?] *stu* of his head. I shall keep healthy his right eye and his left eye. I shall keep healthy his ears. I shall keep healthy his nose. I shall keep healthy [his] mouth. I shall keep healthy his tongue. I shall keep healthy his teeth. I shall keep healthy his throat. I shall keep healthy his neck. [I] shall keep healthy his right shoulder and his left shoulder. I shall keep healthy his belly. I shall keep healthy his heart. I shall keep healthy his lungs. I shall keep healthy his liver. I shall keep healthy his kidneys. I shall keep healthy his intestines. I shall keep healthy his entire abdomen. I shall keep healthy his right foot and his left foot. I shall keep healthy his entire body and all his limbs from his head to the soles of his feet. I shall enable him to grow up. . . . I shall keep him safe from every [kind of] death, every [kind of] illness, every [kind of] disorder, every [kind of] malady, every [kind of] fever, every [kind of] inflammation, every [kind of] *rmn*-sickness and every [kind of] mishap. I shall keep him safe from coughing, from any blindness [?] and from any *hk*. I shall keep him safe from ailment of the head, from a headache and from. . . . I shall keep him safe from any upset [?] and any eye-ailment.[12]

While physical concerns were considerable in ancient Egypt, magical ones were also great. Of the nearly two dozen oracular amuletic papyri, as they are called, almost all mention protection of some sort from evil demons and malicious magic. One papyrus in the Turin Museum indicates that the Egyptians believed that evil demons frequented watering areas:

We shall keep her safe from any action of a demon and from any interference of a demon. We shall keep her safe from any action of a demon of a canal, from any action of a demon of a well, from any action of a demon of [a pool] left [by the inundation], from any action of a demon of a cleft [?] and from any action of a demon of swamps.[13]

It was believed that the god who promised protection could counteract the evil magic of others. Thus, a frequent refrain in the papyri is: "I shall keep her safe from the magic of the Syrians, from the magic of the Ethiopians, from the magic . . . , [from the magic of the Shasu, from the magic of the Libyans, from the magic of the people of Egypt, from a warlock (?)]. . . ." [14]

Many people in Egypt consulted books of fate which, like the Cairo Calendar (see Chapter 15), foretold which days would be favorable and which unfavorable. One purpose of these oracular papyri was to make inoperative the unfavorable predictions. The books of fate most often named were the *Book of Death and Life,* the *Book of the Beginning of the Year,* and the *Book of the End of the Year.*

One of the great values of these written amulets is that they show us just how matter-of-factly the Egyptians took the belief in magic. While they show a tremendous concern for protection from demons, magic, and fate, such anxieties are on a par with nonmagical concerns. Thus, in almost the same line where the god is granting protection from swamp demons, he also grants protection from being crushed by a falling wall or being struck by lightning.

Written amulets such as the ones mentioned here do not seem to have been used throughout Egyptian history. While amulets were used in prehistoric times, written amulets were a relatively late development, probably the result of an abstraction from the image of a god to merely his words of protection. They made their final appearance around the Twenty-first Dynasty (1087–945 B.C.) and were used only for about two hundred years. The reason they went out of fashion is not known.

10. Magical Servant Statues

SMALL FIGURES, usually of wax or clay, were an integral part of
Egyptian magical practices. If a person wanted to destroy his enemy, he could do so by making a small clay figure of the enemy,
saying the proper incantation, then breaking the figure. By sympathetic magic, the figure took the place of the person it represented.
Such miniatures were used not only for malevolent purposes, but
also as aids to the deceased, vital to his existence in the afterlife.

Early in the Old Kingdom, there was a special chamber in the
mastaba called the *serdab*, where a life-size stone statue of the
deceased was housed. The purpose of the statue was to provide a
resting place for the soul in the event that the body of the deceased
was destroyed. These *serdabs* even had small slits in one wall so
that the statue could look out and receive offerings of food and
incense. Many poorer Egyptians were buried with a miniature
statue and coffin (Figure 55). At some point at the beginning of the
Middle Kingdom these miniature statues took on a different function. They became servants which, by magic, would come to life
and do any unpleasant chores the deceased might be called upon to
perform in the afterlife.

Because the daily life of ancient Egyptians centered around
agriculture, they viewed the next world also as primarily agrarian.
They believed that the deceased would have to plant the fields and
maintain irrigation canals, so the little statues buried in tombs began to look more like field workers than mummies. They retained
the mummiform shape so as to be identified with Osiris, the god of
the dead, but their hands were shown protruding from the bandages so as to be able to do work. During the Middle Kingdom the

FIGURE 55. If the body and coffin of Wah-Nefer-Hotep, a nobleman of the Middle Kingdom, were destroyed, these miniatures could serve as substitutes. The Metropolitan Museum of Art, Museum Excavations, 1913–1914, Rogers Fund, 1914

statues began to hold farm implements, often one hoe in each hand. The hoes were held upright with the shorter ends facing outward.

At first the statues were inscribed with only the name of the deceased, but soon they were inscribed with magical spells as well to ensure that they would really come alive to do their chores. Running in horizontal lines around the torso of the figure, the spells commanded the statues to work:

> O shawabti, if the deceased is called upon to do work in the next world, answer "Here I am!" Plough the fields, fill the canals with water and carry the sand of the east to the west.

The word *shawabti* apparently referred to the persea-tree out of which these little figures were occasionally made. Another word for them was *ushabti* which meant "answerer." The idea was that when the deceased was called to work, the figure would answer for him. The figures are called by both names today.

The job of moving sand from the east to the west, mentioned so often on shawabtis, is still a mystery. There was plenty of sand on both sides of the Nile. Why it should have to be brought from one side to the other is not known. Also, while the spells on a great majority of shawabtis mention transporting the sand from east to west, there are also some extant which command bringing the sand west to east. Egyptologists usually refer to these contradictions as errors on the part of scribes, who copied spells incorrectly from earlier figures. This cannot be the explanation because a few shawabtis read: ". . . from east to west and *vice versa* [italics mine]." On the backs of the most detailed figures are sacks, said to have been used for transporting sand. It seems more likely that the sacks represent seed packs for planting in the fields.

Once the main purpose of these figures changed from mummy substitutes to servants, a limit of one was no longer necessary, and it became desirable to have many. During the New Kingdom it was common to have hundreds. Because the number found in tombs is often nearly 365, it is believed by many that the Egyptians intended that there be one for each day. There is no evidence for this, and in fact the number is rarely exactly 365. The pharaoh Taharqa had more than one thousand shawabtis, each one a beautifully carved stone statue.

Shawabtis varied considerably in size and materials, depending upon what the deceased could afford. The least expensive were terra cotta, sometimes only two inches in length, mass-produced from molds. Some shawabtis were so crudely made that they had no facial features and look less like people than fossilized cigars (Figure 56). Such shawabtis, buried with the poor, never had inscriptions. The deceased just had to hope they would know what to do. If he were a bit wealthier, he could have large terra cotta shawabtis, up to nine inches in height. These were more detailed and frequently had the name of the deceased painted on the front in black ink (Figure 57). Another material commonly used was faience. These were made in molds also, and varied considerably in size and quality. The poorest-quality faience shawabtis were quite similar to the poorest-quality terra cotta—small, uninscribed, with minimal features. Some of the larger faience shawabtis were exquisite works of art, the most common glaze being a dark blue. (Even though the primary purpose of such figures was to do work, the Egyptians still attempted to make them beautiful.)

FIGURE 56. The poor man often was provided with crudely fashioned shawabtis, such as these. Photograph by Russell Rudzwick

FIGURE 57. The name of the deceased and a magical formula are written in hieratic on the front of this terra cotta shawabti. Photograph by Russell Rudzwick

FIGURE 58. A fifteen-inch ebony shawabti, belonging to the pharaoh Amenhotep III, was only one of hundreds originally in the tomb. The Metropolitan Museum of Art, Rogers Fund, 1915

By far the most elaborate shawabtis were carved in wood or stone, most commonly in limestone or serpentine. These were reserved for royalty and the high-ranking nobility. Each was an individually carved statue, usually with the magical spell around the torso (Figure 58). A shawabti belonging to Amenhotep II carried not hoes, but an *ankh* in each hand to bring life to the pharaoh in the next world. More often, the shawabtis of kings have farm implements in their hands. Evidently, there was concern that in the next world even the pharaoh could be called upon to work in the fields.

Bronze was by far the rarest material used for shawabtis. Only a few of these extant are known to be authentic, most notably those belonging to the pharaohs Ramses II and Ramses III of the Nineteenth Dynasty and to Psusennes of the Twenty-first Dynasty. There seems to have been no attempt made to shape even these specially made royal shawabtis in the likeness of their owners. The magical spell was considered enough to link the statue with the individual in the next world.

Unique in this respect are the shawabtis of Tutankhamen. Four hundred and thirteen shawabtis of alabaster, limestone, and wood were found in his tomb. The wooden ones are the finest, each a recognizable portrait of the king. Perhaps the reason for the unusually realistic portrayal is that many of these shawabtis were commissioned by Tutankhamen's high officials. They represented a personal link with the king. Carved on the soles of their feet are dedications such as: "Made by the Servant beloved of his Lord, the General Min-nekht, for his Lord, the Osiris, the King, Neb-khepru-Re, justified." [1] Apparently, the servants of Tutankhamen provided him with servants for eternity.

When they began burying shawabtis in tombs in large numbers, the Egyptians foresaw that the shawabtis might become unruly and unable to organize themselves. They needed overseers. Therefore, for every ten or so shawabtis the Egyptians included an overseer, or *reis*. These boss shawabtis were similar to their charges except for two details: Usually, they did not hold the traditional farm implements, but a flail or some other sign of authority; and always they wore the kilted apron, a sign of authority (Figures 59*a* and 59*b*). It was virtually impossible to do manual labor while wearing this highly starched garment. The shawabtis for women were in the form of female mummies holding the traditional agricultural tools. Their overseers were also females.

When only one shawabti, intended as an emergency replace-
ment for the body, was placed in the tomb, it was often laid in or
near the sarcophagus. Later, when the primary function of shawabtis was to serve the deceased and when the figures became numerous, different places had to be found for them.

One such place was a niche carved in the wall of the burial
chamber. The shawabtis were placed there upright in neat rows.
Then the niche was plastered and painted over to conceal the
shawabtis from plunderers. It is an eerie experience for excavators
to uncover one of these niches. When the plaster is removed, there
staring out are hundreds of little servants waiting to do their work.

In the Eighteenth Dynasty the use of these niches changed
slightly because the servant statues took on the additional function
of magical protectors of the deceased as well as servants. Apropos
of this change the priests added a new section to the *Book of the
Dead*, Chapter 151. This chapter explains the placement and function of the protector statues. In each of the four walls of the burial
chamber, about four feet above the floor, there was a niche containing a different protector. Each was mounted on a brick.

The niche in the north wall held a traditional mummiform
shawabti to protect the deceased from enemies who might come to
destroy the body. The magical spell for this guardian of the north
is: "O thou who comest to cast down, I do not permit thee to cast
down. O thou who comest to push aside, I do not permit thee to
push aside. I am the protector of the deceased."

The niche in the south wall held a reed torch. Its flame was to
stop sand from clogging the burial chamber: "It is I who hinders
the sand from choking the secret chamber and who repels the one
who would repel him with the desert flame. I have set aflame the
desert. I have caused the path to be mistaken. I am the protector of
the deceased."

In the niche in the east wall was a small clay statue of Anubis,
frequently depicted lying upon his shrine or on a hill. This is referred to in his magical spell: "Thou watchful one, watchful also is
he-who-is-upon-his-mountain. Thy moment is repelled. I have repelled thy moment of rage. I am thy protector."

The fourth niche, in the west wall, held a *djed*-column of gold
and blue faience. The *djed*-column, an amulet for stability, may
have represented the backbone of Osiris. The magical spell for this

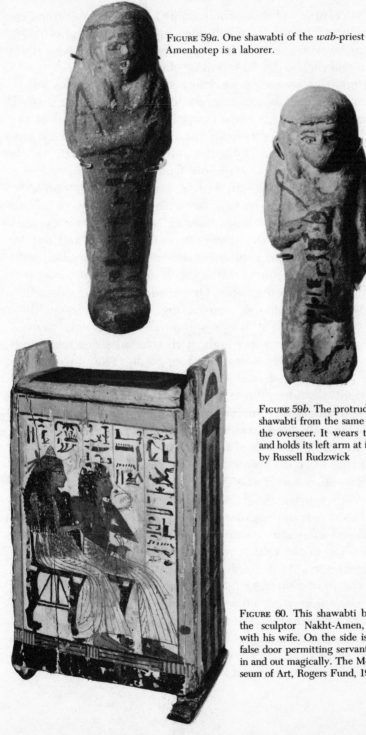

FIGURE 59a. One shawabti of the *wab*-priest Amenhotep is a laborer.

FIGURE 59b. The protruding torso of another shawabti from the same tomb identifies it as the overseer. It wears the kilt of authority and holds its left arm at its side. Photographs by Russell Rudzwick

FIGURE 60. This shawabti box belonged to the sculptor Nakht-Amen, shown seated with his wife. On the side is the traditional false door permitting servant statues to pass in and out magically. The Metropolitan Museum of Art, Rogers Fund, 1947

protector is cryptic: "O thou who comest seeking, whose steps are turned backwards, whose face is hidden but who reveals his hiding place, I am he who stands behind the *dad*, and it is I who stood behind the *dad* on the day of repelling slaughter."

The alternative to storing workmen shawabtis in niches was to house them in a specially constructed box. These boxes, or shrines, as they are often called, became popular toward the end of the Eighteenth Dynasty. They were almost always the shape of a legendary ancient shrine in the Delta town of Buto (Figure 60). While the shrine no longer exists, we know from its depiction in hieroglyphs that it was rectangular with a vaulted ceiling. Similarly, shawabti boxes are usually rectangular with a curved top to imitate the vaulting. Often one or more sides of these boxes was painted with false doors so that the shawabtis could pass in and out by magic. On one side there is often a painting of the deceased with his wife, sometimes in mummiform shape, upright, but sometimes seated in front of an offering table. One of the remaining sides often depicts Anubis, recumbent, protecting the workers within. Shawabti boxes are usually brightly painted, surprisingly gay objects. They are about two feet high, with two sides one and a half feet wide, the other two sides one foot wide. The top was the removable part, so the shawabtis were packed in from there, usually in upright positions. When one looks in from the top one sees rows of tiny heads. Sometimes two or even four of these boxes were needed to house all the shawabtis of a wealthy tomb owner.

While the primary work of these shawabtis was agricultural, in rare instances other occupations are represented. One shawabti, once in the collection of the New York Historical Society, was equipped with a brick mold. Apart from individual instances of nonagricultural occupation, there was sometimes an entire retinue of magical servant statues created to do every conceivable chore for their master in the next world. Unlike mummiform shawabtis, these magical servants were shaped in extremely realistic detail. Some are the most charming pieces of art produced by the Egyptians, and since they were intended to provide for *all* the needs of the deceased's continued existence, they give us a good picture of the daily life of ancient Egypt. These models were considered so vital to the dead Egyptian's well-being that sometimes they were buried in a secret compartment in the tomb. One of these compartments was discovered by H.E. Winlock, who in 1920 was excavating at Thebes with the Egyptian Expedition of the Metropolitan Museum of Art.

Winlock had had a difficult season, having found nothing of value. With the brutal heat of the Upper Egyptian summer just a few months away, his team had little time for further excavating and decided to clear the rubble from a large tomb in the cliffs on the western side of the Nile. The tomb had been excavated previously, but they hoped that it had not been a thorough job and that something worthwhile might be found. After three weeks of work, it looked as if the strategy had been a bad one, and Winlock was faced with the unhappy prospect of reporting to the Metropolitan Museum that nothing had been found. On the early evening of March 17, Winlock left the dig. He was undoubtedly mentally composing his report when a message reached him from the team photographer Harry Burton (who three years later would become the photographer for the Tutankhamen discovery). The note read: "Come *at once* and bring your electric torch. Good luck *at last.*" When Winlock arrived at the tomb, he was shown a small crack at the base of the wall at the floor. One of the workmen who had been clearing the shale chips from the floor noticed that they fell through a crack as fast as he dug. The foreman had been told and Burton called. Burton had had only matches, which did not give off enough light to see into the crack, so when Winlock arrived no one knew what, if anything, was concealed under the floor. Winlock, stretched out on his stomach, aimed his flashlight and looked in. He later wrote:

> . . . I was gazing down into the midst of a myriad of brightly painted little men going this way and that. A tall slender girl gazed across at me perfectly composed; a gang of little men with sticks in their upraised hands drove spotted oxen; rowers tugged at their oars on a fleet of boats, while one ship seemed foundering right in front of me with its bow balanced precariously in the air. And all of this busy going and coming was in uncanny silence, as though the distance back over the forty centuries I looked across was too great for even an echo to reach my ears.[2]

He had discovered the secret compartment for the magical servants of Meket-Re, a wealthy nobleman of the Middle Kingdom

FIGURE 61. The chancellor Meket-Re was to be transported magically to the next world in this model funerary boat. The Metropolitan Museum of Art, Museum excavations, 1919–1920; Rogers Fund, Supplemented by contribution of Edward S. Harkness

(Figure 61). His tomb had been plundered and most of the grave goods robbed, but his tiny servants, hidden so well, had escaped the robbers.

Winlock's find is a permanent exhibit in the Egyptian collection of the Metropolitan Museum of Art. In one model building is a carpenter's shop complete with a small furnace for sharpening tools. Kneeling workmen can be seen squaring timber to make beams for Meket-Re's house, and others are smoothing them with blocks of sandstone. Another building contains both a bakery and a brewery (Figure 62). In one room women grind the grain, and one

FIGURE 62. A bakery and a brewery, miniatures from the tomb of Meket-Re, were to provide their owner with bread and beer in the netherworld. The Metropolitan Museum of Art, Museum excavations, 1919–1920; Rogers Fund, Supplemented by contribution of Edward S. Harkness

man makes flour into dough while another makes mash in a barrel. Tall jars containing the fermenting mash stand by one wall. Still another brewer pours the completed mash into beer jars, so that Meket-Re can enjoy his beer in the next world. On the other side of the wall tiny bakers place loaves of bread into ovens, so that he can have bread with his beer. Weavers produce fabric for Meket-Re's clothing. Nearby are stables where cattle are fattened, and there is a slaughterhouse where they are shown tied up, lying on the floor ready for slaughter (Figure 63). In one corner of the slaughterhouse two men make blood pudding, undoubtedly a favorite of Meket-Re. In another area a scribe records the animals slaughtered so that in the next world Meket-Re's accounts will be accurate.

Meket-Re's wonderful little servant statues are not unique. Any wealthy nobleman of the Middle Kingdom would have wanted an entire entourage of magical servants to meet his every need. They would be expected to prepare his food, weave his cloth, till his land, and see to his needs "for millions of years."

FIGURE 63. Meket-Re's miniature slaughterhouse is complete with hanging sides of beef. The Metropolitan Museum of Art, Museum excavations, 1919–1920; Rogers Fund, Supplemented by contribution of Edward S. Harkness

"Can you see anything?"
"Yes, wonderful things."

—Lord Carnarvon and Howard Carter

11. Magical Objects in Tutankhamen's Tomb

In 1914, having previously stated that he believed there were no more important discoveries to be made, Theodore Davis relinquished his concession to excavate in the Valley of the Kings. This mistaken belief made possible what is probably the single most important discovery in the history of Egyptology—the almost-intact tomb of the pharaoh Tutankhamen.

The Valley of the Kings, which lies on the west bank of the Nile, opposite Luxor, is the burial place of the pharaohs of the New Kingdom. The pharaohs of the Old Kingdom were buried in pyramids, obvious targets for tomb robbers during times of civil distress when they could not be protected. All the pyramids containing pharaohs' bodies were robbed by Eighteenth Dynasty times.

Tuthmose I, in an attempt to safeguard his body, conceived a new plan: He would have a secret tomb cut into the desolate valley on the west bank. So concerned was he for secrecy that evidently the laborers who worked on the tomb were killed. The architect for the tomb, Ineni, recorded on the wall of his tomb with great pride, "I superintended the excavation of the cliff tomb of his Majesty, alone, no one seeing, no one hearing." Howard Carter suggests that the work may have been carried out with foreign prisoners to make the slaughter more acceptable. Pharaohs succeeding Tuthmose I added their tombs to different areas in the Valley of the Kings, but in time most of these, too, were robbed, first by ancient grave robbers, later by modern adventurers, and still later by Egyptologists.

The valley has always been an area of investigation with special mystery about it. The list of excavators who have worked the area

FIGURE 64. This illustration by David Roberts shows the Valley of the Kings in the 1850s. Tutankhamen's undiscovered tomb lies almost exactly at the point of the long stave held by the standing figure.

is long. In the nineteenth century, Belzoni, the Italian strongman-turned-adventurer, did the first systematic excavation of the valley, discovering the tombs of Aye, Ramses I, and Seti I. He left the valley believing that there was no other tomb left to be discovered, though his conviction did not discourage others (Figure 64). Subsequent searchers in the valley included Champollion, Henry Salt, Burton, Lepsius, and many others. In 1898, Loret, who was head of the Service of Antiquities, discovered the tombs of Tuthmose I, Tuthmose III, and Amenhotep II. After Loret, Davis found the tombs of Tuthmose IV, the woman-king Hatshepsut, Horemheb, and other less important tombs. After these discoveries he relinquished his concession.

Howard Carter had excavated in Thebes and been an inspector in the Antiquities Department. He knew the area well and for years had hoped to excavate in the Valley of the Kings. George Edward

Stanhope Molyneux Herbert, the fifth Earl of Carnarvon, had gone to Egypt to recover from a near-fatal automobile accident and while there had become interested in archaeology. In 1907, Carter and Carnarvon formed a partnership: Carnarvon would finance a series of excavations; Carter would direct the work. For several years, then, they excavated, making modest finds. When Davis gave up his concession to the valley, the Carter-Carnarvon team took over.

Their discovery of Tutankhamen's tomb is often assumed to have been a wonderful piece of luck. This is simply not so. When Carter got the concession he specifically had in mind the discovery of this tomb. There were various clues that linked Tutankhamen with the valley: Davis had found under a rock a faience cup with Tutankhamen's name on it. He had also found a small pit with the remains of the king's ritual meal and embalming as well as some gold leaf with Tutankhamen's name on it. Most important, Carter realized that Tutankhamen's tomb had not yet been discovered. With the concession in hand Carter and Carnarvon agreed to conduct what they called "a systematic and exhaustive search" of the Valley of the Kings. It was some time, however, before they could begin. World War I delayed their digging until late in 1917.

The plan was to clear right down to bedrock any area that had not been previously thoroughly excavated. One prime area that contained quite a bit of debris was a triangular area formed by the tombs of Merneptah, Ramses II, and Ramses III. Carter had the upper layers cleared and eventually worked down to the base of the tomb of Ramses VI. Then they found ancient workmen's huts, probably from the construction of the tomb of Ramses VI. Clearing the huts would have closed off access to the tomb of Ramses VI, one of the most popular with tourists, so Carter excavated in another part of the valley and returned to that area during a slack period in tourism.

It was therefore not until November of 1922 that the Carter-Carnarvon excavation began clearing the huts. On November 4, one of the workmen discovered a step cut into the ground. It took another day to clear away enough of the debris to expose all four sides of the stairway. At sunset of November 5, at the twelfth step, the upper part of a sealed doorway was found. The royal necropolis seal was there, so the team knew almost certainly that it was a king's tomb. Through a small hole near the lintel of the door Carter could see that the passage behind the plastered door was filled with rubble. The tomb was intact. The only thing that bothered him was the smallness of the stairway, only six feet wide. Most of the other entrances to kings' tombs are considerably wider.

Carnarvon was in England at the time, so Carter had the stairway filled in again and cabled his patron: "AT LAST HAVE MADE A WONDERFUL DISCOVERY IN VALLEY; A MAGNIFICENT TOMB WITH SEALS INTACT; RE-COVERED SAME FOR YOUR ARRIVAL; CONGRATULATIONS."

By November 25, Carnarvon had arrived and arrangements had been made for opening the sealed door. When the door was removed it was clear that the tomb had been entered previously. In ancient times a narrow path had been made through the rubble, almost certainly by robbers. It took the entire day to clear the thirty-foot-long descending passage from ceiling to floor. In the rubble were some alabaster jars, pottery, and workmen's tools. Finally, a second sealed door was reached. This door showed evidence of having been breached and resealed. Carter made an opening in the upper left-hand corner of the doorway and inserted a candle to test the air. First it flickered because of the escaping hot air, and then Carter could see—"wonderful things"!

Carter was peering into what would later be called the "antechamber." It was piled with funerary furniture, personal belongings of the king, and offerings. Everything was numbered, photographed, and diagrammed. Then one by one the objects were removed to a laboratory set up in the tomb of Seti II, where preservative or restorative procedures were performed.

From the very beginning of the excavation, the tomb became the focus of the attention of occultists. At one point in the removal of the objects from the antechamber, the sky began to darken, and it looked as if one of those rare torrential downpours was about to hit Thebes. Such an event would have been a disaster because water would have poured into the tomb, ruining many of the objects. But the clouds passed. Even so, Carter received the following cable: "IN CASE OF FURTHER TROUBLE, POUR MILK, WINE AND HONEY ON THE THRESHOLD." In his three-volume work on the tomb, Carter wryly comments, "Unfortunately, we had neither wine nor honey with us, so were unable to carry out the directions. In spite of our negligence, however, we escaped the further trouble." [1]

It took the better part of the excavation season to clear the contents of the antechamber. Objects had been piled on top of one another, so that often it was a difficult logistical problem to move one thing without disturbing ten others. Surprisingly few magical objects were in the antechamber. There is an occult tradition that a clay tablet was found which had a curse written on it. In his popular book, *The Curse of the Pharaohs,* Philip Vandenberg mentions the tablet.

> Those at the site, however, especially the scholars, were less euphoric. In fact, they became increasingly nervous. The reason for their concern was an ordinary clay tablet Carter had found in the antechamber. He had it catalogued, as he did the other objects. Then, a few days later, Alan Gardiner decoded the hieroglyphics on it. The inscription read:
>
> > Death will slay with his wings
> > whoever disturbs the peace of
> > the pharaoh.
>
> Neither Carter nor Gardiner nor any of the other scholars present feared the curse then or took it seriously. But they worried that the Egyptian laborers would, and since they were dependent on native helpers, mention of the clay tablet was wiped from the written record of the tomb's discovery. Even the tablet itself disappeared from the artifact collection—but not from the memory of those who read it. (The tablet and the curse on it are cited everywhere, but it was never photographed and is considered lost.) [2]

It is doubtful that such a clay tablet ever existed. There are no reliable references to such a curse and it is not typically Egyptian to speak of death as a being with wings or to write on clay tablets. It is interesting that Vandenberg says in one paragraph that the scholars on the site were not euphoric because of the curse and in the next he says that none of them took the curse seriously.

Of the entire contents of the antechamber perhaps only two objects might be considered magical. On the far end of the antechamber was a sealed door leading to the burial chamber. On either side of this door was a life-size wooden statue of Tutankhamen. The statues represent the pharaoh with black skin, wearing a gold kilt and gold sandals. He is striding, with a staff in his left hand and a mace in his right. The statues were positioned facing each other, so as to guard the door to the burial chamber.

For some reason these two statues were very special to Howard

Carter. At one point he describes them as "Strange and imposing figures these . . . they present an appearance that is almost painfully impressive." [3] By itself this is not terribly surprising, as many objects in the tomb might be described in similar terms. What is surprising is that Carter was extremely reluctant to move them. After every item in the tomb had been removed, the floor swept and the dust sifted for the last bead, the sentinel figures were still in place. When it came time to break down the wall the statues were *still* there. They were in such an awkward place that Carter mentions that workmen had to board them up to protect them. Why not move them? This was such an obvious question that Carter had to say something: "With the exception of the two sentinel statues, left for a *special reason* [author's emphasis], all its contents had been removed. . . ." [4] Carter never told what this special reason was and it remains a puzzle.

One explanation is offered in a book by Barry Wynne, *Behind the Mask of Tutankhamen.* A significant portion of the book is based on interviews with Richard Adamson, a curious man Carter hired to guard the tomb. Adamson says Carter's reason was superstition. He says that, since the statues represented Tutankhamen's *ka*, or spirit, Carter wanted to leave them to guard the body of the pharaoh. In the evenings Carter frequently spoke with everyone around, giving a summary of the day's events. One evening Adamson asked:

> "Those two big statues sir; what are they, and why don't you move them?"
>
> Carter looked at him benignly.
>
> "They are the Royal Kas, the abode of the pharaoh's soul, Richard. They become the refuge for the soul during the period of mummification. It is within those statues that it was believed the pharaoh still lived." [5]

It will be noticed that Carter never really answered the question of why he hadn't moved them. The suggestion that it was out of superstition simply doesn't square with all other descriptions of Carter, nor with his writing, in which he is sharply anti-occult.

The puzzle may be solved in a recent book, *Tutankhamun, The Untold Story,* by Thomas Hoving, the former director of the Metropolitan Museum of Art. Hoving, using museum letters and files to which he, as director, had access, puts forward the theory that Carter broke into the burial chamber and stole some artifacts before the official opening. The crucial evidence is the ancient robber entry on the north wall of the antechamber. Carter reports that he found a discolored area in the middle of the wall near the floor where robbers had broken in. The necropolis officials had resealed it in ancient times. Hoving contends that Carter saw that the repair had been done poorly and was able to remove some of the blocks of stone in the wall and slip into the burial chamber. He was then joined by Lord Carnarvon and Evelyn Herbert, Carnarvon's daughter. To cover their entry, after leaving the burial chamber Carter picked up the lid to a reed basket and leaned it against the wall with a pile of reeds. If Hoving's thesis is correct, then Carter would not want to remove the basket and reveal the breach in the wall. This, in fact, seems to be the case. Plate XLI of the first volume of Carter's three volumes shows the last remaining objects in the tomb, the sentinel statues and the basket and reeds.

There is even further evidence overlooked by Hoving: Carter had a small platform constructed to stand on while removing the wall from the top down. Leaving the statues in place forced the platform to be placed in front of the breach. Plate XLIII shows the platform with Carnarvon and Carter standing on it. There appears to be about one inch between either side of the platform and the guardian statues which have been boarded up. Once Carter had torn down most of the wall, he could quickly dismantle the evidence he wished to hide, which was behind the platform. Plate XLV is extremely revealing in this respect. It shows the platform removed, revealing a small section of the wall intact. It appears that Carter removed the traces of his entry and left as much of the wall standing as possible—as if to say, "See it's OK." The picture also shows reeds strewn all over the floor. This does not support Carter's description of the antechamber: ". . . every inch of its floor had been swept and sifted for the last bead or fallen piece of inlay. . . ." [6]

That Carter was preoccupied with the guardian statues is clear. He mentions them an inordinate number of times, and they appear in a surprising number of plates. What is most surprising is that the very first plate in the three volumes is one of the guardian statues. This is certainly inappropriate. Plate III is the Entrance to the

Valley of the Kings, Plate IV of the valley proper, and so on. Why place the guardian statues first in the layout? Clearly they were on Carter's mind, and for good reason.

Carter's may not have been the only mind on which the guardians preyed. If Hoving's contention is correct, then probably other members of the expedition team knew of the illegal entry. One who may have known and who had an interesting encounter with one of the statues was James Henry Breasted. Hoving tells of the unusual incident:

> Breasted happened to look into the face of one of the two royal guardians. Suddenly one of the sentinels winked! Breasted almost fainted. At length he got the courage to get up and take a look at the statue. Only when he was close at hand did he see the reason for its frightening behavior. Attached to a virtually invisible filament hanging from the King's eyebrow was a tiny piece of dark pigment dropping off in iridescent, micalike flakes. In a gentle breeze that had momentarily passed through the entrance into the Antechamber, the minute flake of ancient paint, shivering slightly, had mirrored the light in such a way that it resembled the wink of the eye.[7]

The reason Breasted was floored by the sentinel statue may have been that he knew Carter's secret. Certainly others knew.

Strong evidence links Lord Carnarvon with an entry into the burial chamber prior to the official opening, and it supports the theory that the statues were kept in place because of the fear that the hole in the wall might be discovered. The evidence comes from a diary kept by Lord Carnarvon's brother, Mervyn Herbert. Herbert tells of driving to the opening with Carnarvon (who was called Porch) and his daughter Evelyn:

> Porch and Evelyn and I started in his Ford and, after we had been going a few minutes, he said that it would really be all right and he could quite well get me in while the tomb was being opened. Then he whispered something to Evelyn and told her to tell me.
>
> This she did under the strictest promise of secrecy—this is a thing I would never give away, in any case, and it is one which I think ought not to be known, at any rate, *for the present*. Here is the secret. They had both already been into the second chamber! After the discovery they had not been able to resist it—they had made a small hole in the wall (which afterwards they filled up again) and afterwards climbed through. She described to me very shortly some of the extraordinary wonders I was about to see.

> It was a most exciting drive. I cannot remember anything like it. The only others who know anything about it are the workmen; none of whom would ever breathe a word to a soul.[8]

It is ambiguous as to whether or not Carter went in with them, but we can deduce that he did, as it would have been difficult to conceal the entry from him. Mervyn Herbert does specifically mention that his brother was nervous at the opening, fearing that the breach would be discovered.

> Porch, poor old fellow, was nervous, like a naughty schoolboy, fearing that they would discover that a hole had already been made.[9]

Think how nervous he would have been if the scaffolding covering the hole had not been there!

While, with the exception of the sentinel statues, there were no magical objects in the antechamber, many were found in the burial chamber. This is logical. Since the main purpose of entombment was the protection of the body, the most important magical objects would be placed near it. Almost the entire burial chamber was taken up by the great shrine that held the mummy of the dead king. There were only about two feet on each side between the shrine and the four walls. It was brought into the burial chamber in sections and assembled there.

The burial chamber is rectangular and oriented to the four cardinal points. The orientation is extremely important in ancient Egyptian burials because the deceased has to head west. In the walls are niches for magical guards of the four cardinal points (mentioned in the chapter, "Magical Servant Statues"). The chamber itself is painted a light gold, which is traditional, the burial chamber being called "The Golden Hall." This is probably because gold does not tarnish, in keeping with the purpose of preservation. The walls of the tomb are sparsely painted, probably because the boy-king died unexpectedly, leaving little time to prepare the tomb. One scene shows Aye, Tutankhamen's successor, acting as high-priest, performing the opening-of-the-mouth ceremony. On a table are the various tools used in this rite. On the east wall is a traditional funerary scene showing the mummy being pulled on a sled to the tomb.

There are actually four shrines, one inside the other, all without floors. Probably the reason for the lack of floors was that, since the shrines contained a heavy stone sarcophagus and an even heavier gold coffin, floors could not have supported such weight. The shrines are made of wood coated with gesso and an outer layer of embossed gold. The body of Tutankhamen still lies in its stone sarcophagus in the tomb, while the golden shrines and outer coffin are in the Cairo Museum. The gold is inscribed with religious texts, such as Chapter 17 of the *Book of the Dead*, which deals with the creation of the world, and the *Book of the Divine Cow*, which tells of the sun god's reign on earth and mankind's punishment for lack of obedience. The *Book of the Divine Cow* consists of magical spells to be uttered to assure the well-being of the deceased. Specific instructions are given as to the conditions under which they are to be said:

> If a man pronounces this spell over himself he should be anointed with oil and unguent, the censer being in his hands with incense. Natron must be behind his ears, *Bed*-natron must be in his mouth, dressed in two new garments, having washed himself in inundation water, shod in white sandals, and the figure of the Truth goddess being painted on his tongue in green painter's colors.[10]

The book also specifies *who* should recite specific spells. Thus, there are certain spells which must be recited by a magician who knows the art well and can properly perform the ritual:

> A magician, his head being purified, should make a female figure standing by his south side. He should represent her a goddess and in the middle of her a snake standing erect on its tail, her hand being placed on its body while its tail is on the ground. Thoth should adore him [the magician], all the dignity of heaven being on him while Shu stretches his arms toward it. [He should recite:]
>
> I am safe from these great and mighty gods, who sit in the eastern part of heaven, who guard the sky, who guard the earth, the mysterious functionaries.[11]

All of these spells are designed to assure a safe journey through the tomb, underworld, and heavens. Thus, "If an accomplished scribe knows these divine words and his spells, he will come out and come down out of the interior heaven."

The texts on the shrines are meant to be read or recited in sequence, starting from the inside of the smallest, innermost shrine and working outward to the outside largest, outermost shrine. Not only the religious and magical texts are important; their shapes are significant. The innermost shrine is shaped like the predynastic Palace of the North, the House of Flame, and thus symbolizes the dead king's reign over Lower Egypt. The two middle shrines represent the Palace of the South, The Great House, and symbolize the king's rule over Upper Egypt. The largest shrine is in the shape of the sanctuary of the Sed Festival, the king's rejuvenation. So the shapes of the shrines go in the same order that the texts are to be read. In the first three shrines are statements of the king's earthly rule. In the fourth is an affirmation of his rejuvenation.

It took Carter the better part of a season to dismantle the shrines, as the sides had in some places been crudely forced together. Another instance of careless handling was that ancient workmen ignored instructions painted on the shrines to orient them so that the doors opened to the west. The doors open on the east. We can only hope that the boy-king had a good sense of direction.

On the floor, surrounding the shrines, were magical objects, some of which are unique and their meaning not fully understood. Between the shrine and the north wall were ten magical oars which were to be used to row the pharaoh's boats to the next world. (These boats were the crescent moon and the ship-constellation.) Also along the wall was a double kiosk made of wood and painted black. Inside each kiosk was a faience cup, one containing natron, the other resin. The two are separated by a stone amulet shaped like Υ , which Carter calls, "Feather of Truth." However, since the contents of the faience cups were ingredients used in the embalming ceremony, it is more likely that the stone amulet represents one of the tools used in the opening-of-the-mouth ceremony (Figure 65).

Surrounding the shrines were magical emblems of Anubis, the god of embalming. These emblems are extremely strange, and it is not completely certain what they are. They are almost six feet high and each consists of a gilded wooden pole from which hangs a wooden carving of an animal skin, also gilded. The curious shape is set into an alabaster pot painted with the royal cartouche.

Along another wall were four wooden sticks covered with gold leaf. They are shaped like $\int$. Nothing like them had ever been found previously. At the time of their discovery Alan Gardiner, who did most of the translation for Carter, suggested that, because they look like the hieroglyph for "to awake," they may have had

FIGURE 65. Among these alabaster models of equipment used in the opening-of-the-mouth ceremony is the tool touched to the mummy's mouth. The Metropolitan Museum of Art

the magical function of awakening the sleeping king. Four small clay troughs found next to them probably have some connected magical function.

After the objects surrounding the shrine were removed and the four shrines dismantled and removed from the burial chamber, the sarcophagus could be opened. Between the innermost shrine and the sarcophagus was a wooden *djed* column, representing the backbone of Osiris and giving stability to the pharaoh. On each corner of the beautifully carved quartzite sarcophagus is a goddess stretching her protective wings. On the northwest corner is Isis, on the southwest, Nephthys, on the northeast, Neith, and on the southeast, Selket. Inside the sarcophagus was a gilded wooden anthropoid coffin in the likeness of Tutankhamen. Inside that was a second anthropoid coffin. Inside that was the famous solid gold coffin containing the mummy of Tutankhamen.

The greatest concentration of magical objects was found within the gold coffin and around the mummy. A black scarab made of resin adorned the neck portion of the gold coffin. Inscribed on the scarab was the magical *Benu*-bird. On the chest of the dead king was a gold cloisonné *ba*-bird, protecting the pharaoh's soul. Hanging from the *ba*-bird were gold plaques bearing magical inscriptions intended to ensure that the gods would welcome Tutankhamen. This is done by putting words into the gods' mouths. For instance, Nut, the sky goddess, says:

"I reckon thy beauties, O Osiris, King Neb Kheperu Re; thy soul livest, thy veins are firm. Thou smellest the air and goest out as a god. . . ."

Seth, the storm god, welcomes Tutankhamen as his son:

"My beloved son, inheritor of the throne of Osiris, the king Neb Kheperu Re; thy nobility is perfect; thy royal palace is powerful. . . ."

Other parts of the plaques say that the four sons of Horus honor Tutankhamen.

When the lid of the gold coffin was removed most present were disappointed because it was clear that the body of the king was in terrible condition. The linens in which the mummy had been wrapped were so saturated with unguents used in the embalming ritual that they were almost totally destroyed. In addition the unguents had run off the body into the bottom of the coffin, and the mummy was stuck fast in a hardened pitch-like morass. Within the wrappings were more than one hundred magical objects, mostly amulets to protect the body.

Wrapped within the head bandages was a small headrest amulet. Such an amulet is mentioned in Chapter 166 of the *Book of the Dead* as having the power to cause the deceased to "rise up from nonexistence." The material out of which such amulets were made was an important part of the ritual. Usually, headrest amulets were made out of hematite, but in a break with this tradition, Tutankhamen's amulet is made of iron. One of the earliest Egyptian uses of iron, it must have been a most treasured object.

About the king's neck were six collars and twenty amulets wound into the six layers of linen. After a "Collar of Horus" done in sheet gold, there was a necklace of four amulets strung on gold wire. First was a red jasper "knot of Isis." According to the *Book of the Dead*, whoever wears such a knot will have the protection of Isis and her son Horus and will be welcomed into the next world.

The red represents the blood, magic, and power of Isis. Then there was a gold *djed*-column with magical inscription. The *Book of the Dead* states that whoever wears the gold *djed* may enter into the next world, eat the food of Osiris, and be justified. There was also a green feldspar papyrus scepter, ensuring the king's fertility in the next world, and a second gold *djed* inlaid with faience. Under all this was yet another layer of amulets in various materials: a green feldspar amulet of Toth, who would record the result of the weighing of Tutankhamen's heart against the feather of truth; a green feldspar amulet of Anubis, who would guard the body of Tutankhamen; a lapis lazuli amulet of Horus; and a red carnelian serpent's head. The *Book of the Dead* specifies what had to be said as the amulets were placed on the mummy and that the spells had to be uttered in a solemn voice.

Near these amulets Carter found a very small papyrus written in white ink. It was too decayed to read, but traces of the names of the gods Isis and Osiris could be made out, so that it may have been the section of the *Book of the Dead* dealing with magical amulets. This small fragment was the only papyrus found in the tomb, which is rather surprising. There were no historical documents or records of the king's reign, nor was there a *Book of the Dead*. Perhaps the texts on the golden shrine were intended as a substitute.

On the right and left thighs of the mummy were the emblems of the north and south—the uraeus of Buto for the north and the vulture Nekhebet for the south. Each of these was properly oriented: Since the king's head was to the west, the goddess of the south was on his right thigh and the goddess of the north on his left side. These emblems also were oriented correctly on the coffins.

On the arms of the king were numerous bracelets, and on his ankle was a gold amulet. While highly decorative, these ornaments probably also had magical protective powers. The hieroglyphic names for such jewelry originally meant protector of the arms and legs.

On the abdomen were numerous amulets that included three made of sheet gold. The significance of these three is still unknown. There were two magical knots, one a Y-shaped amulet placed on a gold oval of sheet gold, and a T-shaped symbol. Such amulets are not mentioned in the various copies of the *Book of the Dead*.

In all, 143 objects were found on the body of Tutankhamen.

Many had magical significance and had been placed there to protect the king's body and to ensure his well-being in the next world.

It took Howard Carter and his team four years to clear the antechamber and burial chamber of their contents (Figure 66). By 1926 there were still two rooms to be explored: a small room off the antechamber known as the "annex" and another off the burial chamber known as the "storeroom." Each had a different specific function. Both had been entered in ancient times.

The storeroom was literally packed with magical things the king would need in the netherworld. On the floor of the entrance, between the paws of a statue of Anubis facing west, was a magical reed torch with a brick stand which had a small hole in the middle in which the reed could be placed. Scratched on the brick was the ominous spell: "It is I who hinder the sand from choking the secret chamber, and who repel he who would repel him with the desert-flame. I have set aflame the desert [?], I have caused the path to be mistaken. I am for the protection of the Osiris." It was the duty of

FIGURE 66. Workers removing the objects from Tutankhamen's tomb. Visitors waited hours for a glimpse of an object as it was taken to the laboratory set up in a nearby tomb.

Anubis to guard this room, which in ancient times was called the "Treasury of the Innermost." Anubis was perched on a shrine that had several compartments. The compartments contained a number of funerary objects, including four blue faience forelegs of a bovine animal, probably having something to do with the ritual last meal or with the sacrifices made at the opening-of-the-mouth ceremony, and two wooden amulets in the shape of a mummy. The strangest objects in the shrine were two alabaster cups, one serving as the top of the other. Inside the bottom one was a mixture of resin, salt, and natron. These obviously had some connection with the embalming process.

Behind the Anubis shrine was the most important object in the room, the canopic shrine containing Tutankhamen's internal organs. It was made of gilded wood. Similar to the stone sarcophagus, on each side was a carving of one of the four protective goddesses. Each of these goddesses was associated with one of the sons of Horus who, in turn, protected the internal organs. Amset was guarded by Isis, Hapi by Nephthys, Duamutef by Neith and Qebesenef by Selket. Inside the wooden shrine was a smaller shrine carved out of alabaster, and inside the alabaster shrine were four jars and four miniature gold coffins containing the king's internal organs. On each coffin was a magical spell invoking the appropriate son of Horus and protective goddess:

> *Words spoken by Isis:* I close my arms over that which is in me. I protect Amset who is in me, Amset Osiris King Neb Kheperu Re, true of voice before the Great God.

> *Words spoken by Nephthys:* I embrace with my arms that which is in me. I protect Hapi Osiris King Neb Kheperu Re, true of voice before the Great God.

> *Words spoken by Neith:* I encircle with my arms that which is in me. I protect Duamutef who is in me, Duamutef Osiris King Neb Kheperu Re, true of voice before the Great God.

> *Words spoken by Selket:* My two arms are on what is in me. I protect Qebesenef who is in me. Qebesenef Osiris King Neb Kheperu Re, true of voice.

It was important that the contents of the canopic shrine be properly oriented to the four cardinal points, and instructions on the shrine gave the direction each goddess should face. However, just as with the golden shrines in the burial chamber, the orientation instructions were not followed. Selket should have faced east and Nephthys, the south, but the workmen reversed them.

All the king's servant statues and models, intended to meet his need in eternity, were stored in this room. There were: a miniature mill for grinding corn, a granary, and 413 shawabti figures. One curious thing about Tutankhamen's shawabtis is that they had extra tools for working in the fields of the next world. More than fifteen hundred miniature hoes, picks, and other implements had been added, as if the king feared that the shawabtis' tools might break from hard work.

One of the most interesting magical objects in this room was a wooden mold in the shape of Osiris. This mold was lined with linen and filled with rich topsoil deposited by the Nile. Seeds, mostly for grain, were planted in the topsoil. When they sprouted, they would be a green, living representation for Osiris, symbolizing resurrection. Tutankhamen had sought to identify himself with Osiris in that way and bring about *his* resurrection.

By the end of 1927, five years after the discovery of the tomb, Carter began clearing the last room of Tutankhamen's tomb, the annex. This little room was only fourteen feet long by eight and one-half feet wide by eight and one-half feet high. It had no decoration whatever. Just as the storeroom had a specific inventory—funerary furniture and magical objects needed by the dead king in eternity— the annex was designed to contain the magical oils and unguents, wine and food needed by Tutankhamen on his journey to the netherworld. The sacred oils must have been especially precious to the ancient Egyptians, as Tutankhamen was buried with thirty-four heavy alabaster vases containing more than one hundred gallons.

There is an interesting parallel from the tomb of Sit-Hat-Hor-Yunet, a princess of the Twelfth Dynasty. She was buried with a large alabaster jar (Figure 67) containing what the inscription called "cool water," which was supposed to be capable of bringing all living things into existence.

Magical unguents were poured on the mummy to preserve it, and these extra vases may have been buried with Tutankhamen for renewals of his state of preservation. (Judging from the residue within the gold coffin, more than five gallons were poured on the coffins and mummy of the king. For some unknown reason, there

FIGURE 67. "Cool water" was kept in this magical jar from the tomb of the princess Sit-Hat-Hor-Yunet. The Metropolitan Museum of Art, Rogers Fund, with a contribution from Henry Walters

was a conscious attempt to avoid anointing the head.) Every single vessel in the annex containing these sacred oils had been emptied by tomb robbers. When Carter removed the rubble from the passageway to the tomb he found several water skins. These may have been used by the thieves to carry off their loot.

By the time the last object was removed from the tomb of Tutankhamen, restored in the laboratory, and sent to the Cairo Museum, nearly ten years had passed since the tomb's discovery. More than ten thousand individual objects were found, a significant number of which had magical import. One of the benefits of finding a royal tomb nearly intact was that it permitted modern scholars to see to what extent royalty adhered to the religion and magical practices of their day. Tutankhamen, at least, would seem to have been grateful for any magical assistance he could get on his journey to the netherworld.

A word should be said about the famous curse of Tutankhamen. Almost everyone knows that it has been claimed that people closely associated with the discovery died soon thereafter as a result of an ancient curse. Perhaps the event that most fostered this belief was the death of Lord Carnarvon soon after he entered the burial chamber. Also, at the approximate time of his death in Cairo, there was a blackout, plunging the city into darkness. While it is true that Lord Carnarvon did die soon after he entered the burial chamber, it is also true that he was a man of poor health. He died of an infected mosquito bite. Further, as any visitor to Cairo knows, blackouts are still quite common and they were even more so in the 1920s.

There has also been talk about germs and bacteria in the tomb carrying illness and death. On the morning after the burial chamber was opened, sterile swabs were used to take cultures from the walls, floor, and shrine. Analysis showed that no life of any kind existed in the burial chamber at the time it was first opened, so that any illness contracted by members of the excavation did not come from ancient bacteria.

Indeed, an objective assessment of the health and well-being of the members of the expedition shows a pattern that might be expected from any excavation team of similar age range. Some members died fairly soon after the initiation of the excavation, and some lived for decades into old age. While Tutankhamen was unquestionably buried with many magical protections, it would seem as if they had no potency against twentieth-century Egyptologists.

As to anything which ye may do against
this, my tomb, the like thereof shall be
done to your property. I was an excellent
and knowing lector-priest; never did any
excellent magic remain secret from me.

—Curse from the tomb of Ankhmaahor

12. Letters to the Dead

THE ANCIENT EGYPTIANS believed a deceased person would continue living in the netherworld pretty much the same way he did
on earth. It is not surprising, then, that they also believed he would
be aware of what happened on earth after his death and that, if
favorably inclined, he could help the living. Sometime before the
Middle Kingdom, the Egyptians instituted the practice of writing
letters to the dead to enlist their help.

Unlike most ancient letters, these were almost always written
on bowls, which possibly contained offerings as well. A bowl was
placed at the tomb of the deceased to whom an appeal was made.
Because the entire text had to go on the bowl, often the letters
were brief and lacked many of the details of the reason for the
request. It was probably assumed that, since the deceased was all-
knowing, he would not have to be told details.

One of the finest examples of a letter to the dead is in the
Louvre. The bowl is almost a perfect hemisphere. The letter is in
hieratic writing, starting at the rim, running around and down,
spiraling toward the bottom of the bowl. Like most letters to the
dead, it consists of five basic parts: the address, some standard formula of greeting, praises of the deceased intended to persuade him
to help, statement of some wrong done to the writer, and the appeal for help.

The Louvre letter to the dead is from a mother, Merti, to her
deceased son, Mereri. The following is a translation of the letter,
broken down into its parts.

Address:

O Mereri, born of Merti.

200

Greeting:

The god Osiris-Khentamenti assures that you shall live for millions of years, by providing for the breath in your nose and by placing bread and beer by the side of Hathor, lady of the horizon. Your condition is like [one who] lives millions of times by order of the gods who are in the sky and on earth.

Praises:

You make obstacles to enemies who have evil characters [and who are] against your house, against your brother, and against your mother [who loves?] her excellent son Mereri. You were excellent on earth and thou are beneficent in the land of the dead. Invocations and offerings are made for you. The Haker Festival is celebrated for you. Bread and beer are placed upon the altar of the god Khentamenti. You sailed downstream in the night-bark [of the sun god]; you sailed upstream in the day-bark [of the sun god]. You are justified in front of every god. Make yourself my favorite dead person!

Wrong:

You know that he said to me, "I shall report against you and your children."

Appeal:

You report against it; you are in the place of justification![1]

The letter lacks information on the wrong done to Merti; apparently, she assumes that Mereri knows the details. It appears as if someone has threatened to accuse Merti and her children, probably in a court of law. She is asking her son to testify in her favor in the divine court before the gods.

The Egyptians were extremely legalistic. They believed that there were divine tribunals in the netherworld which could decide legal matters on earth. One of the functions of the priests was to consult with the gods to settle legal disputes. In this instance, a mother is asking her dead son to plead her case before the gods. Unfortunately, we have no record of what happened to Merti and her accuser.

Sometimes letters to the dead rambled, taking on an almost gossipy tone. A letter in the Haskell Oriental Museum in Chicago makes not one, but three, requests of the deceased. It is written on a pottery stand for a jar with a rounded bottom.

Like the Louvre letter, it is written to a deceased relative, in this case from a son to his father:

> This is an utterance that I said to thee concerning myself: "You know what Idu said concerning his son—'Whatever there may be in the next world, I will not allow him to be afflicted with any affliction.'" Do the same for me!
>
> Behold now, this pottery vessel is brought with respect to a litigation which thy mother is causing. It would be good if thou would support her.
>
> Cause now that there be born to me a healthy male child. Thou art an excellent spirit.
>
> Look now, as for those two maid servants who have caused pain to Seny—Nefertjentet and Itaji—combat them. Destroy every affliction that is against my wife. Thou knowest what I need concerning this; destroy it completely. As thou livest for me, the Great Goddess shall praise thee and happy shall be the face of the Great God over thee. He shall give thee purified bread with his two hands.
>
> I beg for a second healthy male child for thy daughter.[2]

The son asks four favors: (1) help for his grandmother's litigation; (2) that he be granted a male child; (3) that two maidservants who have afflicted his wife be dealt with; and (4) that his sister also be granted a male child. There are, then, three generations in this family who stand to benefit by the intervention of the deceased: his mother, his son, daughter-in-law and daughter, and his future grandsons.

From these two examples, it is clear that the ancient Egyptians believed that the dead could benefit the living. From another, written on papyrus, in the Leiden Museum, it is also clear that the deceased could do harm as well. This letter probably was written on papyrus because it was too long to fit on a bowl. It is from a widower to his wife who had died three years previously. The man was obviously in great misery and believed that his suffering was caused by his wife. He recounted how well he treated her and how he never deserted her, even after he had become well established and served the pharaoh. He reminded her of the fine linen he had provided for her burial, and finally asserted that, even though her sisters were still living in the house, he had not slept with any of them. He had been an exemplary husband, *both* while she was alive and after she was dead. He therefore could not understand why she was causing his miseries.

To the excellent spirit Ankhere! What evil thing have I done to thee, that I should have come into this wretched state in which I am? What have I done to thee? Thou hast laid hands on me, although I had done nothing evil to thee. Since I lived with thee as husband down to this day, what have I done to thee that I must hide [it]? What [have I done] to thee? Thou hast caused me to bring this accusation against thee. What have I done to thee? I will lay a complaint against thee with words of my mouth, in the presence of the Divine Ennead of the West, and it shall be decided betwixt thee and me [by means of] this writing. . . . What have I done to thee?

I made thee a [married] woman when I was a youth. I was with thee when I was performing all [manner of] offices. I was with thee, and did not put thee away. I did not cause thy heart to grieve. And I did it when I was a youth and when I was performing all [manner of] important offices for Pharaoh, without putting thee away but saying, "She has [always] been with [me]—so said I! And everyone who came to me before thee, I did not receive them on thy account, saying, "I will act according to thy desire." And now, behold, thou dost not suffer my heart to take comfort. I will be judged with thee, and one shall discern wrong from right.

Now behold, when I was training officers for the soldiery and the cavalry of Pharaoh, I [caused] them to come and lie on their bellies before thee, bringing all [manner of] good things to lay before thee, and I hid nothing from thee in thy day of life. I did not cause [thee to] suffer pain [in] aught that I did with thee, after the fashion of the lord. Nor didst thou find me disregarding thee after the fashion of a peasant in entering into a strange house. I caused no man to chide me [in] aught that I did with thee. And when they placed me in the position in which I am, I became unable to go abroad in my [wonted] fashion, and I came to do that which one like me does, when he is at home [concerning] thy unguent, and likewise thy provisions, and likewise thy clothes, and they were brought to thee, and I did not put them in a strange place, saying, "The woman is [there(?)]." So said I, and did not disregard thee. But behold, thou dost not know the good that I have done with thee.

I am sending to let thee know that which thou art doing. And when thou didst sicken of the sickness which thou didst have, I [caused to be brought] a master-physician, and he treated thee, and he did everything whereof thou didst say "Do it." And when I followed after Pharaoh journeying to the south, and this condition had come to pass with thee, I spent eight months without eating or drinking like a man. And when I arrived in Memphis, I asked [leave] of Pharaoh, and I [came] to the [place] where thou wast, and I wept exceedingly together with my people in front of [my] street-quarter. And I gave linen clothes to wrap thee, and I caused many clothes to be made, and I left no good thing that it should not be done for thee. And now, behold, I have passed three years dwelling [alone] without entering into a house, though it not be right that one like me should be caused to do it. And behold, I have done it on thy account. But behold, thou dost not know good from bad. It shall be decided betwixt thee and me. And behold, thy sisters in the house, I have not entered into one of them.[3]

While the writer of the letter never specifies exactly what it is that his deceased wife is doing to him, it is reasonable to assume that he believed she was doing it by magic.

One letter to the dead, in the Cairo Museum, indicates that the Egyptians believed diseases were caused by malicious magic and could be cured by the magic of the deceased. An elderly serving maid named Imiu was ill. In her behalf, a member of the household appealed to the deceased former head of the household to combat the bad magic.

Given by Dedi to the priest Antef, born of Iwnakht. As for this serving-maid Imiu who is sick, thou dost not fight for her night and day with every man and woman who does harm to her. Do you want your household to be desolated? Fight for her today anew so that her household may be established and so that water may be poured for thee. If you won't help, then your house will be destroyed. Can it be that you don't recognize that it is this serving-maid who tends your house among men? Fight for her. Watch over her. Save her from everyone who is doing her harm. Then shall thy house and children be established. Good be thy hearing![4]

As these letters to the dead indicate, the Egyptians believed that once a person "went west" his ties with the world were not irrevocably broken. He continued to be aware of what was happening and to be able to influence events important to him.

13. Oracles

AN ANCIENT EGYPTIAN temple was normally composed of three large rooms, one leading into another like a railroad flat. The first room was the open court, an unroofed area where commoners could come to pay respects to the gods. The second was usually roofed over and reserved for the nobility. The third, known as the "holy of holies," was reserved for the priesthood (Figure 68). The holy of holies of different temples had different names. One in a temple built by Tuthmose III was called, "His Great Throne Is Like the Horizon of Heaven."

The temple design was intended to impress upon a visitor that, as he walked farther and farther into the temple, he was nearing a mysterious, sacred place. Between the open court and the enclosed court, there was a ramp or stairway taking the visitor from almost complete openness into an enclosed area. Then, another ramp or stairway led up to the holy of holies, where the ceiling was lower than in the enclosed court. Thus, as the visitor proceeded deeper into the temple complex, the space became smaller and more closed off, and so more mysterious and rarefied.

In the holy of holies were kept oracles—cult statues used for forecasting the future and obtaining divine guidance. Most frequently of Amun (Figure 69), these statues were kept in shrines of stone and were carried about in shrines made of gilded wood, much like the sacred barks sailed on the Nile by the pharaoh during festivals. These portable shrines rested on two long wooden poles, so that they could be carried about on the shoulders of the priests during religious ceremonies.

FIGURE 68. The shrine in the holy of holies in the Temple of Edfu housed the cult statue. The pedestal in front was a resting place for the sacred boat used to transport the statue.

FIGURE 69. The distinguishing crown of double feathers identifies a cult statue of the god Amun. Drawing by Marilyn Papas

According to various ancient texts, oracles could nod their heads and even talk. Since no talking oracle statue has ever been found, we are not certain how this was done. Perhaps the priests surreptitiously pulled strings to make the head nod or, divinely inspired, spoke for the god. This is all conjecture, but we do know that these statues were consulted for all sorts of purposes. There is even a record of one having solved a crime.

The story of the oracle-sleuth is told on a papyrus in the British Museum. The crime took place in Thebes, the capital of Egypt during the New Kingdom. During the Festival of Ipet, the statue of Amun was carried on the shoulders of shaven-headed priests from the Temple of Karnak to the Temple of Luxor. During this festival, which lasted more than a week, the various cult statues of the districts of Thebes also participated. They, too, were brought out from the holy of holies for the people to see. The British Museum papyrus says that the statue of Amun in the Theban district of Pe-Khenty solved the crime.

During the festival a citizen named Amunemwia appeared before his local oracle and reported a theft. Amunemwia's job was to guard the storehouse of a nobleman. Apparently, while he was sleeping on the job at noon, five colored shirts were stolen from the storehouse. Amunemwia asked the statue, "My good and beloved lord, wilt thou give me back their theft?" The papyrus states, "And the god nodded very greatly." Then the guard began to read off a list of all the townspeople, and, when he read the name of the farmer Pethauemdiamun, the god nodded and said, "It is he who stole them." The farmer was present and denied the theft before the oracle. As an appeal, he went before the oracle of his own district and asked if he were guilty. The statue of Amun of Te-Shenyt agreed with the other oracle and condemned the farmer. When he again denied the deed, the oracle of Te-Shenyt ordered that he be brought before a third local oracle, Amun of Bukenen, "in the presence of many witnesses." The papyrus lists the witnesses, but is incomplete here. The farmer probably was condemned a third time. We do know that he finally appeared before the oracle of Pe-Khenty during the later Festival of Khoiakh, a celebration of the accession of the god Horus as ruler over Egypt, and appealed, "Is it I who took the clothes?" The god again nodded very greatly, and the papyrus says that the oracle ". . . inflicted chastisement on him in the presence of the townsmen." This finally broke the farmer's resistance. He confessed to having stolen the shirts and said, "I have them, I will return them." He was then beaten with one hundred blows of a palm-rib and made to swear that, if he went back on his word to return the clothes, he would be thrown to the crocodiles. That is how Amun of Pe-Khenty solved a crime.

Oracles could also act as judges in courts of law. One ancient record tells of an oracle that wrote out its decision. The case involved a dispute over ownership of a tomb. The record of the dispute is a bit cryptic, but fortunately there are two versions, one written on a piece of broken pottery in the British Museum, the other, on a papyrus in the Berlin Museum. (Because papyrus was expensive, records of unimportant matters or first drafts of significant cases frequently were written on pottery.) Between the pottery and the papyrus a fairly coherent record of the case exists.

During the reign of Ramses III a workman named Amenemope claimed to own a tomb known as the tomb of Hai, one of his ancestors who lived during the reign of the pharaoh Horemheb. When the necropolis officials inspected the tomb they found only a coffin with no name and no funerary equipment or offerings. The lack of bodies made the officials suspect Amenemope's claim to the tomb.

Questions over the ownership of tombs frequently arose in Egypt. Grave-robbing was so widespread that it was not unusual for a tomb to be emptied completely soon after an interment. Then, when a hundred years or so had passed and no one from the family was alive, there being little record of ownership, the tomb might be claimed by anyone. This was the situation in the case of Amenemope. The officials were not sure whether the tomb was rightly his.

To settle the matter Amenemope chose to bring the matter before the local god, the deified Amenhotep I. In Thebes during this period the workers of the Theban necropolis worshiped Amenhotep I, and there was a temple for the god with a fairly large cult following. As Amenemope was a tomb builder by profession, it is not surprising that he chose this particular oracle. According to the record, which is Amenemope's account, he stood before the god who "gave me the tomb of Hai by a writing." How could the statue write? One possibility is that two pieces of papyri were placed before the statue, one indicating that the tomb was Amenemope's, the other denying it. When the one affirming the ownership was presented, the statue nodded or, in some similar manner controlled by the priests, indicated that this was the writing with which the god was in agreement.

Amenemope's case is not the only one in which a builder asked Amenhotep I for a legal decision. An ostracon in the British Museum reports a dispute over a house. Kenna, a builder, had found an abandoned house in poor repair. He rebuilt it for himself, but was being prevented from taking up residence by Mersekhmet. Mersekhmet claimed that he had consulted Amenhotep I and had been told by the oracle that he and Kenna should share the house. From the record, which is obviously Kenna's account, Mersekhmet had no claim whatsoever to the house.

Kenna decided to take the case before Amenhotep 1 in the presence of numerous witnesses. Among the witnesses were the "carriers of the god," which indicates that the statue was taken outside the temple in its shrine by the priests. The god spoke: "Give the dwelling to Kenna its owner again . . . no one shall divide it." That is how Kenna got his house.

An illustrated papyrus in the Brooklyn Museum gives the best account of what it must have been like to consult an oracle. Like most other records of oracles, it was drawn up by someone who received a favorable answer. The petitioner, Harsiese, could not be present during the festival when the cult statue of Amun-Re was taken to the open court, so his son, Pemou, put the request before the god in his father's behalf.

The situation was a touchy one. Harsiese was a priest of Amun who wished to leave that god's temple to serve at the Temple of Montu-Re-Horakhty. There is no evidence that his reason was that he had had a great religious conversion. Such changes were usually motivated by mundane considerations, such as a priest's family moving to a new location or better pay. In any event, the priest had to ask the god Amun-Re to relieve him of his obligation.

The shrine was carried by twenty shaven-headed priests to the Hall of Review where anyone who needed a favor, decision, or advice could consult the oracle as it made its rounds of the hall (Figure 70). When the statue came to Pemou and he put forth his father's request, the god agreed to relieve Harsiese from his service. The papyrus clearly indicates that the god gave his consent by moving toward the petitioner. The priests who were carrying the shrine obviously could control this movement. One wonders if any were friends of Harsiese.

It was not unusual for a cult statue to leave its sanctuary. One of the titles of a class of priests was "carrier of the god." Every few days, depending upon the religious calendar followed by the tem-

FIGURE 70. Shaven-headed priests carry the oracle statue in its boat shrine. Two large ostrich-feather fans cool the god. Courtesy of the Brooklyn Museum

ple, the shrine with the statue in it would be carried throughout the town. It would probably be preceded by a priest with incense and followed by lines of other priests dressed in white linen. Every few hundred yards there were small stone pedestals on which the priests could rest the shrine. This was for two reasons: The shrine and statue must have been quite heavy, so that the priests would have needed to rest. Also, the stopping points permitted the people to approach the god and ask for favors or decisions about matters of importance.

The oracles of Egypt were not only for the commoner. Numerous pharaohs have mentioned that they consulted oracles. Tuthmose III, in one of his inscriptions, mentions that when he was a young boy attending a procession, the statue of Amun noticed him and halted. This is told to show that even then he knew he would become pharaoh. Tuthmose III seems to have had an especially

close relationship with the oracle. On a stela found at the Temple of Karnak by Mariette in the nineteenth century, the pharaoh recorded that he built temples to Amun in accordance with an oracular decree:

> The king himself commanded to put in writing, according to the statement of the oracle, to execute monuments before those who are on earth.[1]

Tuthmose was keeping to a family tradition of listening to oracular commands. His aunt, Hatshepsut, the female ruler of Egypt who preferred to be called "king," stated that her trading expeditions to the land of Punt were the result of an oracle's command. The result of this confrontation between oracle and sovereign is carved on the walls of her funerary temple at Deir el Bahari.

The king himself, the King of Upper and Lower Egypt, Makere [Hatshepsut]. The majesty of the court made supplication at the steps of the lord of [gods]; a command was heard from the great throne, an oracle of the god himself, that the ways to Punt should be searched out, that the highways to the Myrrh-terraces should be penetrated. . . . It was done, according to all that the majesty of this reverend god commanded, according to the desire to her majesty [fem.], in order that she might be given life, stability, and satisfaction, like Re, forever.[2]

The grandnephew of Hatshepsut and son of Tuthmose III also recorded his debt to the oracle. Carved on a rock near Philae is an inscription put there by order of Tuthmose IV. The king told how, when he was informed of an uprising in Nubia, he went to the temple to consult the oracle. He made offerings and asked what he should do. The oracle told him what path to pursue and that he would be successful. After hearing this, Tuthmose IV waged war on the Nubians and was triumphant.

Oracle statues not only gave advice, but could also perform miraculous cures. One of the most interesting records is on a stela in the Louvre. This stela was first seen by Champollion when he visited Egypt. It was then lying near the temple of Khonsu at Karnak. Khonsu is the ram-headed god who created humanity on a potter's wheel. The stela recounts a miraculous cure performed by him during the reign of Ramses II but actually it was carved by priests almost one thousand years after the event, because they believed it worth recording for posterity. It is probable, too, that the priests also wanted to increase their own power at that time by showing what their god was capable of doing. On the top of the stela are two carvings of sacred shrines being carried by shaven-headed priests. The one on the right is Khonsu-in-Thebes-Beautiful-Rest, while the one on the left is of Khonsu-the-Plan-Maker-in-Thebes, Great God, Smiter of Evil Spirits.

According to the text that occupies the remainder of the stela, Ramses II was in Naharin, where heads of all foreign countries came with gifts of homage. The king of Bekhten brought his extremely beautiful daughter before the pharaoh, and she became queen. Sometime later, when the royal couple were in Thebes, a messenger from the king of Bekhten arrived informing the pharaoh that his wife's sister was ill with a sickness that had affected her limbs. The king of Bekhten asked that Ramses send one of his wise men to cure her. Ramses sent for priests who were in charge of the secret writings of the House of Life and dispatched one to Bekhten. The priest concluded that the princess was possessed and that he could not help her. Consequently, the king asked Ramses to send an oracle statue to cure his daughter.

Ramses presented the request to Khonsu-in-Thebes-Beautiful-Rest, who apparently was the more powerful oracle. Then the statue of Khonsu-the-Plan-Maker, Great God, Smiter of Evil Spirits, was brought in, and Ramses said, "O thou good lord, if thou inclinest thy face to Khonsu-the-Plan-Maker, the great god, smiting the evil spirits, he shall be conveyed to Bekhten." The oracle nodded vigorously, and so Khonsu-the-Plan-Maker was dispatched to Bekhten.

According to the stela the journeys of both the wise men and the oracle took seventeen months. When the oracle was brought before the princess, the spirit that possessed her left immediately, and she was cured. The spirit, before leaving forever, requested that the oracle ask the king of Bekhten to make a festival day so that the spirit and the oracle could celebrate together!

The king, seeing how powerful the oracle was, decided to keep it in his country. He retained the statue for three years and nine months, until he had a vision. In a dream he saw the oracle coming toward him in the form of a golden falcon that then flew off toward Egypt. The king awoke in a fright and, taking the dream as an omen, ordered that the oracle be returned with a great retinue and gifts to Thebes.

This story is an indication of just how powerful the oracle statues were believed to be, both by foreigners and Egyptians. These statues could heal the sick, solve crimes, settle legal disputes, and send prophetic dreams. Because they had such diverse capabilities, they were called upon whenever a need arose and were an integral part of the ancient Egyptian's life.

> If a man sees himself in a dream sawing
> wood, it is good. It means his enemies are
> dead.
>
> —*Egyptian Dream Book*

14. Dreams

SINCE THE BEGINNINGS of recorded history man has believed his dreams to be a means of knowing the future. The frequency with which dreams are mentioned in the first two books of the Old Testament is an indication of just how important they were in Biblical times. In Genesis alone, there are more than a dozen references to dreams, most of them prophetic.

The story of Joseph and his brothers reveals much about ancient beliefs in prophetic dreams. Joseph was sold into slavery partly because he had dreams that foretold he would rule over his brothers (Gen. 37:5–11). Later, when Joseph was in jail in Egypt with two of the pharaoh's former officials, a cup bearer and a baker, they mentioned that each had had a dream, but that they could find no interpreter. Joseph correctly interpreted the dreams to mean that in three days the cup bearer would be released and the baker would be hanged.

Not only the working people of Egypt but the pharaoh himself believed that properly interpreted dreams could predict the future. Joseph was released from prison only because the pharaoh called upon him to interpret two dreams that the royal magicians had failed to decipher. In the first dream the pharaoh had seen seven fat cows feeding in the Nile rushes. These were approached and devoured by seven lean cows. The second dream paralleled the first, with seven ripe, full ears of corn being swallowed up by seven meager ears (Gen. 41:1–7). Joseph told the pharaoh the dreams meant that seven years of prosperity would be followed by seven years of famine; the people would have to plan accordingly to avoid mass starvation.

Archaeological evidence supports such accounts of ancient beliefs in prophetic dreams. The case of Tuthmose IV (1413–1405 B.C.) is perhaps the most famous. At the foot of the Great Sphinx is a stela that tells of a dream by the young prince who was to become Tuthmose IV. The prince was hunting. At noon he became tired and napped in the desert near where the Great Sphinx lay partially buried in the sand. He dreamed that the Sphinx spoke to him, saying that if he cleared away the sand that encumbered it, the young prince would become pharaoh. The last portion of the story is missing, but undoubtedly it told of how the dream was realized. We know the sand was cleared away and the prince became pharaoh.

The stela does support the impression given in Genesis and Exodus that the ancient Egyptians believed strongly in prophetic dreams. In the story of Joseph, the pharaoh had sufficient confidence in Joseph's interpretation to make provision for the seven years of famine and to allow Joseph to plan the country's economic future for the next fourteen years.

Egyptian sources give another case of a pharaoh taking a dream seriously and acting upon it. Merneptah (1236–1223 B.C.) inherited a kingdom which was in a pronounced state of decline. His father, Ramses II (1304–1237 B.C.), simply lived too long. He became feeble and failed to maintain the strong army needed to protect Egypt's borders. When Merneptah ascended the throne, there were threats on the Libyan border. The details of the crucial battle in which the Libyans were defeated are recorded on one of the walls of the great temple at Karnak. Prior to the battle, the god Ptah, in the form of a statue, appeared to the pharaoh in a dream, told him not to be afraid (". . . banish thou the fearful heart from thee . . ."), and handed him a sword. These words are followed by a description of the victory.

Herodotus tells a somewhat similar version of this story, but the identity of the pharaoh is not clear. Herodotus says that he was told of a pharaoh who neglected the warrior class and so had no one to help defend the country when it was attacked by foreign invaders. This pharaoh, called Sethos by Herodotus, entered a temple and went to the inner sanctuary where the statue of the deity was kept. There he wept and bemoaned his situation and fell asleep. In Sethos' dream the statue told him not to fear, that he should take whoever would follow him and go to battle. Here Herodotus offers a detail lacking in the story of Merneptah. The reason that Sethos was victorious, as the god in his dream had told him, was that the night before the battle, field mice came and ate all of the enemy's quivers and bowstrings.

There is an important difference between the dreams of the Joseph story and those of Merneptah and Tuthmose IV. While the Biblical dreams are symbolic and require explanation, the dreams of the two pharaohs need no interpretation. There is another Egyptian dream, an intermediate between the Joseph dreams and the pharaohs' dreams, for which interpretation was supplied paranormally.

During the period of final decline, Egypt was ruled by foreigners. One was Tanuatamun (664–656 B.C.), an Ethiopian ruler. On a stela he recorded a dream in which he was holding a snake in each hand. When he awoke there were no snakes. As he was wondering what the interpretation of the dream was, he heard these words:

> Upper Egypt belongs to thee, take to thyself, Lower Egypt. The Vulture and Uraeus goddesses have appeared on thy head, and the land is given to thee in its length and breadth, and none shall share with thee.[1]

Apparently the prophecy came true, for a later portion of the stela says that when Tanuatamun was crowned he said, "Lo, the dream is true! It is profitable for him who sets it in his head, evil for him who understands it not."

These examples of ancient Egyptian dreams are isolated cases, and it is impossible to reconstruct from them any system of dream interpretation. Also, because these were royal dreams, it is possible that they were fabricated to establish the divine legitimacy of the pharaohs' claims to the throne.

Fortunately, there exists a relatively complete ancient Egyptian *Dream Book* which provides some sampling of how the ancient Egyptian interpreted his dreams. The book is written on the recto side of a papyrus, some sections of which have been lost. The dating is difficult. The verso side (the side with the horizontal fibers on top) is a description of a battle and a copy of a letter to the vizier of Egypt. This side was undoubtedly written during the Nineteenth

Dynasty, probably around the year 1275 B.C. Since the verso side is always written first, it is certain that the *Dream Book* was written later, but probably soon after the verso. This version of the *Dream Book,* however, may have been copied from a papyrus originally written as early as the Twelfth Dynasty, so it might have originated as early as 2000 B.C.

The beginning and the end of the papyrus are lost so we lack whatever introductory and concluding material there was. What remains is basically a list of dreams and their interpretations. The dreams were all believed to be prophetic—the interpretations tell the future. An interesting question is: For whom was the papyrus intended? Since the common man could not read, one possibility is that, as part of their duties, the priests interpreted dreams. This would be consistent with accounts in the Bible, in which it was possible for anyone to have a dream but only a select few could interpret.

Etymological evidence suggests that the priests of the House of Life (⊓♀ *per ankh*) were the interpreters. Coptic writing, which is ancient Egyptian transcribed in Greek letters with a few characters added, is the strongest connection we have with vocalized ancient Egyptian. In the Coptic (Bohairic) version of the Bible, when the pharaoh calls for his dream interpreters, the word used for "interpreters" is *spheransh.* This is probably a corruption of 𓏏𓏏𓏏 *(sesh per ankh)*—scribe of the House of Life. In support of this theory is the fact that it was common practice for anyone needing divine guidance to spend a night in a temple, in the hope that his dreams would give advice or tell the future. Undoubtedly, the priest would, for a fee, interpret the dream. Sleeping in a temple to obtain dream-oracles was almost a must for any Greek tourist to Egypt, and the Temple of Seti at Abydos was a favorite. On the walls of the back staircase of the temple are names carved by various tourists who slept there. The names are often only a foot or so above the steps, so it seems as if these travelers were uncomfortable and, to pass the hours, chiseled their names. One group recorded, "they caught a fox here."

The *Dream Book* is written in hieratic, a cursive form of hieroglyphs. The text was first translated by Sir Alan Gardiner. Although Gardiner's translation leaves little room for improvement, his commentary is weak. He makes little attempt to make sense of the body of dreams and interpretations and tends to dismiss the text as a bundle of incomprehensible contradictions. There is, in fact, a general trend in Egyptology to view the ancient Egyptians as illogical people who could embrace all manner of silly notions. This approach is unfortunate. A careful attempt at analysis in the light of modern psychoanalytic research can yield insights into ancient dream interpretation.

The text of the *Dream Book* is orderly. Down the right margin (the papyrus reads from right to left) are the words, "If a man sees himself in a dream." Then each horizontal line gives a description of a dream followed by a space and then the interpretation of the dream. Each interpretation begins with either "Good" or "Bad," followed by a fuller explanation.

On comparing this text with the samples of complete dream narratives reviewed in the preceding pages, one is struck by the one-dimensional fragmentary quality of the material presented in the *Dream Book*. Perhaps the book consists of fragments from a wide variety of dreams that the writer/practitioner felt suitable for his particular style of interpretation and which he felt was paradigmatic for a number of similar motifs featured in dreams that had come his way. The *Dream Book* may have been, then, more a teaching device for fledgling dream interpreters—or a do-it-yourself manual for those able to read—than a truly representative compilation of ancient Egyptian dream material.

The occasionally conflicting or inconsistent interpretations are the result either of sloppy workmanship by the scribe who copied the texts or, more likely, the possibility that there were several writers, and each responded to the same motifs or dream fragments with his own idiosyncratic free associations. (This is a pitfall that modern dream interpreters have not always been able to avoid.)

The dream of "sailing downstream" appears three times in the *Dream Book*. Once, early in the text, it has a "Good" interpretation. The two times it appears later, the interpretations are "Bad." It seems unlikely that the same writer believed that the dream portended both good and bad. More likely, two or three writers interpreted the same dream differently. Or perhaps two or three people had similar dreams which were followed by different consequences. To a man living in Upper Egypt, sailing downstream might have meant leaving Thebes and home; to a man living in Lower Egypt, sailing downstream might have meant returning home.

Such considerations aside, the ancient Egyptian dream analyst's approach was apparently guided more by set rules of thumb than by attempts to decode the hidden meaning of a given element in the manifest dream content and its relation to the dreamer's personality or specific life situation. Nevertheless, there is evidence of clear recognition of the symbolic quality of a few recurrent themes that are somewhat similar to principles of modern dream research.

Below is a list of some of the dreams and the events they foreshadow.

Dream	*Prophecy*
Killing an ox	Good. It means the removal of the dreamer's enemies from his presence.
Writing on a palette	Good. It means the establishment of the dreamer's office.
Drinking blood	Good. It means putting an end to his enemies.
Picking dates	Good. It means finding victuals given by his god.
Seeing a large cat	Good. It means a large harvest is coming to the dreamer.
Copulating with a pig	Bad. It means being deprived of possessions.
Uncovering his backside	Bad. It means the dreamer will be an orphan later.
Drinking his own urine	Good. It means eating his son's possessions.
Eating excrement	Good. It means eating his possessions in his house.
Climbing on a mast	Good. It means being suspended aloft by his god.
Drinking wine	Good. It means living in righteousness.
Seeing his face as a leopard	Good. It means gaining authority over his townfolk.
Capturing a female slave	Good. It means something from which he will have satisfaction.

It is difficult to find a common theme or technique of interpretation in these dreams. Some seem rather straightforward, such as the last dream on the list above, but many seem contradictory. For example, if a man sees himself dead, it is good! It means a long life before him.

Several of the dreams are based on the principle of sympathetic

magic: the idea that what one does to a statue or model will happen to the full-size victim. This is why drinking blood means putting an end to your enemies. Similar examples from the *Dream
Book* are: carving an ox with your own hand means killing your
adversary; or veiling yourself indicates removing enemies from
your presence.

What is striking about the dreams and interpretations is the
lack of details. The dream interpreter seemed to care only about
the major theme. It did not matter, then, how one dreamed of one's
death—be it at battle, by disease, or by accident—what was important was the death. Further, it did not seem to matter who had the
dream, it meant the same thing for anyone. Thus, while the Egyptians apparently recognized the symbolic nature of dreams, they
seem to have believed in the objective universality of these symbols. However, one exception involves one of the most puzzling
aspects of the Egyptian religion—the followers of Seth.

The most popular of Egyptian myths involves Seth, the evil
brother of Horus, the falcon god. In Jungian terms, Seth is the
archetype of the devil. He killed his father, Osiris, and then dis-
membered the body. To avenge Osiris' death, Horus does battle
with Seth and defeats him. What is a real mystery concerning the
Egyptian religion, and ultimately the *Dream Book*, is why there
were followers of Seth. Given all the bad attributes of Seth, it is
remarkable that there were large groups of his worshipers. It would
seem as if this is parallel to our modern cults of Satan, but the
followers of Seth were in no way discriminated against in ancient
Egypt. Seth was represented as a curious animal looking much like
a jackal with a U-shaped tail.

These followers of Seth may be the one exception to the universality of the meaning of dreams. Toward the end of the *Dream Book*
papyrus was a section containing interpretations for dreams of the
followers of Seth. All that is left of this section is the introduction,
so unfortunately none of their dreams is preserved. But it does seem
clear that for some reason the dreams of the Sethians were considered different from those of the followers of Horus.

One cannot help but wonder how well the dream interpretations were received. Undoubtedly, it was common for a person to
go to the temple and ask the priest-interpreter for the meaning of
the previous night's dream.

The prophetic powers of the dream were a foregone conclusion. The priest-interpreter had gained possession of the key to unlock the secret meaning of magical texts. In so doing, he acquired knowledge of *past* happenings. By the same token, he was confident that by deciphering and decoding the secret imagery of dreams, he had discovered the key to unlocking the future. He also knew that dreams were inspired by the gods, and while ordinary mortals could not, in their waking hours, fathom the hidden or apparent impact of the dreams on human affairs, the dream interpreter served as a mediator between the dreamer and his god. That in assuming this role the interpreter had himself become the master and manipulator of the secret signs only enhanced his magic powers, and made his services all the more valuable and his pronouncements more consequential. At the same time, the divine origin and unquestioned magic power of his predictions helped to silence doubts and to mute criticism should his prophecies frequently fail to come true. The faith of the petitioner in the validity of the interpretation of his dream may have caused him to act in such a way as to bring about the event predicted.

There was an additional service the interpreter could perform for the dreamer if the dream boded ill. He could give him a magical spell to ensure that the prediction would not come true. An example of such a spell required the dreamer, upon awakening, to ask the goddess Isis, the guardian of magical words, to come and drive off the evils seen in the dream (Figure 71). After the dreamer recited this request, he was given bread moistened with beer and myrrh, which he was to smear on his face. Doing this would drive away the evil seen in the dream.

If a person could not visit the temple to have a prophetic dream, he could consult a magician, who would say a spell and perform a rite to coax a god to visit him in a dream. One spell on a papyrus involves quite a bit of preparation, including magical ink:

> To obtain a vision from [the god] Bes. Make a drawing of Besa, as shown below, on your left hand and envelop your hand in a strip of black cloth that has been consecrated to Isis [?] and lie down to sleep without speaking a word, even in answer to a question. Wind the remainder of the cloth round your neck. The ink with which you write must be composed of the blood of a cow, the blood of a white dove, fresh [?] frankincense, myrrh, black writing-ink, cinnabar,

FIGURE 71. If a dream forewarned of disaster, one could visit the Temple of Isis at Philae and request intervention by the goddess.

mulberry juice, rain-water, and the juice of wormwood and vetch. With this write your petition before the setting sun [saying],

"Send the truthful seer out of the holy shrine, I beseech thee, Lampsier, Sumarta, Baribos, Dardalam, Iorles: O Lord send the sacred deity Anuth, Anuth, Salbana, Chambré, Breïth, now, now, quickly, quickly. Come in this very night." [2]

The Egyptians also believed that it was possible to cause by magic someone else to have oracular dreams. According to the Greek writer pseudo-Callisthenes, the last native king of Egypt, Nectanebo, was a great magician who knew how to cause dreams in others. On one occasion Nectanebo made the Greek queen Olympias dream that the god Amun would make love to her and she would give birth to a god. He did this by gathering desert plants and extracting their juices. He poured these over a wax effigy he had made of the queen and, while doing this, he recited a spell to cause the dream.

When Nectanebo wanted Philip of Macedon to dream that the child who was going to be born to Olympias was the son of the god, he said an incantation over a hawk which then flew to where Philip was sleeping and told him what he would dream. Philip had the dream precisely as the hawk directed, and so the divine origin of Alexander the Great was established.

Just as magic could be used to cause dreams, it could be used to ward off evil dreams or bad events foretold in dreams. A papyrus in the Hermitage Museum in Russia explains that one reason the Great God created magic was so that mankind would have a weapon for combatting the power of events both in dreams at night and during the day.

A late Egyptian manuscript from around the third century gives detailed instructions on how to receive an answer to a question in a dream. Rather than spend the night in a temple, a person could go to a clean, dark cave facing south. A new white lamp containing neither red clay nor gum-water was purified with natron water, then filled with oil. On the wick the word *Bakhukhsikhukh* was written (in Coptic) and magical figures were drawn in myrrh-ink. The word seems to be nonsense, common in magical texts of the late period. It might be a corruption of an earlier Egyptian magical phrase for *Soul of Khukh, son of Khukh.* "Ba" in Egyptian was *soul;* and "si" could be a further corruption of the Egyptian "sa," for *son.* Curiously, the text never says what magical figures to draw on the wick.

The prepared lamp was placed on a brick and the brick on sand which had been spread over the floor of the cave. After frankincense was placed in front of the lamp, the person was to gaze at the flame. When he saw a god, he was to lie down on a rush mat. He was not to speak to anyone. The god would then appear in a dream and answer his questions.

The conditions set up by this magical papyrus could certainly induce a hypnotic, if not hallucinatory, state. The dark cave, the incense, the flame, the solitude, all would contribute to what we today would call an altered state of consciousness. In addition to these preparations, a special ointment was to be placed on the eyes. This ointment was made of flowers of something called "the Greek bean," which was purchased from the garland-seller. The description of how the ointment was prepared and what it looked like is rather bizarre.

The fresh flowers were placed in a glass vessel which was sealed and placed for twenty days in a secret, dark place. When the sealed glass was opened the person would find a pair of testicles with a phallus in it. (That's what the text says!) Perhaps this meant that the flowers would magically assume that shape. The floral genitalia were left for another forty days, after which they would become bloody. This unattractive mess was to be put on a piece of glass in a pottery vessel kept hidden. Then when a person wanted to divine by means of the lamp he smeared it on his eyes.

The extraordinary lengths to which a magician would go to induce a dream indicates how important dreams were to the magical arts. To the ancient sorcerer the dream state was not a psychological phenomenon. It was a little-understood condition in which it was possible for man, for a brief period, to come directly in contact with the gods.

O Re-Atum, O Khopri, I am one who was
born on the First of the Year. . . .

—Coffin Text

15. An Egyptian Horoscope Calendar

JUST AS WE have newspaper horoscope columns that tell us what
will happen to us on a particular day, the ancient Egyptians had
special calendars that told them what to do on each day of the year.
Unlike our modern horoscopes, which apply to individuals, these
calendars applied to everyone. If the calendar advised you not to go
out of your house on a particular day, then *everyone* stayed inside.

The Egyptian calendar was slightly different from ours. There
were only three seasons: (1) *Inundation* (㊂, pronounced *akhet*)
was the season that the Nile overflowed its banks and farmland was
covered with water. This lasted approximately from June 21 to
October 21. (2) *Emergence* (㊂, pronounced *proyet*) was when the
water receded. This season was from October 21 to February 21. (3)
Summer (㊂, pronounced *shomu*) lasted from February 21 to
June 21.

Each of these seasons had four months of thirty days each, so
that there were 360 days to the standard year. While the Egyptians
did not realize that the earth rotates around the sun, they did know
that a calendar of 360 days will soon be out of phase with nature.
For every year that passes, periodic natural phenomena will seem
off by five days. If you are using a 360-day calendar, eventually the
season you call "Inundation" will come when the land is dry, because the Nile starts to overflow its banks every 365 days. To correct for the discrepancy, the Egyptians at the beginning of every
year had five "added days." The hieroglyphs for these days were
㊂, "the yearly five days." Thus, the Egyptian calendar was
really a 365-day calendar.

New Year's Day, which was called "the opening of the year,"

225

dawned with an astronomical event which took place on June 21 in about 3000 B.C. The brilliant star Sirius became visible just before sunrise. This event was called ⏚⟁⚹, "the going up of the goddess Sothis."

In 1943, a rolled-up papyrus was bought by the Cairo Museum from an antiquities dealer. It was written in hieratic and, while portions of it were eaten away by ants, it was clear that the papyrus dealt with the days of the year and what was going to happen on them. The papyrus actually contained three separate books on this theme. The first and the third were badly damaged, but the second is almost complete for each day of the year and has come to be known as the Cairo Calendar.

The title of the Cairo Calendar is ⟋⟍⟋⟍⟍⟍⟍⟍ : "An Introduction to the start of Everlastingness and the end of Eternity."

For each day of the year there is a reading, usually of three parts, in a more or less consistent order:

1. The first part states the day's auspice: "favorable," "mostly favorable," "very favorable," "adverse," "mostly adverse," "very adverse." Most of the days of the Cairo Calendar are either very favorable, ⟊⟊⟊, or very adverse ⟠⟠⟠. A few days, however, seem to be partially favorable and partially adverse.

2. The auspice is determined by the second part, which describes what mythological event took place on that day. For example, on a day when the first part, the auspice, is "very adverse," the second part usually describes an unhappy or even violent happening in the life of the gods, such as Horus fighting with Seth and losing his eye. When the auspice is favorable, the day was generally one of peace or festivity in heaven.

3. The third part of the reading tells how to behave as a result of the auspice and the mythological event. On the day Horus' eye is lost, a bad day, you are told not to go out of your house.

In some places the mythological portions are difficult to follow. Many minor gods are referred to and, while they undoubtedly were recognizable to the ancient Egyptians, they seem remote to the modern reader. Also, the calendar does not tell one sequential mythological story. One theme continues for three or four days and then ends abruptly, to be replaced by a completely different theme.

The Cairo Calendar is difficult to interpret for other reasons as well: The papyrus is damaged in several places making some readings impossible; there are scribal errors; and at times the meaning of the words themselves are obscure. Because of these difficulties some liberties have been taken with the translation, which is based on the transcription from the hieratic by Professor Bakir, who first published the calendar. In some places, totally incomprehensible phrases are omitted—ellipses indicate missing or unreadable text.

On the following pages the Cairo Calendar is reproduced in a form that will enable you to look at each day to see if the Egyptians believed it favorable or unfavorable, what the important mythological event was, and, as a consequence, what actions should or should not be taken. While the Egyptians did not follow our calendar system, an attempt has been made to reconcile the ancient with the modern—though there are inherent difficulties with that, too. The calendar which follows begins on August 1 because Sirius now rises not on June 21, as it did in ancient times, but on August 1. In spite of all the problems, it is hoped that the calendar will give you an understanding of what kinds of magical-religious concerns affected the daily lives of the ancient Egyptians.

FIRST MONTH OF AKHET

August 1 Day 1	August 2 Day 2	August 3 Day 3
First Day of the Year *Very favorable* It is the day of the birth of Re-Horakhty. The Nile begins to rise. All the gods and people celebrate.	*Very favorable* It is the day the Ennead go before Re. If you see anything on this day, it will be good.	*Mostly favorable* . . . Anyone born on this day will die by a crocodile.
August 7 **Day 7**	**August 8** **Day 8**	**August 9** **Day 9**
Very favorable It is the day of welcoming the rising of the river and of offering to the gods. If you see anything, it will be good.	*Mostly favorable* It is the day Re goes forth . . . Do not go out at night on this day.	*Very favorable* It is the day of pacifying the hearts of those in the horizon in front of His Majesty, Re. If you see anything, it will be good.
August 13 **Day 13**	**August 14** **Day 14**	**August 15** **Day 15**
Mostly adverse It is the day of the killing of Meret Shemat [goddess of music]. Anyone born on this day will die of blindness.	. . . . . . Make offerings to the gods of your city.	*Mostly adverse* It is the day of the rage of Seth battling Horus. Do not go in a boat on this day.
August 19 **Day 19**	**August 20** **Day 20**	**August 21** **Day 21**
Very favorable The Ennead is in festivity in front of Re, a happy day in heaven. Burn incense.	*Very adverse* It is the day the great ones—the followers of Seth and Horus—are in conflict. Do not do any work on this day.	*Very favorable* . . . . Make offerings to the followers of Re. Do not kill a bull or even let it cross your path. It is a day to be cautious of bulls.
August 25 **Day 25**	**August 26** **Day 26**	**August 27** **Day 27**
Mostly favorable It is the day of the going forth of Sekhmet to the Eastern district and of the repelling of the confederates of Seth. Do not go out of your home or on any road at night.	*Very adverse* It is the day of Horus fighting with Seth. Do not do anything today.	*Very favorable* It is the day of peace between Horus and Seth. Make a holiday today. Do not kill any *ankhy*-reptile.

August 4	Day 4	August 5	Day 5	August 6	Day 6
Mostly favorable		*Very favorable*		*Mostly adverse*	

The gods go in a contrary wind.

Do not navigate a boat today. Do not do anything on this day.

The gods are peaceful in heaven, navigating the great barque.

If you see anything, it will be good.

Anyone born on this day will die trampled by a bull.

. . .

August 10	Day 10	August 11	Day 11	August 12	Day 12
Very favorable		*Very adverse*		*Very adverse*	

It is the day of the going forth of Hedj-Hotep [goddess of weaving]. All is festivity.

Anyone born on this day will die honored in old age.

It is the day of the going forth of the Great Flame [the fire-spitting cobra goddess].

Kindle the fire today. Do not look at a bull. Do not copulate today.

It is the day anyone disobeying Re in his house will fall down at once.

Do not go out today. Wait till Re sets in his horizon.

August 16	Day 16	August 17	Day 17	August 18	Day 18
Very adverse		*Very adverse*		*Very favorable*	

. . .

Anyone born on this day will die of a crocodile.

It is the day the offering to Sobek was taken away.

Do not eat any *mehyet*-fish today.

It is the day Horus was judged greater than his brother Seth.

If you see anything on this day, it will be good.

August 22	Day 22	August 23	Day 23	August 24	Day 24
Very adverse		*Very adverse*		*Very favorable*	

It is the day Re swallows all the gods. When they move about he kills them and vomits them out into the water. Their bodies turn to fish and their souls to birds.

Do not eat fish today. Do not warm oil. Do not eat birds.

It is the day of causing the heart of the enemy of Re to suffer.

Anyone born on this day will not live. Do not listen to singing or watch dancing on this day.

The God [Re] sails peacefully with a favorable wind.

Anyone born in this day will die honored in old age.

August 28	Day 28	August 29	Day 29	August 30	Day 30
Very favorable		*Mostly favorable*		Last Day of the Month *Very favorable*	

The gods are happy when they see the children of Nut [Horus and Seth].

If you see anything it will be good.

. . .

Do not kindle fire in the house today. Do not burn incense. Do not go out at night.

House of Re, House of Osiris, House of Horus.

If you see anything on this day, it will be good.

SECOND MONTH OF AKHET

August 31 Day 1	September 1 Day 2	September 2 Day 3
Very favorable The Ennead is in festivity on this day. The heir is established. . . .	It is the day of the procession of Horus the Elder of Sais to his mother Neith. Make offerings to all gods. This is important.	*Very favorable* Toth [god of writing] is in the presence of Re in the inaccessible shrine. He gives the order for the healing of Horus' injured eye. If you see anything on this day, it will be good.
September 6 Day 7	**September 7 Day 8**	**September 8 Day 9**
Very adverse On this day Re goes forth to countries which he created to kill the children of the rebellion. He returns and kills them in front of the Ennead. Anyone born on this day will die in foreign lands. Do not do anything on this day.	*Very favorable* . . . If you see anything on this day, it will be good.	*Very favorable* It is the day of jubilation in the heart of Re. His Ennead is in festivity. All enemies are killed. Anyone born on this day will die at a good old age.
September 12 Day 13	**September 13 Day 14**	**September 14 Day 15**
Very favorable It is the day of satisfying the hearts of the great gods with a feast, and of saluting their lord who overthrew the enemies, who exist no more. . . .	*Very favorable* It is the day of the receiving of the white crown of the majesty of Horus. His Ennead is in great festivity. Make offerings to your local gods and pacify the spirits.	*Mostly adverse* It is the day of the going forth of Re at night with his followers. If anyone sees them, he will die immediately. Do not leave your house at night.
September 18 Day 19	**September 19 Day 20**	**September 20 Day 21**
Very favorable It is the day of the going forth of Nun to set up the *djed*-pillar in its place to compensate the gods in its presence. . . .	*Very adverse* It is the day of reckoning in the presence of Re, overseen by Toth. It makes an example of the rebels, carrying them below. . . .	*Mostly adverse* It is the day of the going forth of the Upper Egyptian goddess, Neith, in the presence of His Majesty Atum—Re-Horakhty—may he live and be prosperous. It is the goddess' eyes which guide Toth in appeasing and praising her. . . .
September 24 Day 25	**September 25 Day 26**	**September 26 Day 27**
Very adverse It is the day of the finding of the children of the rebellion wrapped in a burial mat. Do not go out on any road on this day.	*Very adverse* It is the day of the opening and sealing of the windows of the palace of Busiris. Do not lay the foundation of a house. Do not put a ship in a shipyard. Do not do any work on this day.	*Very adverse* . . . Do not go out. Do not do any labor till the sun sets. Anyone born on this day will die of a snake.

September 3 **Day 4**	**September 4** **Day 5**	**September 5** **Day 6**
Mostly adverse	*Very adverse*	*Very favorable*
Anubis goes forth to inspect the embalming place for the protection of the god. Anyone born on this day will die of a skin rash.	It is the day of offering in the presence of Hedj-Hotep [goddess of weaving] and Montu [god of war]. Anyone born on this day will die of copulation. Do not go out of your house on any road today.	It is a happy day for Re in heaven. The gods are pacified in his presence. The Ennead is making glorification in front of the Lord of the Universe. Anyone born on this day will die in a state of drunkenness.
September 9 **Day 10**	**September 10** **Day 11**	**September 11** **Day 12**
Very favorable	*Very favorable*	*Very adverse*
It is the day of the procession of Bastet, goddess of Ankh-Towe, and the informing of Re in Heliopolis about her paying tribute to the August Tree [which has the names of kings inscribed on its leaves]. . . .	It is the day of fixing the front piece of the prow on the sacred boat. Life and property are before the august one. Everything is good on this day	It is the day on which he who rebelled against his lord reared his head. His utterance has annihilated the speech of Seth, son of Nut. The separation of his head is inflicted on him who conspired against his lord. . . .
September 15 **Day 16**	**September 16** **Day 17**	**September 17** **Day 18**
. . .	*Very favorable*	*Very adverse*
It is the day of the feast of Osiris-Onnophris. The gods who are in his retinue are in great festivity. The Ennead is pleased. If you see anything on this day, it will be good.	The Great and Little Ennead come forth from the chaotic waters of Nun. Make offerings of bread and beer. Burn incense. It is important.	It is the day Anubis inspects the funerary tent while he performs a transformation into lizards in the sight of all men . . . Then he weeps . . . The male and female gods place their hands on their heads. Do not do anything on this day.
September 21 **Day 22**	**September 22** **Day 23**	**September 23** **Day 24**
Very adverse	*Mostly adverse*	*Very adverse*
It is the day of the cutting of the tongue of Sobek, son of Neith. Do not bathe today.	. . . Anyone born on this day will die of a crocodile.	It is the day of the going forth of the executioners from Sais in the Delta to look for the children of the rebellion. Do not go out of your house in any wind until Re sets.
September 27 **Day 28**	**September 28** **Day 29**	**September 29** **Day 30**
Very favorable	*Very favorable*	Last Day of the Month *Very favorable*
. . . If you see anything on this day, it will be good.	. . . Anyone born on this day will die an honored man among his people.	The land is in festivity on this day. House of Re, House of Osiris, House of Horus. . . .

THIRD MONTH OF AKHET

September 30 Day 1	October 1 Day 2	October 2 Day 3
Very favorable	. . .	*Very favorable*
It is the day of the feast of the members of heaven, honoring Hathor, mistress of all the female gods.	It is the day of the return of Wedjoyet from Dep.	. . .
. . .	. . .	If you see anything on this day, it will be good.
October 6 Day 7	**October 7** Day 8	**October 8** Day 9
Very favorable	. . .	*Very adverse*
. . .	It is the day Isis goes forth, her heart is pleased on this day because the heritage is granted to her son.	It is the day of the blaming of the great ones.
If you see anything on this day, it will be good.	. . .	Do not go outside your house on any road. Do not let light fall on your face until Re sets in his horizon.
October 12 Day 13	**October 13** Day 14	**October 14** Day 15
Very adverse	*Very adverse*	*Very adverse*
It is the day Osiris is sailing upstream to Abydos, to his great town. He is transformed into a little old person. He gives the fare to Anty and says, "Ferry me over to the west . . ."	It is the day when the hearts of the gods are sad because of what [Seth] the enemy of Anty has done.	It is the day of the inspecting of Ba-neb-dedet [god of sexual fertility] in the temple.
. . .	Do not do anything on this day.	. . .
October 18 Day 19	**October 19** Day 20	**October 20** Day 21
Very adverse	*Very adverse*	*Very favorable*
It is the day of the children of the storm [demon].	It is the day of the going forth of Bastet, mistress of Ankh-towe in front of Re, she being angry.	It is the day of the feast of Shu, son of Re.
Do not sail downstream or upstream on the river. Do not navigate any boat on this day.	Anyone born on this day will die in the year of pestilence.	. . .
October 24 Day 25	**October 25** Day 26 *Very favorable*	**October 26** Day 27 *Very favorable*
Very favorable	It is the day of establishing of the *djed*-pillar of Atum in heaven and on the land of Heliopolis at the moment of uproar. The two lords are reconciled, causing the land to be in peace. All Egypt is given to Horus, all of the desert to Seth. Toth goes forth to judge before Re.	It is the day of the judging of Seth and Horus, stopping the fighting. The rowers are hunted down and an end is put to the uproar. The two lords are satisfied, causing the doors to open.
. . .		
If you see anything today, it will be pleasing to the hearts of the gods.		. . .

October 3	Day 4	October 4	Day 5	October 5	Day 6

October 3   **Day 4**

Very adverse

It is the day of the trembling of the earth under Nun.

If anyone navigates on this day, his house will be destroyed.

October 4   **Day 5**

Very adverse

It is the day of the blaming by his majesty of this god.

Do not keep a fire burning in the house on this day. Do not look at a fire.

October 5   **Day 6**

Very favorable

It is the day of the encouragement of the gods of the two lands.

. . .

October 9   **Day 10**

Very favorable

It is the day of great rejoicing in heaven. The crew of Re are in peace. His Ennead is cheerful. Those in the fields are working.

. . .

October 10   **Day 11** .

Very favorable

. . .

If you see anything on this day, it will be good.

October 11   **Day 12**

. . .

It is the day of the pacification of the hearts of the gods, wherever they are. The Udjat-eye is again in the head of Re.

. . .

October 15   **Day 16**

Very favorable

It is the day of the appearance of the great eight gods [the Ennead] in Ashmuneim.

It is a happy day of infinity and eternity.

October 16   **Day 17**

Very adverse

It is the day of the landing of the great ones, the upper and lower ones, at Abydos. Isis and Nephthys weep and wail loudly over [the death] of Osiris.

. . .

October 17   **Day 18**

Very adverse

It is the day of strife for the children of Geb.

Do not approach any road to make a journey.

October 21   **Day 22**

. . .

It is the day of the raising [of the statue] of Maat in order to see Re when she is summoned by the gods to his presence. A uraeus is placed in her hand and another below her, being fixed at the front of the *mesektet*-boat.

. . .

October 22   **Day 23**

Very adverse

It is the day Re judges.

Anyone born on this day will not live.

October 23   **Day 24**

Very favorable

It is the day of the going forth of Isis, and her heart is happy. Nephthys is in jubilation. They see Osiris. He has given his throne to his son, Horus, in front of Re.

. . .

October 27   **Day 28**

Very favorable

It is the day the gods are in jubilation when the decree is written for Horus, son of Osiris. The land is in festivity and the gods are pleased.

If you see anything on this day, it will be good.

October 28   **Day 29**

Very favorable

It is the day of the going forth of the three noble ladies who are in the *Ta-nenet* sanctuary in the presence of Ptah, lovely of face, while giving praise to Re, who belongs to the throne of truth of the temple of the goddess. The white crown is given to Horus, the red one to Seth. Their hearts are thus pleased.

October 29   **Day 30**

Last Day of the Month
Very favorable

It is the day of the Houses of Re and of Osiris.

If you see anything on this day, it will be good.

FOURTH MONTH OF AKHET

October 30 Day 1	October 31 Day 2	November 1 Day 3
Very favorable	*Very favorable*	*Very adverse*
It is the day when Re is joyful in his beauty. His Ennead is in festivity. Everyone, every lion and every single one among the *ankhy*-reptiles, the gods, goddesses, spirits, dead, and those who came into being in the primordial age, Nun's form is in their bodies. . . .	It is the day the gods and goddesses are in festivity. The heavens and the land are in joy. If you see anything on this day, it will be good.	It is the day of smashing into the ears of Bata in his own inaccessible temple. Do not do anything on this day. Anyone born on this day will die of his ears.

November 5 Day 7	November 6 Day 8	November 7 Day 9
Very adverse	*Very favorable*	*Very favorable*
. . . Do not eat *mehyet*-fish today.	. . . If you see anything on this day, it will be good.	It is the day of the action performed by Toth, and of the speech given by his majesty Re in the presence of the great ones. Thereupon these gods, with Toth, cause the enemy of Seth to kill himself in his sanctuary. It is this that has been done by the executioners of Kesert today. . . .

November 11 Day 13	November 12 Day 14	November 13 Day 15
Very favorable	*Very favorable*	. . .
It is the day of the going forth of the white one, or the majesty of heaven [Hathor], her heart being pleased in the presence of Re. The great Ennead is in festivity. Make a holiday in your house today.	Hedj-Hotep and Tayet [two goddesses of weaving] come forth from the temple of Benben today. They hand over their things to Neith. Their hearts are happy. . . .	It is the day of the feast of Sekhmet and Bastet. . . .

November 17 Day 19	November 18 Day 20	November 19 Day 21
Very adverse	*Very adverse*	*Mostly adverse*
It is the day of the presenting of offering in the Hewet Desert and of making ointment for Osiris before the hall of embalming. Do not taste bread or beer. Drink grape juice till Re sets.	It is the day of looking in the direction of the Akhet-eye [sun disk]. Do not go out on the road today. Do not anoint yourself with ointment. Do not go out at noon.	It is the day of the going forth of the mysterious great ones to look for the Akhet-eye [sun disk]. Do not go out of your house in daytime.

November 23 Day 25	November 24 Day 26	November 25 Day 27
(Papyrus damaged)	*Favorable*	*Mostly favorable*
	Toth establishes the . . . in an elevated position in Letopolis. . . .	. . . If you see anything today, it will be good. Do not go out at night.

November 2 **Day 4** *Very favorable* . . . Perform the rituals of Sobek in his temple and in thy house today, with all provisions in the necropolis. This will be pleasant to the gods today.	**November 3** **Day 5** *Very favorable* It is the day of the going forth of Hathor in the presence of the great ones in Kher-aba. Life, stability, and welfare are given to her and the Ennead and the gods of Kher-aba. The majesty of Inundation. . . .	**November 4** **Day 6** *Very adverse* The barque of Re is established to overthrow the enemies from one moment to another on this day. Do not go out today.
November 8 **Day 10** *Very favorable* . . . Anyone born on this day will die in old age as beer enters his mouth.	**November 9** **Day 11** *Very favorable* It is the day of the feast of Osiris in Abydos in the great *neshmet*-boat. The dead are in jubilation. . . .	**November 10** **Day 12** *Very adverse* It is the day of the transformation into the Benu [the phoenix]. Offer to the Benu in your house today. Do not go out on the road in any wind today.
November 14 **Day 16** (Papyrus damaged)	**November 15** **Day 17** *Mostly adverse* It is the day the people and gods judge the speech of the crew in Heliopolis when Horus arrives in Kher-aba. Do not go out at midday today.	**November 16** **Day 18** *Very adverse* It is the day of overthrowing the boat of the god. . . .
November 20 **Day 22** *Mostly favorable* . . . If you see anything on this day, it will be good.	**November 21** **Day 23** *Mostly favorable* It is the day [they] wait to annihilate Horus, who is the savior of his father. Do not go out during the night. If you see a lion, he will kill you.	**November 22** **Day 24** (Papyrus damaged)
November 26 **Day 28** *Very adverse* It is the day of the going forth of the *bab-mehyet*-fish which is in Busiris, its form being a dolphin. Do not eat any *mehyet*-fish on this day. Do not offer it today.	**November 27** **Day 29** *Very adverse* . . . Do not eat or smell any *mehyet*-fish while throwing the flames from offerings into the water. Do not let any *mehyet*-fish or any other fish touch your hands.	**November 28** **Day 30** Last Day of the Month *Very favorable* It is the day of pleasure for the great Ennead. House of Re, House of Osiris, House of Horus. Anything on this day will be pleasing to the hearts of the gods. Offer to the gods and assistants of the Ennead. Make an invocation and offering to the spirits, give food.

FIRST MONTH OF PROYET

November 29 Day 1	November 30 Day 2	December 1 Day 3
Very favorable . . . Double the offerings and present the gifts of Neb-kau [lord of kas]. If you see anything today, it will be good.	*Favorable* . . . Make a holiday in your house.	. . . . . . Do not burn fire in the presence of Re.
December 5 **Day 7**	**December 6** **Day 8**	**December 7** **Day 9**
Very adverse . . . Do not copulate with any woman or any person in front of the Great Flame [sun].	*Very favorable* . . . If you see anything on this day, it will be good.	*Very favorable* It is the day the gods are joyful with the offerings of Sekhmet. Make *pawet*-cakes and repeat the offerings. It will please the gods and spirits.
December 11 **Day 13**	**December 12** **Day 14**	**December 13** **Day 15**
Very favorable It is the day of prolonging life and of making beneficial the goddess of truth in the temple. . . .	*Very adverse* It is the day Isis and Nephthys weep for Osiris in Busiris in remembrance of what he had been. Do not listen to singing or chanting today.	*Very favorable* It is the day of the going forth of Nun through the cavern to the place where the gods are in darkness. If you see anything on this day, it will be good.
December 17 **Day 19**	**December 18** **Day 20**	**December 19** **Day 21**
Very adverse It is the day the great gods are in heaven with the pestilence of the year. There are many deaths. If a sick man does not get well by the end of this day, he will not recover from his illness.	*Very adverse* It is the day of the going forth of Bastet who protects the two lands and cares for him who comes in darkness. Beware of passing on land until Re sets. Do not do anything on this day.	*Very favorable* It is the day Bastet guards the two lands. Make *abet*-offerings to the followers of Re today.
December 23 **Day 25**	**December 24** **Day 26**	**December 25** **Day 27**
. . . It is the day of the establishing of the great cow in the presence of the majesty of Re. Do not drink milk on this day. Drink and eat honey on this day.	*Very adverse* . . . Do not go out today until Re sets when offerings are diminished in Busiris . . . They will be much blamed about it. . . .	*Very favorable* Great festivity in Hefau. . . .

December 2 — Day 4	December 3 — Day 5	December 4 — Day 6
Very favorable . . . Anyone born on this day will die old among his people. He will spend a long lifetime and will be received by his father. If you see anything on this day, it will be good.	*Mostly adverse* It is the day Sekhmet places the flame in front of the great ones. She presides over the sanctuary in Lower Egypt and is violent because of her detention by Maat, Ptah, Toth, Hu, and Sia. . . .	*Very favorable* . . . Repeat the food offerings of He-Who-Dwells-in-Weret. Also repeat the offerings to Khenty-Irety. The offerings to the gods are doubled on this day.
December 8 — Day 10	**December 9 — Day 11**	**December 10 — Day 12**
Very adverse It is the day of the coming forth of flame together with Horus from the marshes. Do not burn papyrus on this day.	*Very adverse* . . . Do not approach flame on this day.	*Very adverse* It is the day of answering every speech of Sekhmet. If you see any dog, do not approach him today.
December 14 — Day 16	**December 15 — Day 17**	**December 16 — Day 18**
Very favorable It is the day of the going forth of Shu to count the crew of the *mesektet*-boat. . . .	*Very adverse* It is the day of the going forth of Nun to the place where the gods are. Those who are above and below come into existence. The land is still in darkness. Do not wash yourself with water today.	*Very favorable* It is the day of holiday in Rostau and of the going forth of the gods to Abydos. . . .
December 20 — Day 22	**December 21 — Day 23**	**December 22 — Day 24**
Very favorable . . . If you see anything on this day, it will be good.	*Very favorable* . . . Anyone born on this day will die in great old age, rich in everything good.	*Very favorable* It is the day everything has been placed behind him in the presence of the Ennead. It is the day of being loyal to the executioners of Re. Happiness is in heaven and on earth today.
December 26 — Day 28	**December 27 — Day 29**	**December 28 — Day 30** Last Day of the Month
Very favorable It is the day Toth takes a solemn oath in Ashmuneim. It is the going forth of the Noble One. The land is in festivity on this day. Make a holiday in your house.	*Very favorable* It is the day of an appearance in the sight of Hu. Toth will send this command south so that Bastet, together with the sole mistress, Sekhmet, can guide the two lands. The gods are happy. If you see anything on this day, it will be good.	*Very favorable* Today is the day of the crossing over in the presence of Nun from the temple of Hapi [the Nile], the father of the gods and of the Ennead. Do not leave anyone out who is on the list to offer incense to. House of Re, House of Osiris, House of Horus.

SECOND MONTH OF PROYET

December 29 Day 1	December 30 Day 2	December 31 Day 3
Very favorable	*Very favorable*	*Very adverse*
The gods and goddesses are in festivity. It is the day of the feast of Ptah's lifting of the heaven of Re with his hands. Make a holiday.	It is the day the gods receive Re. The hearts of the two lands are festive. . . .	It is the day of the going forth of Seth and his confederates to the eastern horizon, and of the navigation of Maat to the place where the gods are. Do not go out of your house on any road today.
January 4 Day 7	**January 5** Day 8	**January 6** Day 9
Very favorable	*Very favorable*	*Very favorable*
. . . Make invocation offerings in your house to the spirits. Make *abet*-offerings to the gods and they will be accepted on this day.	It is the day the gods and goddesses are in festivity. Make a holiday in Letopolis.	It is the day the god enters to distribute the ration of all the gods of Kher-aba. If you see anything on this day, it will be good.
January 10 Day 13	**January 11** Day 14	**January 12** Day 15
Very adverse	*Mostly favorable*	. . .
It is the day of the proceeding of Sekhmet to Letopolis. Her great executioners pass by the offering of Letopolis on this day. Do not go out of your house on any road today.	It is the day of seeing the rebel and killing him by Seth at the prow of the great barque. Do not go out at dawn on this day.	The gods go forth for him in heaven. His two hands hold the *ankh* and *was*-scepter which he offers to the nose of Khenty-Irety at the time of his reckoning. . . .
January 16 Day 19	**January 17** Day 20	**January 18** Day 21
Mostly adverse	*Very adverse*	. . .
It is the day of the mourning of the God. Do not go out by yourself in the daytime.	It is the day of the proceeding of the female goddesses of heaven southward to the road.	It is the day of the birth of cattle. They go to the place where the meadows are in the neighborhood of the foremost god. . . .
January 22 Day 25	**January 23** Day 26	**January 24** Day 27
Very favorable	. . .	. . .
. . . If you see anything on this day, it will be good.	Today is the going forth of Min to Coptos. He is guided to it, boasting of his beauty. Isis sees that his face is beautiful. . . .	It is the day of the Feast of Sokar in Rostau before that of Onnophris [a form of Osiris] in Abydos. . . .

January 1 Day 4	January 2 Day 5	January 3 Day 6
Very favorable . . . Show your heart to your local gods. Propitiate your spirits. Exalt your crew on this day.	*Very favorable* . . . If you see anything on this day, it will be good.	*Very adverse* It is the day of the putting up of the *djed*-pillar of Osiris. The gods are sad with their faces downward when they remember Osiris. . . .
January 7 **Day 10**	**January 8** **Day 11**	**January 9** **Day 12**
Very adverse It is the day of the going forth of the Udjat-eye for singing in Heliopolis. It is the day of elevating the female deity of the sanctuary of Mnevis. Re raises Maat again and again to Atum.	*Very favorable* It is the day of the feast of Neith, of the taking of the writing material that is in her house and of the going forth of Sobek to guide her majesty. You will see good from her hands.	*Very favorable* . . . If you see anything on this day, it will be good.
January 13 **Day 16**	**January 14** **Day 17**	**January 15** **Day 18**
. . . It is the day of the awakening of Isis by the majesty of Re . . . when the son Horus saves his father. He has beaten Seth and his confederates. . . .	*Very favorable* It is the day of keeping those things of the *wabet* of Osiris which have been placed in the hands of Anubis. . . .	*Very adverse* It is the day of the going forth of the seven executioners. Their fingers are searching for the Akhet-eye in the towns of Iyet and Letopolis. . . .
January 19 **Day 22**	**January 20** **Day 23**	**January 21** **Day 24**
Very favorable . . . If you see anything on this day, it will be good.	*Very favorable* . . . If you see anything on this day, it will be good.	*Very adverse* The gods are descending into the river. Anyone who approaches the river on this day will not live. Do not sail a boat on this day.
January 25 **Day 28**	**January 26** **Day 29**	**January 27** **Day 30**
Very favorable Onnophris is pleased and the spirits are joyful. The dead are also in festivity. . . .	*Very adverse* It is the day of the instigation of fighting, of the creation of rebellion, and of making uproar among the children of Geb. Do not do anything on this day.	Last Day of the Month *Very adverse* House of Re, House of Osiris, House of Horus. Do not talk with anybody on this day.

THIRD MONTH OF PROYET

January 28 Day 1	January 29 Day 2	January 30 Day 3
Very favorable It is the day of the feast of entering into heaven and the two banks. Horus is in jubilation. . . .	*Very favorable* . . . If you see anything on this day, it will be good.	(Papyrus damaged)
February 3 **Day 7** *Very adverse* It is the day when the eye of Re calls the followers and they reach him in the evening. Beware of it! Do not go out of your house till Re sets.	**February 4** **Day 8** *Very favorable* It is the day of making way for the gods by Khnum who presides over those who remove themselves from him. If you see anything on this day, it will be good.	**February 5** **Day 9** *Very favorable* It is the day of judgment in Heliopolis. . . .
February 9 **Day 13** *Very favorable* It is the day that Toth and his spirits go forth. Any ritual act performed on this day will be good.	**February 10** **Day 14** *Very adverse* It is the day of making health. Do not go out of your house on any road today.	**February 11** **Day 15** *Very adverse* It is the day of rebellion in the shrine. Do not do any work on this day.
February 15 **Day 19** . . . It is the day of the birth of Nut anew. Do not go out of your house. Do not look into the light.	**February 16** **Day 20** *Very adverse* . . . Do not go out of your house on any road. Do not look into the light.	**February 17** **Day 21** (omitted by scribal error)
February 21 **Day 25** . . . Today is the day of the great cry which the gods of the desert make, having come this day. Do not do anything on this day.	**February 22** **Day 26** *Very adverse* It is the day he is sent into the cave without the knowledge of the great ones to look for the occasion of coming. . . .	**February 23** **Day 27** *Very adverse* . . . Do not do anything on this day.

January 31 Day 4	February 1 Day 5	February 2 Day 6
Mostly adverse It is the day of the announcement of fighting and the call [to battle] in Heliopolis by Seth. His voice is in heaven and on earth and is in great fury. . . .	*Very favorable* It is the day Neith goes forth from Sais and when they see her beauty in the night for four and one half hours. Do not go out during these four and one half hours.	*Very favorable* It is the day of jubilation of Osiris in Busiris and of the going forth of Anubis with his adorers following him. He receives everyone in the hall. Make the ritual!
February 6 **Day 10** *Very adverse* It is the day of the coming of Toth. They guide the very great flame [Nesert] into her house of the desert of eternity. She finds a way among them. Anyone who approaches her on this day will not be separated from her by violence.	**February 7** **Day 11** *Very favorable* It is the day the dead go about in the necropolis in order to repel the anger of the enemy who is in the land named. . . .	**February 8** **Day 12** *Very favorable* It is the day Osiris-Het [the Nile] comes from Nun. Give food on this day.
February 12 **Day 16** *Very adverse* It is the day of the opening of the windows and court and looking into the doorways of the Temple of Karnak, where his [Osiris'] place is. Do not look at anything in the darkness today.	**February 13** **Day 17** *Very adverse* . . . Do not pronounce the name of Seth on this day. Anyone who pronounces his name without his knowledge will fight eternally in his house.	**February 14** **Day 18** *Very favorable* It is the day of the feast of Nut, who counts the days. Make a holiday in your house.
February 18 **Day 22** *Very adverse* It is the day of the birth of the mysterious one [Apophis], the snake with limbs. Do not think of pronouncing the names of the snakes. Catch snakes in Dep.	**February 19** **Day 23** *Very favorable* It is the day of the feast of Horus in Kemwer and of his years and his beautiful images. . . .	**February 20** **Day 24** *Very adverse* . . . Do not go out of your house on any road on this day.
February 24 **Day 28** *Very favorable* It is the day of the feast of Osiris in Abydos. . . .	**February 25** **Day 29** *Very favorable* . . . If you see anything on this day, it will be good.	**February 26** **Day 30** Last Day of the Month . . . It is the day of the feast in Busiris. The names of the doorways [of the horizon] come into existence. House of Re, House of Osiris, House of Horus.

FOURTH MONTH OF ΡROYET

February 27 Day 1	February 28 Day 2	March 1 Day 3
Very favorable It is the day of smiting the enemies who rebelled against their mistress. There is a great feast in heaven. . . .	*Very favorable* It is the day His Majesty Geb proceeds to the throne of Busiris to see Anubis, who commands the council, to learn the day's requirements. . . .	*Very adverse* It is the day the great ones and the uraeus fought, appointing her to regenerate the eye of Horus the elder. Any lion who pronounces the name of the constellation Orion will die at once. Do not do anything on this day.
March 5 Day 7	**March 6** Day 8	**March 7** Day 9
Very favorable It is the day of the going forth of Min into the tent in festivity. The gods are jubilating. Pay attention to incense on the fire. Smell sweet myrrh.	*Very favorable* It is the day the Ennead is in adoration when they see the eye of Horus the elder in its place. All its parts—½, ¼, ⅛, 1/16, 1/32, 1/64—are accounted for by its master. . . .	*Very adverse* . . . Do not go out in darkness when Re goes.
March 11 Day 13	**March 12** Day 14	**March 13** Day 15
Very adverse It is the day of conducting Osiris in his ship to Abydos. Avoid any wind.	*Very adverse* It is the day the crew goes with the gods to look for the confederates of Seth. Do not be courageous on this day.	*Very favorable* It is a happy day in the eastern horizon of heaven. Instructions are given to the followers of the gods in their temples in the presence of the great ones in the two horizons. . . .
March 17 Day 19	**March 18** Day 20	**March 19** Day 21
Very favorable It is the day his majesty Re goes forth in his barque across heaven. There is feasting in Heliopolis. If you see anything on this day, it will be good.	*Very adverse* It is the day Re repels those who rebel against their master. The soul of anyone who passes rebels will suffer for eternity. Do not do any work on this day.	*Very adverse* . . . Do not go out on any road on this day.
March 23 Day 25	**March 24** Day 26	**March 25** Day 27
Very adverse It is the day of cutting out the tongue of Sobek. Do not eat anything which is on the water.	(Papyrus damaged)	*Very adverse* It is the day the majesty of the goddess Sekhmet is angry in the land of Temhu. Behold she goes about walking and standing. Do not go out until Re sets.

March 2 Day 4	March 3 Day 5	March 4 Day 6
Very favorable	. . .	*Very adverse*
It is the day the gods and goddesses are satisfied when they see the children of Geb sitting in their places. If you see anything on this day, it will be good.	It is the day His Majesty Horus is well when the red one sees his form. For anyone who approaches on this day, anger will come of it.	It is the day the stars go forth bitterly and openly. If anyone sees small cattle on this day, he will die at once.

March 8 Day 10	March 9 Day 11	March 10 Day 12
. . .	*Very adverse*	*Very adverse*
It is the day of introducing the great ones to the whole eye of Horus (the Udjat). If you see anything on this day, it will be good.	. . . . . .	. . . . . .

March 14 Day 16	March 15 Day 17	March 16 Day 18
Very favorable	*Very adverse*	*Very adverse*
It is the day of the going forth of Khepri [the scarab], who hears the words of his followers. Every town is in joy.	It is the day of the going forth of Seth, son of Nut, to disturb the great ones who check him in his town of Sew. These gods recognize him and repel his followers until none remains. . . .	. . . Do not approach in the morning. Do not wash yourself with water on this day.

March 20 Day 22	March 21 Day 23	March 22 Day 24
Very adverse	*Mostly adverse*	*Very adverse*
It is the day of the killing of the children of Bedesh. Anyone born on this day will not live.	It is the day of making offerings at Abydos to the spirits.. . . .	It is the day of the rebellion Seth made against Onnophris. Do not mention the name of Seth loudly today. Anyone who mentions his name will have strife in his house forever.

March 26 Day 28	March 27 Day 29	March 28 Day 30
Very favorable	*Very favorable*	Last Day of the Month *Very favorable*
. . . If you see anything on this day, it will be good.	It is the day the gods are satisfied when they give adoration to Onnophris, incense being on the fire, and your local gods [offer] myrrh. It is pleasant on this day.	House of Re, House of Osiris, House of Horus. Make offerings to Ptah-Sokar-Osiris-Atum, lord of the two lands of Heliopolis. Offer to all gods on this day.

FIRST MONTH OF SHOMU

March 29 Day 1	March 30 Day 2	March 31 Day 3
Very favorable	*Very adverse*	*Very favorable*
It is the day of the feast of Horus, son of Isis, and his followers. . . .	. . . Do not sail in any wind on this day.	. . . If you see anything on this day, it will be good.
April 4 Day 7	**April 5** Day 8	**April 6** Day 9
Very favorable	. . .	*Very favorable*
It is the day the crew follows Horus in the foreign lands . . . where he kills he who rebelled against his master. Every heart is glad. Every land is happy.	. . . If you see anything on this day, it will be good.	. . . If you see anything on this day, it will be good.
April 10 Day 13	**April 11** Day 14	**April 12** Day 15
. (Papyrus damaged) .	*Very adverse* It is the day of the cutting out of the tongue of Sobek. . . .	. (Papyrus damaged) .
April 16 Day 19	**April 17** Day 20	**April 18** Day 21
Very favorable	*Very adverse*	*Very adverse*
It is the day of counting by Toth, who heard Maat, the great one. All gods are in festivity. . . .	It is the day Maat judges in front of the gods who become angry in the island of the sanctuary of Letopolis. His majesty Horus revised it. . . .	It is the day of the vomiting of things which come back from the boat, so that no followers of Re remain in attendance. . . .
April 22 Day 25	**April 23** Day 26	**April 24** Day 27
. (Papyrus damaged) .	*Very favorable* . . . If you see anything on this day, it will be good.	*Very adverse* . . .

April 1	Day 4	April 2	Day 5	April 3	Day 6
Very adverse . . . Do not go out of your house on any road this day. Follow Horus on this day.		*Very adverse* It is the day of the feast of Ba-neb-dedet [god of sexual fertility]. If anyone goes out of his house today, disease will waste him till he dies.		*Very favorable* It is the day of the coming of the great ones from the House of Re. They rejoice on this day when they and their followers receive the Udjat-eye. If you see anything on this day, it will be good.	

April 7	Day 10	April 8	Day 11	April 9	Day 12
Very adverse It is the day the White One of Heaven proceeds upstream to be at the front, among those who rebelled against their master in the Delta. . . .		. (Papyrus damaged) .		*Adverse*	

April 13	Day 16	April 14	Day 17	April 15	Day 18
Very adverse . . . Anyone born on this day will die. Do not go out of your house until Re sets in the horizon.		*Very favorable* . . . If you see anything on this day, it will be good.		*Very favorable* The Ennead is in joy and the crew of Re is in festivity. If you see anything on this day, it will be good.	

April 19	Day 22	April 20	Day 23	April 21	Day 24
Very favorable . . . Anyone born on this day will die in old age.		*Very favorable* . . . If you see anything on this day, it will be good.		. (Papyrus damaged) .	

April 25	Day 28	April 26	Day 29	April 27	Day 30
Very favorable . . . If you see anything on this day, it will be good.		. (Papyrus damaged) .		Last Day of the Month *Very favorable* House of Re, House of Osiris, House of Horus. . . .	

SECOND MONTH OF SHOMU

April 28 Day 1	April 29 Day 2	April 30 Day
Very favorable	. . . It is the day the heart of the gods listens very well. The crew of Re is in festivity. . . .	*Very favorable* The day is fixed in heaven and on earth as a feast. It is the month of the followers of Re. . . .
May 4 **Day 7** *Very adverse* It is the day of the executioners of Sekhmet. Do not go out of your house during waking time while Re is in the horizon.	**May 5** **Day 8** *Very favorable* . . . Make a holiday for Re and his followers. Make a good day on this day.	**May 6** **Day** *Very favorable* . . . Make incense of different kinds of sweet herbs for Re's followers which will please him on this day.
May 10 **Day 13** *Very favorable* It is the day of the feast of Udjat in Dep. Her followers are also in festival when singing and chanting take place on this day of offering incense and all kinds of sweet herbs. Make offerings.	**May 11** **Day 14** *Very favorable* . . . If you see anything on this day, it will be good.	**May 12** **Day 1** *Very adverse* It is the day of fighting. Do not judge yourself on this day.
May 16 **Day 19** *Very adverse* It is the day the Ennead sails repeatedly in the entire land. Today is the day of the judging of the great ones. If a lion is seen, he will pass away at once.	**May 17** **Day 20** *Very adverse* It is the day many will die if they come with an adverse wind. Do not go out in any wind on this day.	**May 18** **Day 2** *Mostly adverse* It is the day of the living children of Nut. Do not go out until daybreak.
May 22 **Day 25** *Very favorable* It is the day everybody and everything is pacified by the Akhet-eye. It is pleasant to the gods and Re. . . .	**May 23** **Day 26** *Very adverse* It is the day of the going forth of Neith. She walks on this day in the flood, in order to look for the belongings of Sobek. If any lion sees them, he will pass away immediately.	**May 24** **Day 27** *Very adverse* It is the day of the cutting of the heads and tying of the throats [of the crew]. There is an uproar among the gods. Do not do any work on this day.

May 1 **Day 4**	**May 2** **Day 5**	**May 3** **Day 6**
Very adverse It is the day that what Geb and Nut have done is judged in the presence of the gods. Do not shout at anyone on this day.	*Very favorable* . . . If you see anything on this day, it will be good.	. . . It is the day Horus proceeds to avenge what was done to his father and to inquire from the followers of his father Onnophris. . . .
May 7 **Day 10**	**May 8** **Day 11**	**May 9** **Day 12**
Very favorable . . . Anyone born on this day will be noble.	*Very adverse* It is the day of catching birds and fish by the followers of Re. Do not sail in a boat on the river. Anyone who sails on the river will not live.	*Very favorable* . . . If you see anything on this day, it will be good.
May 13 **Day 16**	**May 14** **Day 17**	**May 15** **Day 18**
Very favorable . . . Anyone born on this day will die a great magistrate among all people.	*Very adverse* . . . Do not go out on this day. Do not do anything or any work on this day.	*Very adverse* It is the day of the going forth of Khesti [Osiris] from the god's house, when he goes to the august mountain. Do not eat any lion's meat on this day. All who smell death and have a skin rash will never recover.
May 19 **Day 22**	**May 20** **Day 23**	**May 21** **Day 24**
Very adverse It is the day Shu complains to Re about the great ones of infinity. There is disturbance below and an uproar of the gods of the *kri*-shrines. Do not go out on this day.	*Very favorable* It is the day the crew rests when it sees the enemy of its master. . . .	*Very favorable* . . . If you see anything on this day, it will be good.
May 25 **Day 28**	**May 26** **Day 29**	**May 27** **Day 30**
Very favorable Today is the day of purifying things and making offerings in Busiris. The gods spend the day in festivity. Act in accordance with events today.	*Very favorable* . . . If you see anything on this day, it will be good.	Last Day of the Month *Very favorable* It is the day of the going forth of Shu to bring back the Udjat-eye and of the appearing of Toth. House of Re, House of Osiris, House of Horus. . . .

THIRD MONTH OF SHOMU

May 28 Day 1	May 29 Day 2	May 30 Day 3
Very favorable It is the day of a great feast in the southern heaven. Every land and every body are in jubilation. Ipet-Hemet [Hathor] and every land are in festivity. . . .	*Very favorable* It is the day every god and goddess spends the day in festivity and great awe in the sacred temple. . . .	*Very adverse* It is the day of the anger of the Divine Majesty. Do not do anything on this day.
June 3 Day 7	**June 4** Day 8	**June 5** Day 9
Very adverse It is the day of the sailing of the gods after the majesty of the goddess. . . .	*Very adverse* It is the day of the massacre of the followers of the majesty of the goddess. Do not beat anybody.	*Very favorable* It is the day the gods are content and they are happy because Re is at peace with the Akhet-eye. Every god is in festivity. . . .
June 9 Day 13	**June 10** Day 14	**June 11** Day 15
Very adverse It is the day His Majesty Re sails westward to see the beauty of Onnophris. . . .	*Very adverse* It is the day of the anger of the eye of Horus the Elder. Do not burn anything that glows with a flame in your house on this day.	*Very favorable* On this day Horus hears your words in the presence of all gods and goddesses. You will see all good things in your house. If you see anything on this day, it will be good.
June 15 Day 19	**June 16** Day 20	**June 17** Day 21
Very adverse . . . Do not embrace anyone or do any work on this day.	*Very adverse* . . . Do not go out of your house on any road on this day.	*Very favorable* . . . If you see anything on this day, it will be good.
June 21 Day 25	**June 22** Day 26	**June 23** Day 27
Mostly favorable It is the day the great enemy is in the temple of Sekhmet. Do not go out at midday.	*Very favorable* . . . If you see anything on this day, it will be good.	*Very adverse* It is the day of sailing on the river and of tearing down the enclosure wall. Do not go out of your house on this day.

May 31	**Day 4**

Very favorable

. . .

If you see anything on this day, it will be good.

June 1	**Day 5**

Very adverse

It is the day of departure of this goddess [Hathor] to the place from where she came. The gods are very sad.

Do not go out of your house. Do not go on a boat. Do not do any work.

June 2	**Day 6**

Very adverse

It is the day every temple of the goddess is in an uproar.

Do not fight or make an uproar in your house.

June 6	**Day 10**

Very adverse

It is the day of creating enmity according to the event. The hearts of the gods who are in the shrine are sad.

. . .

June 7	**Day 11**

Very adverse

It is the day of the introduction of the great ones by Re to the booth to see what he saw through the eye of Horus the Elder. They are with heads bent down when they see an eye of Horus being angry in front of Re.

Do not perform any ritual on this day.

June 8	**Day 12**

Very favorable

It is a holiday, the reception of Re. His followers are in festivity; everyone is in festivity.

. . .

June 12	**Day 16**

Very adverse

It is the day of transporting Maat to the shrine by his Majesty Re, of Heliopolis. Gods learn that Maat is blamed for it.

. . .

June 13	**Day 17**

Very adverse

It is the day of the escape of the fugitive eye. The gods are deprived of Re who had come to hand over the rebels to it.

. . .

June 14	**Day 18**

Very adverse

It is the day Maat and Re go forth in secret.

Do not go out of your house on any road on this day.

June 18	**Day 22**

Very adverse

It is the day of Sepa of Tura coming from Heliopolis.

Do not look at any digging, skin-rash, or fever on this day.

June 19	**Day 23**

Very adverse

It is the day of quarreling and reproaching *m* with Onnophris.

Anyone born on this day will not live.

June 20	**Day 24**

Very favorable

It is the day of the children of Bedesh. The god kills them when he comes. Then he sails south.

. . .

June 24	**Day 28**

Very adverse

It is the day of creating misery and bringing terror into existence in conformity with the custom of what is in the year.

. . .

June 25	**Day 29**

Very favorable

Today is the festival of Mut in Shera [the lake at the Temple of Karnak]. It is the day of feeding the gods and her followers.

. . .

June 26	**Day 30**

Last Day of the Month
Very favorable

House of Re, House of Osiris, House of Horus.

If you see anything on this day, it will be good.

FOURTH MONTH OF SHOMU

June 27 Day 1	June 28 Day 2	June 29 Day 3
Very favorable It is the day of sending *abet*-offerings to those in heaven. All gods and goddesses spend the day in the feast of Onnophris. . . .	*Very favorable* It is the day Maat and all the gods perform the rites as one who is in heaven. . . .	*Very adverse* It is the day her majesty the goddess goes to Heliopolis of Re. A feast is made on this day. Do not go out to do anything on this day.
July 3 **Day 7**	**July 4** **Day 8**	**July 5** **Day 9**
Very adverse It is the day the dead one goes about in the cemetery and arrives on earth. Whoever approaches him will die by being trampled by a bull.	*Very favorable* . . . If you see anything on this day, it will be good.	*Very favorable* . . . Anyone born on this day will have noble honor.
July 9 **Day 13**	**July 10** **Day 14**	**July 11** **Day 15**
Very favorable It is the day of holiday because of defending the son of Osiris [Horus]. . . .	*Very favorable*	*Very adverse* It is the day Re goes forth to propitiate Nun in his cavern in the presence of his followers and the Ennead. Do not do anything. Do not go out on any road on this day.
July 15 **Day 19**	**July 16** **Day 20**	**July 17** **Day 21**
Very favorable It is the day the eye of Horus (the Udjat-eye) has returned complete, nothing is missing from it. Celebrate the feast of your local god. Appease your spirit.	*Very adverse* It is the day of the cleansing and renewal of the noble ones. There is silence because of it on earth in order to propitiate the Udjat-eye on this day. Do not kill any *ankhyt*-reptile on this day.	*Very favorable* . . . If you see anything on this day, it will be good.
July 21 **Day 25**	**July 22** **Day 26**	**July 23** **Day 27**
Very favorable It is the day God is established in front of the crew of Re who is happy in the Hewet Desert. . . .	*Mostly favorable* It is the day the gods sail. Do not go out on this day at midday. . . .	*Very adverse* . . . Do not do anything on this day.

June 30 Day 4	July 1 Day 5	July 2 Day 6

June 30   Day 4

Mostly adverse

It is the day of the procession of Sopdu together with his followers in a state of youth and staying the course of the day. She will never be able to find a living soul.

. . .

July 1   Day 5

Very favorable

It is the day the temple becomes festive, because Min is at Akhmim.

If you see anything on this day, it will be good.

July 2   Day 6

Very adverse

It is the day of transporting the rejuvenated one [Onnophris] to Rostau and of hiding the mysteries of the conspirators.

Do not do anything on this day.

July 6   Day 10

Very favorable

It is the day of the repelling of the crew which was in the Delta. It is the day of the entering of the eye of Re in his horizon when he sees his beauty.

. . .

July 7   Day 11

Very adverse

It is the day destructiveness is created in the presence of the followers of Re, and of repelling the confederates of Seth into the eastern country.

. . .

July 8   Day 12

Very favorable

It is the day of jubilation throughout the entire land. The hearts of those in the shrine are happy.

. . .

July 12   Day 16

Very favorable

. . .

Pour ritual water for those in the next world. It is pleasant for your male and female ancestors who are in the cemetery.

July 13   Day 17

Very favorable

. . .

If you see anything on this day, it will be good.

July 14   Day 18

Mostly adverse

It is the day the crew leads the rebels.

Do not go out in the morning. If any lion goes out on this day on the earth he will be blind and they will say: "He shall not live."

July 18   Day 22

Very favorable

It is the day of the feast of Anubis who is on his mountain. The children of Geb and Nut spend the day in festivity, which is a holiday because of the good purification of the gods on this day.

. . .

July 19   Day 23

Very adverse

. . .

Do not taste bread or beer on this day.

July 20   Day 24

Very favorable

. . .

Make *abet*-offerings to the gods in the presence of Re. Make a holiday in your house.

July 24   Day 28

Very favorable

It is the day of the feast of Min.

If you see anything on this day, it will be good.

July 25   Day 29

Very favorable

It is the day of a holiday in the temple of Sokar, on the estate of Ptah. Those who are on this estate are in great festivity, because they are healthy.

. . .

July 26   Day 30

Last Day of the Year
Very favorable

Anything which comes forth on this day from the estate of Ptah will be good.

Anything, any rite, or anybody on this day, will be good throughout the year. Sing and make many offerings.

The Five Additional Days of the Year

The great ones are born. As to the great ones whose forms are not mysterious, beware of them. . . . Birth of Osiris, Birth of Horus, Birth of Seth, Birth of Isis, Birth of Nephthys. Anyone who knows the names of the five additional days shall not be hungry, shall not be thirsty. Bastet shall not overpower him. He will not enter into the great law court, he will not die through an enemy of the king and will not die through the pestilence of the year. He will last every day till death arrives, no illness will take possession of him. As to he who knows the names of the five additional days, he shall be prosperous. His speech shall be important, heard in the presence of Re.

July 27 First Day Birth of Osiris	*July 28 Second Day Birth of Horus*	*July 29 Third Day Birth of Seth*
Words to be said:	Words to be said:	Words to be said:
O Osiris, bull in his cavern whose name is hidden. . . . Hail to thee; I am thy son, O father Osiris. The name of this day is The Pure One . . .	O Horus of Letopolis. . . . The name of this day is Powerful is the Heart.	O Seth, son of Nut, great of strength . . . protection is at the hands of thy holiness. I am thy son. The name of this day is Powerful of Heart.
July 30 Fourth Day Birth of Isis	*July 31 Fifth Day Birth of Nepthys*	
Words to be said:	Words to be said:	
O this Isis, daughter of Nut, the eldest, mistress of magic, provider of the book, mistress who appeases the two lords, her face is glorious. I am the brother and the sister. The name of this day is He Who Makes Terror.	O Nephthys, daughter of Nut, sister of Seth, she whose father sees a healthy daughter. . . . I am the divine power in the womb of my mother Nut. The name of this day is The Child Who is in his Nest.	

Words to be spoken at the end of the five additional days:

Hail to you! O great ones according to their names, children of a goddess who have come forth from the sacred womb, lords by virtue of their father, goddesses by virtue of their mother, who do not know the necropolis. Behold, may you protect me and save me. May you make me prosperous and protect me. I am one who is on their list.—This spell is to be said four times.

Make for yourself an amulet for protection to be worn about the neck for the five additional days in the names of these gods. Have the figures of Osiris, Horus, Seth, Isis, and Nephthys drawn on linen.

How are magical practices to be explained? By sympathy, by the existence of a concordance of like things and a contrariety of unlike things, and by a diversity of many operative powers in the one driving universe. Without any external contrivance, there is much drawing and spell-binding. The true magic is Love and Strife in the universe. In magical practices men turn all this to their own uses.

—Plotinus

16. Greco-Roman and Coptic Magic

WHEN ALEXANDER THE GREAT conquered Egypt in 332 B.C., Egypt already had been defeated by the Assyrians and Persians and was in a greatly weakened state. Most conquering nations would have imposed their cultures on the suppressed Egyptians but the Greeks had always revered them for their wisdom and technical skills and wanted to preserve Egyptian culture. In fact, although Egyptian civilization eventually did die out, it left a greater impression on its Greek occupants than vice versa.

The Greeks especially admired the Egyptians for their magical skills. They quickly equated their gods with those of the Egyptians—it is quite usual to find the names of Egyptian gods in Greek magical papyri. Also, many Greco-Roman spells were merely versions of much older Egyptian texts.

Another aspect of Egyptian magic the Greeks borrowed was the use and significance of stone in the production of amulets. To the Egyptians the stone a charm was made of was important. A white stone amulet might promote the flow of milk in a mother nursing her child, or a red stone amulet might be used to overcome the effects of drinking too much wine. The Greeks continued the use of colored stone amulets, but they eliminated the use of shape—*djed*-column, *ankh*-sign, Eye-of-Horus, etc.—as an indication of an amulet's purpose. Instead, they inscribed a magical text on the stone, which was usually an oval.

One particularly interesting category of Greek amulets became known as "gnostic gems." These amulets normally date from the second or third century A.D. and are called "gnostic" because they were associated with the religious philosophy of spiritual knowledge considered heretical by the early Christian Church. These amulets, made of semi-precious and other stones worn as pendants, normally called upon non-Christian gods for protection and help. While there is no known inscribed magical gem from pre-Christian times, they must have existed in Greece. Greek playwrights frequently mention magical stones and rings. For instance, in *Plutus,* a play written by Aristophanes in the fourth century B.C., the Just Man is threatened with blackmail and replies that he does not worry about such things because he has bought a magical ring from Eudamus for a drachma.

Inscribed magical gems were probably derived from Egyptian oracular papyri, which evolved as a kind of substitution for amulets late in the New Kingdom. Inscribed stones usually are carved with the figure of either a traditional Greek god or a Hellenized Egyptian god, such as Isis or Anubis, and a brief inscription such as, "Preserve me," or "Do my bidding." Sometimes stones were inscribed for a particular purpose. For instance, one carved for a sailor to protect him from shipwreck has a figure of Poseidon resting his foot on a dolphin. For the stones to have full power they had to be consecrated. The limited evidence we have suggests that this ceremony involved the burning of incense, libations, and animal sacrifices.

The inscriptions on these magical gem stones are almost always in Greek letters, but often they are meaningless syllables intended to impress the purchaser by their strangeness of sound. A typical example of such a formula is: *aththa, baththa, ibi, abi, selti, belti.* Sometimes a series of letters that reads the same forward and backward would be inscribed, such as $\alpha\beta\alpha\nu\alpha\theta\alpha\nu\alpha\lambda\beta\alpha$. In some instances the numerical value rather than the phonetic value of the letters is important. When each Greek letter is given its numerical value ($\alpha = 1$, $\beta = 2$, $\rho = 100$, $\chi = 600$, etc.), the total of all the letters gives some magically significant number. An especially interesting example is a gem of red jasper with the following Greek inscription:

ΧΑΒΡΑΧ

ΦΝΕΙΕΧΗΡ

ΦΙΧΡΟ

ΦΝΤΡΩ

ΦΩΧΩ

ΒΩΧ

These words have no meaning in Greek, but the first line contains the rudiments of a magical word familiar to us all—*abracadabra*. This word was believed to have magical powers; stones inscribed with it are called "abraxis stones." The origins of the word are uncertain, but it appears for the first time in a poem of the second century A.D. The first word of the above inscription would be pronounced in English "xabrax." Clearly the first *x* does not seem to fit, at least phonetically. However, it is there because of its numerical value. When each letter is replaced by its numerical value the inscription looks as follows:

$$
\begin{array}{lcl}
600 + 1 + 2 + 100 + 1 + 600 & = & 1304 \\
500 + 50 + 5 + 200 + 600 + 8 + 100 & = & 1463 \\
500 + 10 + 600 + 100 + 70 & = & 1280 \\
500 + 50 + 400 + 100 + 800 & = & 1850 \\
500 + 800 + 600 + 800 & = & 2700 \\
2 + 800 + 600 & = & \underline{1402} \\
& & 9999
\end{array}
$$

The number 9999 frequently appears on Greco-Egyptian inscribed stones.

One of the most popular spells from this period was called the "Sword of Dardanus," used to make someone fall in love. Dardanus was a fictitious ancient magician whose books of magic supposedly were buried with him and later discovered by Democritus. The "Sword of Dardanus" was to be inscribed on a magnetic stone. (Such stones were said to contain the breath of life, perhaps because they could move inanimate metallic objects.) One side of the stone was to be engraved with the figure of Aphrodite sitting on a soul represented as a butterfly. Under her was Eros, standing on a globe and applying a flaming torch to Psyche. Underneath this scene were magical names. The stone was to be placed under the tongue of the user and turned round and round while he recited an incantation (a feat which in itself sounds like magic).

The "Sword of Dardanus" could also be inscribed on a gold leaf, although the instructions for its use are rather bizarre. The inscribed leaf had to be swallowed by a partridge. You then killed the bird and recovered the leaf. You wore the leaf, along with the paideros plant, around your neck. Then you could command a spirit to aid you. To enlist Eros, you carved an image of him out of mulberry wood, making the back hollow. You lined the hollow place with gold foil inscribed with the name of the loved one. The name had to be written with a Cyprian stylus that had been heated and then hardened by being plunged into cold water. You then went to the loved one's home, knocked on her door with the image, and said a spell to cause her to dream. Eros appeared in her dream as the god she venerated most and assisted you. When you returned home, you burned incense to Eros on a table covered with clean linen. This had to be done before flowers and the image of Eros. He would then appear and help you.

In addition to inscribed stones, magical papyri have survived from the Greek occupation of Egypt. While these papyri have many characteristics in common with Egyptian magical papyri, they also have distinct traits of their own. One typically Greek feature is that they contain numerous spells for communicating with the gods. Such close personal contact with the gods was rarely attempted by the Egyptians. The London-Leiden magical papyrus describes a method that is the precursor of the crystal ball. It involves a young boy and a bowl of oil.

In a darkened room the boy gazes into a bowl filled with oil. He then closes his eyes, and the magician recites the following spell:

> Grow, O light, come forth O light.
> Rise O light, ascend O light.
> Thou who art without, come in.[1]

If, when the boy opens his eyes, he does not see the light, the magician tells him to close his eyes again and the following formula is recited:

> O darkness, remove thyself from before him.
> O light, bring the light to me.
> Pshai that is in the abyss, bring in the light to me.
> O Osiris who is in the Neshem-boat, bring
>   in the light to me.
> These four winds that are without, bring in the
>   light to me.
> O thou in whose hand is the moment that belongeth
>   to these hours, bring in the light to me.
> Anubis, the good oxherd, bring in the light to me. . . .
> O great god whose name is great, appear to this
>   child without alarming or deceiving, truthfully.
> SAY THIS SPELL SEVEN TIMES [2]

If, after the second spell, the boy does see light and Anubis appears, there is another spell to greet him.

> . . . Hail Anubis, come to me. The High and Mighty,
> the Chief over the mysteries of those in the
> Underworld, the Pharaoh of those in Amenti, the
> Chief Physician, the fair [son] of Osiris, he
> whose face is strong among the gods, thou manifest
> thyself in the Underworld before the hand of Osiris. . . .
> Come to earth, show thyself to me here today. . . . Come to
> the mouths of my vessel today and do thou tell me
> answer in truth to everything that I shall inquire
> about without falsehood therein. . . .[3]

As the seance continues, the magician continues to ask the boy if the gods have come in yet, and he provides for them a table, bread, and beer. From among the gods present, the boy requests one to stand up and answer the magician's questions. Once the boy identifies the god standing, the magician can ask any question he wishes.

If the magician wanted to make sure the bowl used for divination would work quickly, he could burn a crocodile egg on a flame. This would cause the bowl to perform instantly. If he wanted to bring in the gods by force, he could mix the bile of a crocodile with frankincense on a brazier. If he wanted to converse with entities other than the gods, he could burn other substances on the brazier, depending on the entity desired: If he wanted to talk to a spirit, he burned a hyaena or hare heart; to a drowned man, a *karob*-stone; to a murdered man, asses' dung and an amulet of Nephthys; and if, for some reason, to a thief, crocus powder and alum. If the spells worked as hoped, he would need another to dismiss all the spirits conjured up. To make them go away, he burned ape's dung on the brazier and said, "Good dispatch, joyful dispatch."

A second method of divination, more direct and not involving a youth, caused a priest in fine linen to appear. In the middle of a clean room, the magician placed a four-legged table made of olive wood at which no man had ever sat. He covered the table with a cloth, then placed four bricks underneath. On a clay censer in front of the table he burned olive-wood charcoal. He then formed into balls a mixture of wild goose fat, myrrh, and *qs-ankh* (a plant). Placing one of the balls on the censer, he said the following spell in Greek three times:

> I invoke thee who art seated in the invisible darkness and who art
> in the midst of the great gods sinking and receiving the sun's rays
> and sending forth the luminous goddess Neboutosoualeth, the great
> god Barzan Boubarzna Narzazouzan Barzabouzath the sun; send up
> to me this night thy archangel Zebourthanunen; answer with truth,
> truthfully, without falsehood, without ambiguity concerning this
> matter, for I conjure thee by him who is seated in the flaming ves-
> ture on the silver [?] head of Agathodaemon, the almighty four-faced
> daemon, the highest darkling and soul-bringing [?] Phox; do not dis-
> regard me, but send up speedily in this night an injunction [?] of the
> god.[4]

Then, without speaking to anyone, the magician lay down in the
room. Soon the linen-clad priest appeared and answered his questions.

While magical papyri of the Greco-Roman period assert that
the technique of basin-divination, called "lekanomancy," works,
there are few eye-witness accounts of its use. One is the report of
Thessalos, a Greek who lived in the first century A.D., who claimed
to have studied magic in the temples of Egypt. His somewhat pom-
pous account of his contact with the gods is fascinating:

> To Caesar Augustus, Greeting! Many have tried during their life,
> Augustus Caesar, to deliver up the secrets of lots of marvellous
> things, but none of them has been able to complete his project be-
> cause of the fatal darkness that came to overwhelm his spirit; and I
> then seem to be the only one of all those who have lived since the
> beginning of time to have composed a marvellous treatise. Indeed,
> though I had undertaken a task that goes beyond the limits of human
> powers, I have been able to crown it with the end that is required—
> not, it is true, without many trials and dangers. . . .
>
> So I began to travel about Egypt, driven on by this goad that
> wounded my soul, seeking some way of making my rash hope, or if I
> failed, resolved to abandon life by suicide. As my soul predicted to
> me ceaselessly that I'd have communication with the gods, I went on
> raising my hands to heaven, begging the gods to accord me, by a
> dream-vision or by an inspiration from on high, some favour of
> which I might be proud, returning, joyous, to Alexandria and my
> homeland.
>
> Thus I arrived at Diospolis [Thebes], the most ancient capital of
> Egypt, which possesses a host of temples; and there I established
> myself. In effect there lived there priests, friends of letters and

learned in many sciences. Time passed. My friendship with the priests went on increasing all the while. One day I asked them if something of the operative force of magic survived. I noticed that most of them were shocked at my boldness in conceiving such hopes; but one, who inspired confidence by the gravity of his manners and his great age, did not disappoint my friendship. He assured me that he had the power of producing visions by means of a basin filled with water.

I then invited him to stroll with me in the most deserted part of the city without telling him what I wanted. We came to a woodland environed with a profound peace, and there I suddenly threw myself down on the ground, and, weeping, embraced his feet. And as he, bewildered at this unexpected act, asked me why I had done it, I declared that my life was in his hands, that it was absolutely necessary for me to converse with a god, and that, if this desire was not satisfied, I was ready to give up living. Raising me up from the earth, he quieted me with the most amiable discourse, promised cordially to yield to my prayer, and bade me fast for three days.

As for me, my soul was completely melted at the declaration of these promises. I kissed his hand and heaped him with thanks, weeping like a fountain. For it's a law of nature that an unhoped-for joy provokes more tears than grief. Then, emerging from the wood, we began to fast; and those three days, in my impatient condition, seemed to me as many years.

When the third day was come, from the moment of dawn, I went to greet the priest. He had prepared a suitable chamber with everything needed for the consultation. On my side, always prepared, I had brought, without informing the priest, paper and ink for taking notes, if I had the chance, of anything said. The priest asked if I wanted to talk with the ghost of a dead man or with a god.

"With Asklepios," I told him, adding that he would crown his kindness if he let me converse with the god on my own. He agreed without pleasure, as I could tell clearly from his face, but at least he promised. Then he shut me in the chamber, bade me sit down opposite the throne where the god would take his seat, and invoked Asklepios, thanks to the virtue of mysterious words. After that he hurried out, locking the door with a key.

And there I was seated, annihilated in body and soul at the sight of so wonderful a thing—for no human word could render the features of that face or the splendours of the ornaments that set it off—when the god, lifting his right hand, saluted me thus:

"O Blessed Thessalos, today a god honours you, and soon, when men learn of your success, they will hold you in reverence as a god yourself. Ask me what you please, I will reply to you faithfully in all matters."

I could scarcely speak, so much was I carried out of myself and so much fascinated by the god's beauty. Still I asked him why I had failed in trying the recipes of Nechepso.

The god answered me, "King Nechepso, highly intelligent man as he was, and possessing every magic power, had not however received from any divine voice the secrets that you want to learn. Endowed with a natural sagacity, he had grasped the affinities [*sympatheiai*] of stones and plants with the stars; but he did not know the moments or the places where the plants must be gathered. The growth or the withering of all fruits of the season depend on the efflux [*aporrhoia*] of the stars. Further, the divine spirit [pneuma], which in its extreme subtlety passes through every substance, is spread in particular abundance in the spots which the astral influx successively reached in the course of the cosmic revolution.[5]

While Thessalos' account is clearly self-serving, it is possible that he actually did participate in lekanomancy. One cannot help but wonder what actually happened.

Although the Greeks admired and were influenced by the magicians of Egypt, they also added much of their own to the magical corpus. One typically Greek aspect is the careful attention paid to the position of the heavenly bodies when gathering plants used in potions, or even when invoking the heavenly bodies for assistance.

One kind of spell, known in Greek as *Diabole*, involves slandering your enemy to the moon. You can tell the moon about the evils done by your rival in the hope that the moon will punish him. One such spell was reputed to have been so effective that the Roman emperor Hadrian doubled the salary of the magician, Pachrates, who by use of the spell brought a man to the court within one hour, made him ill within two hours, and killed him in seven. The same spell also caused the king himself to have a dream. The use of spells to impress and influence monarchs became such an important part of magic in the Roman period that a frequent annotation to spells in magical papyri was, "It works on kings."

In spite of their great technical achievements, and careful craftsmanship, the Egyptians did not make the kind of cause-effect observations and experiments by which we define science. The idea that specific positions of planets could affect a magical spell is a typically Greek contribution. Alchemy had its start in ancient Egypt. The word "alchemy" is a corruption of the Arabic *al ki-miya,* which means the art of transmutation. This Arabic derivation comes from the ancient Egyptian word for "Egypt," which was *khemt* and which meant *the black land.* The Greeks built alchemy into a network of connections between planets, metals, and human events. They believed that for each planet there was a corresponding metal that also corresponded to a human emotion. For instance, quicksilver corresponded to the planet Mercury, and its emotion was changeability.

The practice of alchemy in the Middle Ages, although far more sophisticated than anything in Egypt of the Ptolemaic period, had its roots first in the ancient Egyptian crafts and second in Greek science. The alchemists' purposes were greatly misunderstood in the Middle Ages, and even today their ultimate goal is not recognized. While some did in fact intend to change lead into gold, this was really a metaphor. The ultimate goal was that the alchemist's *soul* be tranformed from base to pure. Metals were "tormented" by the fire of the crucible, while the alchemist was tormented psychologically by the suffering of his soul.

The one theme that seems to appear repeatedly in Greek magical papyri is love. The Greeks had innumerable spells to make people fall in love. Often these love incantations involved both words and wax figures. One typical Greek love spell involved two figures, one of Ares and one of the woman to be charmed. The woman was to be represented kneeling, with both her hands tied behind her back, while Ares held his sword to her throat. Various demons were to be summoned to cause her to fall in love, their names inscribed on the legs of the figure of the woman. Thirteen bronze needles were to be stuck into its limbs while the man said: "I pierce [woman's name] that she may think of me." After this, various magical words were to be written on a lead plate which was to be tied to the figures by a cord with 365 knots in it to assure that she would love the man every day of the year. The figures with the plate were to be buried in the grave of someone who died young or who was killed violently.

The Egyptian tradition of magic carried on by the Greeks extended into the period of Roman occupation of Egypt. Even though the Roman emperor Diocletian ordered all magical texts destroyed, a considerable practice of magical arts continued in Egypt during the first few centuries of the Christian era. A great many of the practitioners were the Copts.

The Copts are the Christian sect of Egypt. The word "Copt" is probably a corruption of the Greek word for Egypt. When St. Mark began preaching Christianity in Egypt during the first century, he found the Egyptians ready converts. Since the Egyptian gods had always formed trinities, when St. Mark preached of another, it probably was not difficult to accept. Although Christians, the Copts were also Egyptian, so it is not surprising that they continued the practice of magic.

The concerns of Coptic magical texts are basically the same as their Egyptian (non-Christian), Greek, and Roman counterparts— health, wealth, and love. One Coptic magical text in the British Museum contains a love incantation that is at times poetic and at times nearly pornographic. It involves calling upon demons to cause a woman to desire a man:

> . . . Kok Tpatkokok, he whose head is in the abyss, his feet in hell, we are come to thee this day, we put trust in thee for [name], that thou mayest give her the food that I may become honey in her belly, manna upon her tongue, and that she desire me as it were the sun and love me as it were the moon and wait for me [lit. hang upon me] like a drop of water hanging upon a jar and that she be like unto a honey [-bee] seeking [honey], a bitch prowling, a cat going from house to house, like unto a mare going beneath horses in heat. Now, now, now, quickly, by all the might of hell!
>
> Kok Kocharotoch Parsobol Anael. I asked him and he sent a demon whose name is Theumatha, whose head is in the abyss, whose feet are in hell, the Gehenna of fire. He took fiery prongs, wherewith to smite the head of [name] until she came to me, to any place that I wish. She shall draw her garment up to her neck and shall call to me saying, "Come hither." By the might of Adael! Now, now, quickly, quickly! [6]

Coptic spells were somewhat different from their earlier counterparts. Although spirits still were called upon for assistance, they were angels; and, instead of a host of gods to be invoked, there was only one. There is a Coptic wizard's book of magical spells in the library of the University of Michigan that dates from around the seventh century. It contains a general, all-purpose spell that could be used on a variety of occasions:

> O God, O Lord, O Lord, O Omnipotent
> Whose body is the color of fire
> Who is light in the hidden
> Whose name no flesh-born man knoweth
> Save only himself
> The whole way of wisdom
> This one from among the eons of light
> This inscrutable one
> Surround by all the powers
> Each being appointed over his work and his service
> Perform for me every labor pertaining to this spell
> And every operation which I shall undertake
> These seven angels
> Each being appointed over his work and his service
> Perform for me
> I am Seth the son of Adam. . . .[7]

This incantation is more like a Christian prayer than a magical spell. It calls upon God and his angels for help, but it does contain one clearly magical element: The magician asserts that he is Seth, the son of Adam, and, as with earlier magical spells, saying it makes it so. This spell continues with an assertion that the magician has specially purified himself and that not everyone could do what he does. Interestingly, in another place the text claims that much of the power of the spell comes from the fact that secret names are in Hebrew. In fact, they are not, but are made-up sounds intended to impress.

> I have purified myself forty days
> Till its power is manifest
> And the power of its Hebrew and all its executions
> That it may assist in every task which I shall undertake
> Employ it while being pure and reverential
> I am Seth the son of Adam
> To whom have been revealed the virtues and mysteries and
>   its executions and the power of these arts, more
>   honored than the spells. . . .

> Not every man can bear it
> Save only those that are sufficiently pure
> Who are perfected in all its appellations and its powers
> For this causes a spirit to dwell upon him
> And a wisdom more than any man.[8]

The magician's claim to being special and, further, that not just anyone who obtained his spells could use them, probably arose from a very practical concern. During this period, there were many copies of this particular text circulating. Possibly, the magician wanted to scare off anyone from simply purchasing a pirated text and becoming his own magician. Therefore, he warned that one needed purification, wisdom, etc.

This general spell was to be recited seven times over some honey and licorice root. Additional very detailed instructions were to be carried out for particular circumstances. If you purified yourself for forty days, put on clean garments, and then fried a hawk's egg in honey, the spell would have three effects: (1) it would dissipate the anger of every married man, (2) heal the bites of insects and animals, and (3) save you from hate and from evil plots against you. The spell was also used in preparing written amulets. It could be written on a piece of papyrus and tied to your right arm; then if a monarch were angry with you, your life would be spared. For protection on a sea or ocean voyage the papyrus would be tied to the tip of the mast.

Depending upon how the general spell was recited, it could have different effects. If it were recited over water, a person stung by an insect could drink the water and be cured. If it were recited over water with laurel in it, a sufferer of jaundice could be cured by drinking the water and washing with it. Recited over oil, the spell could cure a problem of the spleen—the afflicted was anointed with the purified oil. If someone could not sleep, the spell was recited over water and the surroundings where he slept were washed with the water. If someone had nightmares, the spell was recited over rain-water and the person washed with it. Treated water, while primarily used against unseen foes and demons, could also be used against mundane physical enemies. If the water were sprinkled over your house and all the paths leading to it, your enemies could do you no harm. All of this anointing with magically purified water is close to the modern Christian concept of the power of holy water.

These examples of Coptic magic illustrate the continuation of the eclectic nature of Egyptian magic throughout its three-thousand-year history. The Egyptians tended to view competitive belief-systems not as rivals but as knowledge to be assimilated. It is not surprising, then, that the Egyptians simultaneously worshiped the one God, called upon demons and angels for special help, and used magical rituals, all the while incorporating the practices of their Greek conquerers.

One example of this type of eclecticism is a papyrus containing a horoscope written on April 13, 95 A.D. Though badly damaged, the papyrus gives clearly detailed positions of the planets, the stars, and the moon. The sun and Mercury are viewed as benevolent influences that can ward off the influence of malevolent planets. The author of the horoscope, though undoubtedly a Christian, believed that the heavenly bodies could influence such specific events in his life as whether his wife would become pregnant or what his future profession would be. While his Egyptian ancestors of the New Kingdom never thought of such possibilities, they certainly would have been able to appreciate the magical principles underlying his belief.

O my sister, as thou be not asleep, Tell
us one of thy pleasant stories, to beguile
the watches of the night. . . ."
"With all my heart, if the good king
leave me."
"Tell on."

—Sheherazade and the King
The Thousand and One Nights

17. Tales of Magic

BECAUSE MAGIC PLAYED such a large role in the daily life of the ancient Egyptians, it is not surprising that it influenced their literature. They were particularly fond of stories with magical themes. Two of the most famous of these narratives are "King Cheops and the Magicians" and "The Shipwrecked Sailor." In this section Professor William Kelly Simpson's translations are reprinted along with his introductions and notes from his *The Literature of Ancient Egypt* with corrections made especially for this book.

King Cheops and the Magicians

This cycle of stories about the marvels performed by the lector priests is cast in the form of a series of tales told at the court of Cheops by his sons. The name of the first son is missing together with most of the story. The second son, Khaefre, later became king and is known as the builder of the Second Pyramid at Giza. The third son, Bauefre, is known from other sources; a later text indicates that he may have also become king for a short time. The fourth son, Hardedef, is known as one of the sages of the past, and part of his instruction has survived.

The text derives from a single manuscript of which the beginning and conclusion are missing. The papyrus was inscribed in the Hyksos period before Dynasty 18, but the composition appears to belong to Dynasty 12; the events described are set in the Old Kingdom. The last story is a prophecy of the end of Cheops's line through the birth of the three kings who founded Dynasty 5. The story of their actual birth is presented as a sort of annex. Elements of the miraculous royal birth are represented in later Egyptian and Near Eastern literature and even are reflected in the biblical accounts. The device of providing stories for the diversion of the king is also represented in The Prophecies of Neferti, The Admonitions, and The Eloquent Peasant, as well as several later compositions. The real substance of the composition is certainly the prophecy of the birth of the kings, and the other tales merely lead up to it. For bibliography and commentary on King Cheops and the Magicians (Papyrus Westcar), see Lefebvre, Romans et contes, pp. 70–90, and Erman, The Ancient Egyptians, pp. xxiv, lxviii–lxix, 36–49.

W.K.S.

First Tale: End of the Marvel in the Time of King Djoser

[. . . His Majesty] the King of Upper and Lower Egypt, Khufu (Cheops), the vindicated [said: Let there be given . . .], one hundred jugs of beer, an ox [. . . to] the King of Upper and Lower Egypt, Djoser, the vindicated [and may there be given . . .], a haunch of beef [. . . to the lector priest . . .]. [For I] have seen an example of his skill. And [they] did according as [His Majesty] commanded.[1]

Second Tale: The Marvel Which Happened in the Time of King Nebka

The king's son Khaefre (Chephren) arose [to speak, and he said: I should like to relate to Your Majesty] another marvel, one which happened in the time of [your] father, [the King of Upper and Lower Egypt] Nebka, the vindicated, as he proceeded to the temple of [Ptah, Lord of] Ankh-towy.[2]

Now when His Majesty went to [. . .], His Majesty made an [appeal? . . . to] the chief [lector] Webaoner [. . .]. But the wife of Webaoner [. . . was enamored of a townsman. She caused to be brought (?)] to him a chest filled with garments [. . .], and he returned with [the] servant.[3] [Now several] days [passed by . . .]. There was a greenhouse [4] [on the estate] of Webaoner. The townsman [said to the wife of Weba]oner: Is there a greenhouse [. . .]?

[Come], let us pass time in it. [Then said the wife of] Webaoner to the caretaker who [cared for the estate]: Let the greenhouse be prepared [. . .] and she spent the day there drinking [with the townsman . . . and] [resting] [. . .]. Now after [evening came . . .] he [went to . . .] the caretaker, and [the] servant girl [. . .].

[When] day broke, and the second day [came, the caretaker informed Webaoner of] this matter [. . .]. He gave it to his [. . .] of the water. Then [he (?)] lit [a fire]. [He said to his caretaker]: Bring me [. . . my chest] of ebony and gold [and he made . . . and he opened . . . and made] a crocodile [of wax . . .] seven [fingers long . . .]. He read out his [magic words saying . . .]: [If anyone] comes [to] bathe [in] my lake [. . .] the townsman. Then he gave it to [the caretaker], and he said to him: After the townsman goes down to the pool, as is his daily fashion, you shall cast [the] crocodile after him. The [caretaker] went forth and he took the crocodile of wax with him.

Now the [wife] of Webaoner sent to the caretaker who was in charge of the [garden] saying: Let the greenhouse be prepared for I have come to stay in it. The greenhouse was prepared [with] every good thing. They (the wife and the maidservant?) went forth, and they (spent) a pleasant day with the townsman. After night fell, the townsman returned as was his daily fashion, and the caretaker threw the crocodile of wax behind him into the water. [At once it grew] into a crocodile of seven cubits,[5] and it took hold of the townsman.

Webaoner tarried with His Majesty the King of Upper and Lower Egypt, Nebka, the vindicated, for seven days, all the while the townsman was in the [lake without] breathing. After seven days had passed, His Majesty the King of Upper and Lower Egypt, Nebka, the vindicated [came forth], and the chief lector Webaoner placed himself in [his] presence and [he] said [to him]: May Your Majesty come and see the marvel which has taken place in Your Majesty's time. [His Majesty went with] Webaoner. [He called out to the] crocodile and said: Bring back the townsman. [The crocodile] came [out of the water . . . .]. Then the [chief] lector [Webaoner] said: [Open up]! And he [opened up]. Then he placed [. . . .]. Said His Majesty the King of Upper and Lower Egypt, Nebka, the vindicated: this crocodile is indeed fearful! But Webaoner bent down, and he caught it and it became a crocodile of wax in his hand. The chief lector Webaoner told His Majesty the King of Upper and Lower Egypt, Nebka, the vindicated, about this affair which the townsman had in his house with his wife. And His Majesty said to the crocodile: Take what belongs to you! The crocodile then went down to the [depths] of the lake, and no one knew the place where he went with him.

His [Majesty the King of Upper] and Lower Egypt, Nebka, the vindicated, had the wife of Webaoner taken to a plot north of the capital, and he set fire to her [. . . in] the river.

Such is a marvel which happened [in] the time of your father, the King of Upper and Lower Egypt, Nebka, one which the chief lector Webaoner performed. His Majesty the King of Upper and Lower Egypt, Khufu, the vindicated, said: Let there be offered to the King of Upper and Lower Egypt, Nebka, the vindicated, one thousand loaves of bread, one hundred jugs of beer, an ox, and two cones of incense, and let there be offered to the chief lector Webaoner a large cake, a jug of beer, a joint of meat, and one cone of incense, for I have [seen] an example of his skill. And it was done according to all His Majesty commanded.

Third Tale: The Marvel Which Happened in the Reign of King Snefru

Bauefre arose to speak, and he said: Let me have [Your] Majesty hear a marvel which took place in the time of your (own) father King Snefru, the vindicated, [one] which the chief lector Djadjaemonkh [made] and which had not taken place [before] . . . [Now His Majesty had searched out the chambers] of the palace, l.p.h.,[6] to seek for him [some diversion . . . and he said]: Hasten, bring me the chief lector and scribe, [. . . Djadjaem]onkh! He was brought to him immediately. [His] Majesty said to him: [I have looked through the chambers of the] palace, l.p.h., to seek for myself some refreshing matter, but I cannot find any. Djadjaemonkh said to him: Let Your Majesty proceed to the lake of the palace, l.p.h., and equip for yourself a boat with all the beauties who are in your palace chamber. The heart of Your Majesty shall be refreshed at the sight of their rowing as they row up and down. You can see the beautiful fish pools of your lake, and you can see the beautiful fields around it. Your heart will be refreshed at this. His Majesty said: I will indeed fit out my rowing excursion. Let there be brought to me twenty oars made of ebony, fitted with gold, with the butts of sandalwood (?) fitted with white gold. Let there be brought to me twenty women, the most beautiful in form, with hair well braided, with firm breasts, not yet having opened up to give birth. Let there be brought to me twenty bead garments, and let these bead garments be given to these women when they have taken off their clothes. Then it was done according to all that His Majesty commanded, and they rowed up and down. The heart of His Majesty was happy at the sight of their rowing.[7]

Now one of the strokes combed her tresses, and a fish-shaped charm of new turquoise fell in the water. She became silent and did not row, and her side of the boat became silent and did not row. His Majesty said: Are you not rowing? And they said: Our stroke is silent and does not row. Then [His] Majesty said to her: [Why] do [you] not row? She said: A fish-shaped charm of new [turquoise] fell into the water. And [His Majesty said to her]: Would you like one to replace [it]? But [she said]: I [prefer] my own [to a look-alike].[8] His Majesty said: [Let there be brought again] the chief lector [Djadjaemonkh, and he was brought at once]. His Majesty said: Djadjaemonkh, my brother,[9] I have done as you have said, and the heart of His Majesty was refreshed at the sight of their rowing. But a fish-shaped charm of new turquoise, belonging to one of the leaders, fell into the water. She was silent and did not row. And it came to pass that she ruined her side. I said to her: Why have you stopped rowing? She said to me: It is because a fish-shaped charm of new turquoise has fallen into the water. I said to her: Row! I will replace it! She said to me: I prefer my own to a look-alike. Then said the chief lector Djadjaemonkh his magic sayings. He placed one side of the water of the lake upon the other, and lying upon a postsherd he found the fish-shaped charm. Then he brought it back and gave it to its owner. Now as for the water, it was twelve cubits deep, and it amounted to twenty-four cubits after it was folded back. He said his magic sayings, and he brought back the water of the lake to its position. His Majesty passed a holiday with the entire palace, l.p.h. When he came forth, he rewarded the chief lector Djadjaemonkh with all good things.

Such is a marvel which took place in the time of your father, the King of Upper and Lower Egypt, Snefru, the vindicated, something done by the chief lector, scribe of the document, Djadjaemonkh. And His Majesty the King of Upper and Lower Egypt, Khufu, the vindicated, said: Let there be an offering made to His Majesty the King of Upper and Lower Egypt, Snefru, the vindicated, consisting of one thousand loaves of bread, one hundred jugs of beer, an ox, and two cones of incense, and let there be given a large cake, a jug of beer, and one cone of incense to the chief lector, scribe of the document, Djadjaemonkh. For I have seen an example of his skill. It was done according to all His Majesty commanded.

The Fourth Tale: A Marvel in the Time of King Khufu Himself

The king's son Hardedef arose to speak, and he said: [You have heard examples of] the skill of those who have passed away, but there one cannot know truth [from falsehood]. [But there is with] Your Majesty, in your own time, one who is not known [to you . . .]. His Majesty said: What is this, Har[dedef, my son? Then said Har]dedef: There is a townsman named Dedi. He lives in Ded-Snefru, the vindicated. He is a villager of 110 years, and he eats 500 loaves, a shoulder of beef as meat, and as drink 100 jugs up to this day.[10] He knows how to reattach a head which has been cut off, and he knows how to make a lion go behind him, its tether on the ground. He knows the shrines of the secret chambers of the enclosure of Thot. Now His Majesty the King of Upper and Lower Egypt, Khufu, the vindicated, had spent much time in seeking for himself these secret chambers of the enclosure of Thot to fashion for himself their likeness for his horizon. His Majesty said: You yourself, Hardedef, my son, you shall bring him to me. Boats were prepared for the king's son, Hardedef, and he sailed south to Ded-Snefru, the vindicated. After these boats were moored at the river bank, he went by land. He sat in a carrying chair of ebony, its poles made of *sesnedjem*-wood and sheathed in gold leaf.[11] When he reached Dedi, the carrying chair was put down, and he proceeded to address him. It was lying down on a mat at the threshold of his house that he found him, a servant at his head massaging him and another wiping his feet. The king's son Hardedef said: Your condition is like that of a person sleeping until daybreak, free from ailments, and there is no coughing in your throat [for old age is death, burial, and interment]. Greetings, O honored one! It is to summon you on the business of my father, King Khufu, the vindicated, that I have come here, and that you may eat the delicacies of the king's giving, the food of those who are in his following, and that he may send you in good time to your fathers who are in the cemetery. And this Dedi said: In peace, in peace, Hardedef, king's son, beloved by his father! May your father King Khufu, the vindicated, favor you! May he advance your station among the venerables. May your Ka contend with your enemy, and may your Ba learn the way to the Portal of the One Who Clothes the Weary One.[12] Greetings to you, O king's son!

The king's son Hardedef stretched out his hands to him and raised him up.[13] He went with him to the riverbank, giving him his arm. Dedi said: Let me have a *kakau*-boat that it may bring me (my) students and my writings. There were made to attend him two boats and their crews.

Dedi went northward in the barge in which the king's son Hardedef was. When he reached the capital, the king's son Hardedef entered to report to His Majesty the King of Upper and Lower Egypt, Khufu, the vindicated. The king's son Hardedef said: Sovereign, my lord, I have brought Dedi. His Majesty said: Hasten, bring him to me. His Majesty proceeded to the pillared hall of the palace, l.p.h., and Dedi was ushered in to him. His Majesty said: What is this, Dedi, my not having seen you (before)? And Dedi said: It is only the one who is summoned who comes, Sovereign, l.p.h. I have been summoned and see I have come. His Majesty said: Is it true, the saying that you know how to reattach a head which has been cut off? Dedi said: Yes, I do know how, Sovereign, l.p.h., my lord. His Majesty said: Let there be brought to me the prisoner who is in confinement, that his punishment may be inflicted. And Dedi said: But not indeed to a man, Sovereign, l.p.h., my lord. For the doing of the like is not commanded unto the august cattle. So there was brought to him a goose, and its head was severed. Then the goose was placed on the western side of the pillared court, and its head on the eastern side of the pillared court. Dedi said his say of magic words. The goose arose and waddled and so did its head.

The one (part) reached the other, and the goose stood up and cackled. Next he caused a waterfowl to be brought, and the like was done with it. Then His Majesty caused that there be brought him an ox, and its head was felled to the ground. Dedi said his say of magic words, and the ox stood up behind him with its tether fallen to the ground. [The scribe has obviously omitted a paragraph here dealing with a lion.]

Then [His Majesty] King Khufu, the vindicated, said: Now as for the rumor that you know the shrines of the secret chambers of the enclosure of [Thot]? Dedi said: By your favor, I do not know their shrines, Sovereign, l.p.h., my lord, but I do know the place where they are. His Majesty said: Where are they? And Dedi said: There is a passage of flint in a chamber called the Inventory in Heliopolis: in that passage.[14] [His Majesty said: Hasten, Bring it to me!] Dedi said: Sovereign, l.p.h., my lord, it is not I who can bring it to you. His Majesty said: Who then can bring it to me? Dedi said: It is the eldest of the three children who are in the womb of Reddedet; he will bring it to you. His Majesty said: I desire this indeed. But [as for] what you say, who is this Reddedet? Dedi said: She is the wife of a *wab*-priest of Re, Lord of Sakhbu, and will give birth to three children of Re, Lord of Sakhbu, of whom it is said that they shall exercise this magisterial office in the entire land. The eldest of them will be chief seer in Heliopolis.[15]

As for His Majesty, his heart became very sad at this, and Dedi said: What now is this mood, Sovereign, l.p.h., my lord? Is it because of the three children? I say: First your son, then his son, then one of them.[16] His Majesty said: At what time shall she give birth, this Reddedet? She shall give birth in the first month of Proyet on the fifteenth day. His Majesty said: Then the sandbanks of the Two Fishes Canal will be cut off, my servant, (otherwise) I myself could visit it and then I could see the temple of Re, Lord of Sakhbu. Dedi said: I shall cause there to be water four cubits deep on the sandbanks of the Two Fishes Canal. His Majesty proceeded to his palace, and His Majesty said: Let it be commanded to Dedi to (go to) the house of the king's son Hardedef that he may live there with him. Fix his rations at one thousand loaves of bread, one hundred jugs of beer, an ox, and one hundred bundles of greens. And one did according to all His Majesty had commanded.

The Birth of the Kings

One of these days it happened that Reddedet took sick and it was with difficulty that she gave birth. The Majesty of Re, Lord of Sakhbu, said to Isis, Nephthys, Meskhenet, Heket, and Khnum: [17] May you proceed that you may deliver Reddedet of the three children who are in her womb; they who shall exercise this magisterial office in the entire land. For they shall build the shrines in your towns, they shall provision your altars, they shall renew your offering tables, and they shall increase your divine offerings.[18] These goddesses proceeded, and they transformed themselves into musicians, with Khnum accompanying them carrying the birthing-stool. When they reached the house of Rewosre, they found him standing with his apron untied.[19] They proffered to him their necklaces and (their) rattles. But he said to them: My ladies, see, there is a woman in labor, and it is with difficulty that she gives birth. They said to him: Let [us] see her, for we are knowledgeable about childbirth. So he said to them: Proceed! And they entered into the presence of Reddedet. Then they locked the room on her and on themselves. Isis placed herself in front of her, Nephthys behind her, and Heket hastened the childbirth. Isis then said: Do not be strong *(wsr)* in her womb in this your name of Worsef *(wsr rf)*.[20] This child slipped forth upon her hands as a child one cubit long, whose bones were firm, the covering of whose limbs was of gold, and whose headdress was of real [21] lapis lazuli. They washed him, his umbilical cord was cut, and he was placed upon a cushion on bricks. Then Meskhenet approached him, and she said: A king who will exercise the kingship in this entire land! Khnum caused his limbs to move.

Next Isis placed herself in front of her (Reddedet), Nephthys behind her, and Heket hastened the childbirth. Isis said: Do not kick *(sah)* in her womb in this your name of Sahure *(sāhu-Re)*. And this child slipped out on her hands as a child one cubit long, whose bones were firm, the covering of whose limbs was of gold, and whose headdress was of real lapis lazuli. They washed him, his umbilical cord was cut, and he was placed on a cushion on bricks. Then Meskhenet approached him and she said: A king who will exercise the kingship in this entire land! Khnum caused his limbs to move.

Then Isis placed herself before her, Nephthys behind her, and

Heket hastened the childbirth. Isis said: Do not be dark (kkw) in her womb in this your name of Keku. And this child slipped forth upon her hands as a child one cubit long, whose bones were firm, the covering of whose limbs was of gold, and whose headdress was of real lapis lazuli. Then Meskhenet approached him, and she said: A king who will exercise the kingship in this entire land! Khnum caused his limbs to move. They washed him, his umbilical cord was cut, and he was placed on a cushion on bricks.

Now these goddesses came forth after they had delivered this Reddedet of the three children, and they said: May you be pleased, Rewosre, for there have been born to you three children. And he said to them: My ladies, what can I do for you? Please give this corn to your birthing-stool bearer, and take it as a payment for making beer. And Khnum placed the sack on his back. So they proceeded to the place from which they came. But Isis said to these goddesses: What is this, that we are returning without performing a marvel for these children and can report to their father who caused us to come? So they fashioned three royal crowns, l.p.h., and they placed them in the corn. Then they caused the heavens to turn into a storm and rain, and they turned back to the house and said: Would you please put the corn here in a locked room until we can come back on our northward journey? So they placed the corn in a locked room.[22]

Reddedet cleansed herself in a purification of fourteen days, and she said to her maidservant: Is the house prepared? She replied: It is outfitted with everything except for jars (for beer-making), for they have not been brought. Reddedet said: Why is it that jars have not been brought? The servant replied: There is not anything here for (beer-) making, except for some corn of these musicians, which is in the room with their seal. So Reddedet said: Go and bring some of it, for Rewosre will give them its equivalent when he returns. The servant went and she opened the room. And she heard the sound of singing, music, dancing, and exultations—everything which is done for a king—in the room. She returned and she repeated everything that she had heard to Reddedet. So she (too) went around the room but could not find the place in which it was being done. Then she put her forehead to the bin and discovered it was being done in it. (Then she placed it) in a chest which was (in turn) placed in another sealed box tied with leather thongs, and she put it in a room with her stores and she sealed it off. When Rewosre came back, returning from the fields, Reddedet related this business to him, and his heart was more pleased than anything. They sat down and celebrated.

After some days had passed, Reddedet had an argument with the maidservant, and she had her punished with a beating. So the maidservant said to the people who were in the house: Shall this be tolerated? She has given birth to three kings, and I am going and I will tell it to His Majesty the King of Upper and Lower Egypt, Khufu, the vindicated! So she started out, and she came upon her eldest brother, on her mother's side, tying flax yarn on the threshing floor. He said to her: Where is it that you have been going, little girl? And she told him about this business. Her brother said to her: Is this indeed something to be done, your coming to me thus? And am I to agree to [this] denunciation? Then he took a whip of flax to her, and he gave her a real beating. The maidservant ran to get herself a drink of water and a crocodile caught her. [Her brother] went to tell it to Reddedet, and her brother found her sitting with her head on her knee,[23] her heart very sad. He said to her: My lady, why is it that you are so sad? She said to him: That little girl who grew up in this house, see, she has gone away saying: I am going and I will denounce. Then he put his head down and said: My lady, she stopped by, in going away, to tell me [. . .] that she might go off with me. And I gave her a sound beating, and she went to get some water, and a crocodile caught her . . .

(Here the papyrus breaks off.)

The Shipwrecked Sailor

The tale of the sailor is preserved in a single manuscript of the early Middle Kingdom, and it has been suggested that it was written in Dynasty 11. Unlike so many other compositions extant through only one text, it seems to be complete from beginning to end, although the real beginning may be cut off. It begins abruptly with an expedition commander's aide addressing him to console him on an unsuccessful expedition to the south. In trying to cheer him up, the aide relates a set of similar experiences which he had. In the course of these a serpent relates a story. There is a story within a story within a story. The nature and location of the Island of the Ka, the enchanted island reached by the sailor, are still subjects for discussion. Some view the entire tale as a sort of psychological journey. At the end of the story the commander speaks his only words; they suggest that he is downcast at the thought of reporting on his unsuccessful mission. The tale represents one of the earliest examples of a narrative of the unreal. The beginning is couched in terms of a standard quarrying report such as might be found in the Hammamat Valley or the Sinai. The real import of the tale perhaps escapes us. It has recently been suggested that the sailor serves as a model for the man of the times in the same way as does Sinuhe. For bibliographical references and commentary, consult Lefebvre, Romans et contes, pp. 29–40, and Erman, The Ancient Egyptians, pp. xxiii–xxiv, 29–35.

W.K.S.

The astute assistant spoke: May your wish be satisfied, commander. See, we have reached home. The mallet has been taken, the mooring post driven in, and the prow rope set upon the ground. Praise has been rendered, God has been thanked, and every man embraces his companion. Our crew is returned safe without loss to our troops. Now that we have reached the limits of Wawat and we have passed by Senmut, we have returned in peace, and we have attained our land.[1]

Listen to me, commander. I am devoid of exaggeration. Wash yourself; place water on your fingers. Then you can reply when you are interrogated and speak to the king with self-assurance. You will answer without stammering. For the speech of a man saves him, and his words gain him indulgence. It is in your own interest that you should act. Yet speaking to you (in this fashion) is wearisome.

Let me tell you of a similar thing which happened to me myself.[2] I went to the mining country for the sovereign. I went down to the sea[3] in a boat 120 cubits long and 40 cubits wide.[4] One hundred twenty sailors from among the best of Egypt were in it. Whether they looked at the sky or whether they looked at the land, their hearts were fiercer than those of lions. They could foretell a storm-wind before it came and a downpour before it happened.

A stormwind broke out while we were at sea, before we had touched land. The wind was lifted up,[5] but it repeated with a wave of eight cubits in it. There was a plank which struck it (the wave) for me.[6] Then the boat died. And of those who were in it not a single one survived.

Next I was set upon an island by the surf of the sea, and I spent three days alone, my heart as my companion. I slept inside of a cabin of wood; [7] I embraced the shade. I stretched forth my two legs to learn what I might put in my mouth. There I found figs and dates, and all excellent kinds of vegetables. Sycamore figs were there and notched sycamore figs. And cucumbers as if they were cultivated. Fish were there and birds. There was not anything which was not within it. Then I ate to satisfaction, and I put (some aside) on the ground because it was too much for my arms. When I had cut a fire drill and lit a fire, I made a burnt offering for the gods.

Then I heard the sound of a thunderclap, but I thought it was the surf of the sea. The brush was breaking and the ground was quaking. When I uncovered my face, I discovered that it was a serpent coming along. He was thirty cubits, it being more than two cubits that his beard extended, and his body was plated with gold. His two eyebrows were of real lapis lazuli, and he was coiled up in front.[8]

He opened his mouth to me while I was on my belly in his presence, and he said to me: Who is it who has brought you, who is it who has brought you, little one, who is it who has brought you? If you delay in telling me who it is who has brought you to this island, I shall see that you find yourself as ashes, transformed into one who is not seen.

Although he was speaking to me, I did not hear it; when I was in his presence, I did not know myself. He placed me in his mouth, and he took me off to his rest house. He set me down without touching me, and I was intact, without anything being taken away from me.

He opened his mouth to me while I was on my belly in his presence, and he said to me: Who is it who has brought you, who is it who has brought you, little one, who is it who has brought you to this island of the sea, the two sides of which are in waves? And I answered him, my arms bent in his presence, and I said to him: It is

I (myself) who have gone down to the mines on a mission of the sovereign in a boat 120 cubits long and 40 cubits wide.[9] One hundred twenty sailors from among the best of Egypt were in it. Whether they looked at the sky or whether they looked at the land, their hearts were fiercer than those of lions. They could foretell a storm-wind before it came and a downpour before it happened. Each one of them, his heart was fiercer and his arm more valorous than his fellow's, without a fool among them. A storm-wind came forth while we were at sea, before we could make land. The wind was lifted up, but it repeated with a wave of eight cubits in it. There was a plank which struck it (the wave) for me. Then the boat died. And of those that were in it not a single one remained except for me. Behold me at your side. Then I was brought to this island by the surf of the sea.

He said to me: Do not fear, do not fear, little one, do not turn white. You have reached me. Behold, it is by bringing you to this island of the *Ka*,[10] within which there is nothing that does not exist, that the God has allowed you to live. It is full of all good things. See, you shall spend month after month until you complete four months within this island. A boat shall come back from home with sailors in it whom you know. You shall go home with them, and you shall die in your village.[11]

How joyful is the one who relates what he has tasted after painful affairs are past. Let me relate to you something similar which took place in this island when I was on it with my brothers and sisters and the children among them.[12] We were seventy-five serpents, my children and my brothers and sisters. And I will not call to mind to you a little daughter whom I as a wise man (knowing what would happen) brought away.[13]

Then a star fell, and because of it these went up in fire.[14] It happened completely. Yet I did not burn, for I was not among them. But I died for them when I found them in a single heap of corpses.[15]

If it be the case that you have courage, regulate your desire. Then you will fill your embrace with your children, you will kiss your wife, and you will see your house (again); for it is better than anything. You will reach the home in which you (once) were in the midst of your brothers and sisters.

As I was stretched out on my belly and touching the ground in his presence, I said to him: I shall relate your prowess to the sovereign, and I shall inform him of your greatness. I shall have brought to you ladanum, *heknu*-oil, *iudeneb,* cassia, and incense for the temples with which to satisfy every god. I shall indeed relate what has happened to me through what I have seen of your prowess. You will be thanked in (my) town in the presence of the magistrates of the entire land. I shall sacrifice to you oxen as a burnt offering, and I shall wring the necks of birds for you. I shall have brought to you transport ships loaded with all the specialties of Egypt, as should be done for a god who loves the Egyptians in a distant land which the Egyptians do not know.

Then he laughed at me because of these things which I had said, out of the craftiness of his heart. And he said to me: Myrrh is not abundant with you, although you have become a possessor of incense. Indeed, I am the Prince of Punt; myrrh belongs to me. That *heknu*-oil, of which you spoke about bringing me, why it is the main product of this island! Should it happen that you separate yourself from this place, it will be impossible for you to see this island, since it will have turned into waves.

Then that boat came, as he had foretold before. I went and I set myself on a high tree, and I recognized those who were in it. I went to report it, but I found that he knew it. And he said to me: Farewell, farewell, little one, to your home! You will see your children. Place my good repute in your town; this is all I ask from you.

I placed myself on my belly, my arms bent in his presence. And he gave me a cargo consisting of myrrh, *heknu*-oil, *iudeneb,* cassia, *tishepses, shasekh,* black eye-paint, giraffe tails, large cakes of incense, elephant tusks, hounds, apes, baboons, and every kind of precious thing. I then loaded them onto this boat. It then came to pass that I placed myself upon my belly to thank him, and he said to me: You will arrive home within two months. You will fill your embrace with your children. You will become young again at home, and you will be (properly) buried.

I went down to the shore in the vicinity of this ship, and I called out to the troops who were in this ship. I gave praise upon the shore to the lord of this island, and those who were in it (the ship) did likewise.

We sailed northward to the Residence city of the sovereign, and we arrived at the Residence in two months, according to everything he had said. Then I entered before the sovereign, and I presented to him this produce which I had brought back from within this island. He thanked me before the magistrates of the entire land. I was appointed lieutenant, and I was assigned two hundred people. Look at me, now that I have touched land, after I have seen what I have experienced. Listen to my speech. It is good for men to hearken.

He said to me: Do not act the part of the astute man, friend. What is the good of giving water to a goose just before it is being killed? [16]

This is how it comes, from its beginning to its end, as it has been found in writing, in the writing of the scribe excellent of fingers, Ameny's son Amen-aa, l.p.h.

In the midst of the word he was trying to say,
　　In the midst of his laughter and glee,
He had softly and suddenly vanished away—
　　For the Snark *was* a Boojum, you see.

　　　　　　　　　　—The Hunting of the Snark
　　　　　　　　　　Fit the Eighth

18. Spells for All Occasions

BY NOW IT MUST be clear that magic was used by the ancient Egyptians for just about every occasion. If something undesirable happened or was foretold, magic might be used to change or avoid the situation. If an object or occurrence was desired, magic could be used to bring it about.

In this chapter a variety of spells is presented so that the reader can see the kind of magical incantations, charms, and potions that were available in Egypt for daily use. These come from a variety of sources, most of which have been mentioned throughout the book: The *Book of the Dead,* the Coffin Texts, magical papyri, and in a few cases, secondary sources. No attempt has been made to distinguish the spells as to date; they range from the Old Kingdom pyramid texts to Greek papyri of the fourth century A.D. They have been grouped according to subject matter, with sections for Health, Prosperity, Love, Malicious Magic, and, finally, Assorted Spells that do not fit the other categories. These spells are the result of more than three thousand years of magical practice. Their range and diversity testify to the inventiveness of the ancient Egyptian.

Health

Headache

This is a remedy which Isis prepared for Re's headache:
Take equal parts of the following: berry of the coriander, berry of the poppy-plant, wormwood, berry of the *sames*-plant,

berry of the juniper-plant, honey. Mix the ingredients together and a paste will form. Smear the afflicted person with the paste and he will instantly become well.

Papyrus Ebers

Cataracts
Mix brain-of-tortoise with honey. Place on the eyes and say:
There is a shouting in the southern sky in darkness.
There is an uproar in the northern sky.
The Hall of Pillars falls into the waters.
The crew of the sun god bent their oars so that the heads at his side fall into the water.
Who leads hither what he finds?
I lead forth what I find.
I lead forth your heads.
I lift up your necks.
I fasten what has been cut from you in its place.
I lead you forth to drive away the God of Fevers and all possibly deadly arts.

Papyrus Ebers

Bone in the Throat
I am he whose head reaches the sky and his feet reach the abyss, who hath raised up [?] this crocodile . . . in Pizeme [?] of Thebes; for I am Sa, Sime, Tamaho, is my correct name, Anouk, saying, hawk's egg is that which is in my mouth, ibis-egg is that which is in my belly; saying, bone of god, bone of man, bone of bird, bone of fish, bone of animal, bone of everything, there being nothing besides; saying, that which is in thy belly let it come to thy heart; that which is in thy heart, let it come to thy mouth; that which is in thy mouth, let it come to my hand here today; for I am he who is in the seven heavens, who standeth in the seven sanctuaries; for I am the son of the god who liveth.
Say the spell seven times over a cup of water and have the woman drink it.

London-Leiden Papyrus

Indigestion

Crush a hog's tooth and put it inside four sugar cakes. Eat for four days.

                                                    Papyrus Ebers

To Relieve Retention of Urine in a Child

Cook an old papyrus in oil and smear on the body of the child.

                                                    Papyrus Ebers

Diarrhea

Mix ⅛ measure of figs, ⅛ measure of grapes, 1/32 measure of bread dough, 1/32 measure of pit-corn, 1/64 fresh lead-earth, 1/32 measure of onion, ⅛ measure of elderberry.
  Sing: O, Hetu!
  Again: O, Hetu!

                                                    Papyrus Ebers

Constipation

Mix half an onion in the froth of beer. Drink it. This is also a delightful remedy against death.

                                                    Papyrus Ebers

Displaced Uterus

Place a wax ibis on coals and allow the smoke to penetrate the sex-organs.

                                                    Papyrus Ebers

Power in the Legs

Ho [name]! You shall go forth into the day, you shall have power in your legs in the morning, you shall have power in your legs in the evening, you shall have power in your legs at the lamp-lighting, you shall have power in your legs at all seasons, at any hour in which you desire to go forth. . . .

                                                    Coffin Texts, Spell 22

Lesions of the Skin

After the scab has fallen off put on it: Scribe's excrement. Mix in fresh milk and apply as a poultice.

Papyrus Ebers

Burns

Make a mixture of milk of a woman who has borne a male child, gum, and ram's hair. While administering to the patient say:

Thy son Horus is burnt in the desert.

Is there any water there?

There is no water.

I have water in my mouth and a Nile between my thighs. I have come to extinguish the fire.

Papyrus Ebers

Antidote for Poison

Hail to him! Yablou, the golden cup of Osiris. Isis [and] Osiris [and] the great Agathodaemon have drunk from thee; the three gods have drunk, I have drunk after them myself; for dost thou make me drunk? Dost thou make me suffer shipwreck? Dost thou make me perish? Dost thou cause me confusion? Dost thou cause me to be vexed of heart? Dost thou cause my mouth to speak blasphemy? May I be healed of all poison, pus [and] venom which have been . . . to my heart; when I drink thee may I cause them to be cast up in the name of Sarbitha, the daughter of the Agathodaemon; for I am Sabra, Briatha, Brisara, Her is my name. I am Horus Sharon [?] when he comes from receiving acclamation [?], Yaho, the child is my name as my real name.

Say this spell seven times over a cup of wine with fresh rue in it. Have the man who has taken the poison drink it in the morning before he has eaten.

London-Leiden Papyrus

Dog Bite

I have come from Arkhah, my mouth being full of flood of a black dog. I spit it out the . . . of a dog. O this dog, who is among the ten days which belong to Anubis, the son of his body, extract thy venom, remove thy saliva [?] from me [?] again. If thou dost not extract thy venom and remove thy saliva [?] I will take thee up to the court of the temple of Osiris, my watch-tower [?]. I will do for thee the *parapage* [?] of birds [?] like the voice of Isis, the sorceress [?], the mistress of sorcery [?], who bewitches [?] everything and is not bewitched [?] in her name of Isis the sorceress [?]

Pound garlic with *kmou* [?] and place it on the wound. Recite the spell daily till better.

London-Leiden Papyrus

Splinters

Catch one mole, kill and cook it and drain the oil. Take worm's blood, cook and crush in oil. Mix in ass' dung and fresh milk. Apply to the opening. The splinter will be drawn out.

Papyrus Ebers

To Tell if a Child Will Live on the Day It Is Born

If it cries "ni" it will live.
If it cries "ba" it will die.

Papyrus Ebers

Replacing a Head

My head is knit on for me by Shu, my neck is made firm for me by Tefnut on that day when the heads of the gods were knit on to them. My eyes have been given to me that I may see with them, I have received my spinal cord through Ptah-Sokar, my mother has given me her hidden power, my son has extended his arms over me, in order to put an end to the injury which Seth did in the secret thing which he did against me in this my name of [name].

Book of the Dead, Spell 532

Spell to Become a Child Again

I have indeed become a child, whom my father begot and of whom my mother spoke. Such am I.

Book of the Dead, Spell 291

Prosperity

To Achieve Great Acclaim Wherever You Go
Take an oxyrhynchus fish and place it in oil with styrax, frankincense and seeds of the "great of love plant." Place all the ingredients in a vase and anoint a wreath of flowers with the contents of the vase. Recite a magical spell before the sun without speaking to anyone. [The text doesn't give the spell!] Anoint your face with what is in the vase and place the wreath in your hand.

You can go anywhere, among any people and you will be greatly praised. This spell is from King Darius and there is none better.

London-Leiden Papyrus

Spell to Be a God
Ho [name]! You are a god and you shall be a god, you shall have no foes or opponents with Re who is in the sky or with Osiris the great god who is in Abydos.

Coffin Texts, Spell 19

To Have Power over the Winds
These winds have been given to me by these maidens. Such is the north-wind which circulates about the Isles, which opens its arms to the limits of the earth and which rests when it has brought the things which I daily desire. The north wind is the breath of life, and what it has granted to me is that I may live by means of it. . . .

Book of the Dead, Spell 162

Spell to Have Food
O [name], I have filled your stockhouses, I have brought in your jar stands, I have given to you bread and beer which does not grow mouldy and your beer which does not grow sour.

Book of the Dead, Spell 67

Love

A *Love Potion*

Take a lock of hair from the head of a man who has died a violent death, seven grains of barley that has been buried in the grave of a dead man and pound them with ten *oipe*, or nine, of apple seeds. Mix in the blood of a worm, of a black dog, some blood from your second finger and some blood from the center of your left hand, and your semen. Mix together and place in a cup of wine and add three *utch* of the first pressing of the grapes. Before you pour the drink, recite the following spell seven times:

I am he of Abydos in truth, by formation [?] and birth in her [?] name of Isis the bringer [?] of fire, she of the mercy-seat of the Agathodaemon. I am this figure of the sun, Sitamearo is my name. I am this figure of a Captain of the host, very valiant, this Sword [?], this Overthrower [?], the Great Flame is my name. I am this figure of Horus, this Fortress [?], this Sword [?], this Overthrower [?] is my name. I am this figure of One drowned, that testifieth by writing, that resteth on the other side [?] here under the great offering-table of Abydos; as to which the blood of Osiris bore witness to her [?] name of Isis when it was poured into the cup, this wine. Give it, blood of Osiris that he gave to Isis to make her feel love in her heart for him night and day at any time, there not being time of deficiency. Give it, the blood of [name] born of [name] to give it to [name] born of [name] in this cup, this bowl of wine to-day, to cause her to feel love for him in her heart, the love that Isis felt for Osiris, when she was seeking after him everywhere, let [name] the daughter of [name] feel it, she seeking after [name] the son of [name] everywhere; the longing that Isis felt for Horus of Edfu, let [name] born of [name] feel it, she loving him, mad after him, inflamed by him, seeking him everywhere, there being a flame of fire in her heart in her moment of not seeing him.

London-Leiden Papyrus

A *Love Charm*

Make a figure of a dog eight fingers long out of wax and gum. Write magical words on the figure where the ribs are. On a separate lead tablet, write the names of the demons who are being called upon to assist. Then place the tablet on a tripod and the dog on the tablet. Recite the words of power written on the side of the dog and the names written on the tablet.

If the dog snarls the spell will not be successful.

If it barks it will be a success.

Greek papyrus

A Love Spell
Hail to thee, O Re-Harakhte, Father of the Gods!
Hail to you, O ye Seven Hathors
Who are adorned with strings of red thread!
Hail to you, ye Gods lords of heaven and earth!
Come [make] so-and-so [f.] born of so-and-so come after me,
Like an ox after grass,
Like a servant after her children,
Like a drover after his herd!
If you do not make her come after me,
Then I will set [fire to] Busiris and burn up [Osiris].

Written on a Twentieth Dynasty pottery fragment

Spell to Seduce a Married Woman
Unas cohabits with his phallus,
Unas is the lord of seed,
he who takes the women from their husbands,
whenever Unas wants, according to the wish of his heart.

Pyramid Texts, Spell 510

Spell to Make Love Day and Night (in the Next World)
Copulating by a man in the realm of the dead.
My eyes are the lion, my phallus Babi,
I am the Outcast, seed is in my mouth, my
    head is in the sky, my head is on earth.
I am one having power in my heart. . . .
I am one who ejaculates when he knits together [?],
I ejaculate seed as that one and this one.

AS FOR ANY MAN WHO SHALL KNOW THIS SPELL,
HE SHALL COPULATE IN THIS LAND BY NIGHT AND

DAY, AND DESIRE SHALL COME TO THE WOMAN
BENEATH HIM WHENEVER HE COPULATES. TO BE
RECITED OVER A BEAD OF CARNELIAN OR OF
AMETHYST, TO BE PLACED ON THE RIGHT ARM OF
THE DECEASED.

Book of the Dead, Spell 576

Malicious Magic

To Make a Man Blind
Drown a shrew-mouse in water and give the water to the victim
to drink.

London-Leiden Papyrus

To Cause Skin Disease
Take a *hantous*-lizard and a *hafleele*-lizard and cook them with
oil. Wash the person you want to have the skin disease with it.

London-Leiden Papyrus

To Make a Man Die
Grind up a shrew-mouse and place it in a man's food. He will
swell up and die.

If you don't have a shrew-mouse, drown a hawk in a measure
of wine and give it to a man to drink. He will die.

London-Leiden Papyrus

Assorted Spells

To Drive Off a Cockroach
Keep away from me, lips of crookedness. I am Khonsu, lord of
the circuit, who brings the words of the Gods to Re; I report the
message to its Lord.

Book of the Dead, Spell 36

Drive Off Snakes
Back, invisible [snake], make thyself invisible and let Unas not

see thee. Come not to the place where Unas is, lest he pronounce against thee this by name, Nemy, son of Nemyt.

Pyramid Texts, Spell 434

Protection from Fire
I am the *nehew*-serpent, Bull of the Enneads, who obeys no magic, who is not scorched because of fire, who is not wet because of water. I will never obey magic, I will never be scorched because of fire, I will never be wet because of water. . . .

Coffin Texts, Spell 88

Fighting a Sovereign
Do not pursue me, thou!
I am Papisetpu Metoubanes.
I am carrying the mummy of Osiris
and I am proceeding to take it to Abydos,
to take it to Tastai [?] and to deposit
it in Alkhai; If [name] deal blows at me,
I will cast it at him.

London-Leiden Papyrus

To Get Out of Jail
Ho [name]! You shall not be examined,
you shall not be imprisoned,
you shall not be restrained,
you shall not be fettered,
you shall not be put under guard. . . .

Book of the Dead, Spell 23

Spell to Avoid Decapitation
. . . My head will not be cut off,
my neck will not be severed,
my name will not be unknown among spirits. . . .

Book of the Dead, Spell 229

To Avoid Execution
I am Shu fully equipped, I have not been taken to the god's place of execution, for I am covered with the *kny*-garment. I have not

been made to enter into the god's place of execution, for I am covered with the *kny*. . . . I am a great one, baboon-shaped, I have not entered into the god's place of execution, the knife has no power over me.

Coffin Texts, Spell 114

Not to Die a Second Time

O You who take away and bring days to an end, do not take away my years or bring my days to an end, for I am Horus, Lord of the Netherworld, Monarch of the Western Horizon. I will not die in the West, and the messengers of Osiris have no power over me, for I am Horus, son of Osiris. I will not die in *On, Kherehaha,* or the East, and the messengers of *Soped* have no power over me, for I am Horus, son of Osiris. I will not die in the South, and the messengers of Horus have no power over me, for I am Horus, son of Osiris. I will not die in the North and the messengers of the Outcast have no power over me, for I am Horus, son of Osiris. I will not die in the waters, and the messengers of those who are in the waters have no power over me, for I am Horus, son of Osiris.

I will not die in the Abyss, and the messengers of those who are in the Abyss have no power over me, for I am Horus, son of Osiris.

I will not die a second time, and the dwellers in the Netherworld have no power over me. I will not eat their fish, their fowl shall not scream over me, for I am Horus, son of Osiris.

Coffin Texts, Spell 423

Spell to Dispel the Gods' Anger

To dispel anger in the heart of a god against me.

Woe to you, O you who send out power and who preside over all mysteries. See, a word is spoken against me by a god who is angry with me, but wrongdoing is washed away, and it falls into the hands of the Lord of Justice, since you evilly do harm to me. He who is respected [?] has joined with Maat, his god is gracious to me, and my impediment is imposed on someone else. O Lord of offerings in *Gn-wr* [?] see, I am brought to you, and life is provided by means of it; may you partake of it. Be gracious to me and dispel all anger which is in your heart against me.

Coffin Texts, Spell 272

To Communicate with the God Anubis

Engrave the figure of Anubis on a bronze bowl. Fill it with water and keep it away from the sun. Coat the surface of the water with oil. Place the bowl on three new bricks which had their bottom sides sprinkled with sand. Spread out four other bricks and have a child lie down on his stomach on them, with his chin on the brick on which the bowl is resting.

Have the child look into the oil while he has a cloth spread over his head. There must be a lighted lamp on his right and a censer with fire on his left. Place a leaf of the Anubis-plant on the lamp and place incense made of frankincense, wax, styrax, turpentine, datestone and wine rolled into a ball on the censer. Say:

Open my eyes	4 times
Open my eyes, open thy eyes	3 times
Open Tat, Open Nap	3 times
Open unto me	3 times

For I am Artamo, born of Hame-o, the great basilisk of the East, rising in glory together with thy father at dawn; hail, Heh, open to me Hah.

Artamo, open to me Hah; if thou dost not open to me Hah, I will make thee open to me Hah. O Ibis, sprinkle that I may see the great god Anubis, the power, that is about my head, the great protector of the Uzat, the power, Anubis, the good Ox-herd, at every opening [?] [of the eye?] which I have made, reveal thyself to me, for I am Nostham, Naszot, Nashoteb, Borilammai, Mastinx, Anubis, Megiste, Arian, thou who art great, Arian, Pi-anuzy, Arian, he who is without. Hail, Phrix, Ix, Anaxibrox, Ambrox, Eborx, Xon, Nbrakhria, the great child, Anubis; for I am that soldier. O ye of the Atef-crown, ye of Pephnun, Masphonke; hail! Let all that I have said come to pass here today; say hail! thou art Tham, Thamthom, Thamathom, Thamathomthom, Thamathouthi, Amon, thy correct name, whom they call Thom, Anakthom; thou art Itth; Thouthi is thy name, Sithom, Anithom Op-sao, Shatensro black; open to me the mouths of my vessel here today; come to me to the mouths of my vessel, my bandage [?], let my cup make the reflection of heaven; may the hounds of *hulot* give me that which is just in the abyss;

may they tell me that about which I inquire here today truly, there being no falsehood in them ⲁⲉⲏⲓⲟⲩⲱ, Makhopneuma.

Recite this seven times and ask the child to open his eyes and look into the bowl. Say, "Is the god coming in?" If the boy answers "yes," Say:

> Thy bull [?] Mao, ho! Anubis, this soldier [?], this kam, this kem . . . Pisreithi, Greithi, Abrithi is thy name, by thy correct name.

Then you can ask the god whatsoever you wish. When you want him to go say:

> Farewell, Anubis, the good oxherd, Anubis, the son of a jackal and a dog. . . .

> London-Leiden Papyrus

Charm to Have Dreams

Take a clean linen bag and write upon it the names given below. Fold it up and make it into a lamp-wick, and set it alight, pouring pure oil over it. The words to be written are: Armiuth, Larlamchouch, Arsenophrephren, Phtha, Archentechtha. Then in the evening, when you are going to bed, which you must do without touching food [or pure from all defilement], do thus. Approach the lamp and repeat seven times the formula given below; then extinguish it and lie down to sleep. The formula is this: Sachmu . . . epaema Ligotereench: The Aeon, the Thunderer, Thou hast swallowed the snake and dost exhaust the moon, and dost raise up the orb of the sun in his season, Chthetho is thy name; I require, O lords of the gods, Seth, Chreps, give me the information I desire.

> Budge, *Egyptian Magic*

To Become a Lotus Flower

I am this pure lotus that has ascended by the Sunlight and is at Re's nose. I spend my [time] shedding it [i.e., the sunlight] on Horus. I am the pure [lotus] that ascended from the field.

> *Book of the Dead*, Spell 81

To Become a Snake

I am a *nehew*-snake, a bull snake who leads, who swallowed his seven uraei, and his seven neck-vertebrae came into being; who gave orders to his seven Enneads which hear the word of the monarch. My mother is the Pelican, and I am her son; I have come that I may inhale myrrh, and accept myrrh; my nostrils [?] are [full of] myrrh, my fingernail is [full of] myrrh. I have taken away your divinity, you gods; serve me when I confer your powers. I am Nehebkau.

Coffin Texts, Spell 374

To Drive Off a Snake
Go forth, O snake, at the monuments of Shu [?]. You have eaten a mouse, which Re abominates; you have chewed the bones of a putrid she-cat.

Coffin Texts, Spell 369

To Preserve Bread
. . . This bread of his cannot grow mouldy, this beer of his cannot go bad. . . .

Coffin Texts, Spell 327

Pure Water Spell
Ho [name]! Come, that you may ascend to the sky; the ladder of the side of Re is put together for you among the gods, who remove the pestilence of the streams so that you may drink water from them.

Coffin Texts, Spell 21

Spell for Not Eating or Stepping in Excrement
My abomination is my abomination; I will not eat my abomination. Dung is my abomination; I will not eat it. Ordure—none shall drop into my belly. I will not touch it with my hands; I will not step on it with the soles of my feet.

Book of the Dead, Spell 52

Protection Against Robbers
Doer, doer, passerby, passerby,
[May thy] face look backward.
Beware of the great door!

Coffin Texts, Spell 421

Protection Against Fire

I am one invisible of form in the midst of the sunshine, I enter into the fire, I come forth from the fire, the sunshine has not pierced me, thou who find the Great One have not burned me, mine is the knife which cuts down him who is in the hands of Thoth. . . .

Coffin Texts, Spell 246

Spell to Wake the Dead

Turn about, turn about, O sleeper, turn about in this place which you do not know, but I know it. . . .

Coffin Texts, Spell 74

Notes

Notes to Chapter 2

1. *Journal of Humanity,* Vol. 1, No. 11 (August 5, 1829):44.
2. Thomas George Allen, *The Book of the Dead* (Chicago: University of Chicago Press, 1974), p. 77.

Notes to Chapter 3

1. Serge Sauneron, *The Priests of Ancient Egypt* (New York: Grove Press, 1960), p. 50.
2. Ibid., pp. 20–21.
3. W.M. Flinders Petrie, *Ten Years' Digging in Egypt* (Chicago: Ares Publishers, Inc., 1976), p. 125.

Notes to Chapter 4

1. J. Grafton Milne, "The Sanatorium of Der-el-Bahri," *Journal of Egyptian Archaeology* Vol. 2, Part 1 (April 1914): 96–98.
2. James Henry Breasted, *The Edwin Smith Surgical Papyrus,* 2 vols. (Chicago: University of Chicago Press, 1930), Vol. 1, p. 220.
3. Ibid., p. 477.
4. Paul Ghalioungui, *Magic and Medical Science in Ancient Egypt* (Amsterdam: B.M. Israël, 1973), p. 143.

Notes to Chapter 5

1. Brian M. Fagan, *Rape of the Nile* (New York: Charles Scribner's Sons, 1975), pp. 162–64.
2. Warren R. Dawson, "Pettigrew's Demonstrations upon Mummies. A Chap-

ter in the History of Egyptology," *Journal of Egyptian Archaeology* 20 (1934): 177–78.

3. Warren R. Dawson, "Making a Mummy," *Journal of Egyptian Archaeology* 13 (1927): 43.

4. A. Lucas, "The Use of Natron in Mummification," *Journal of Egyptian Archaeology* 18 (1932): pp. 125–40.

5. E.A. Wallis Budge, *Egyptian Magic* (London: Kegan Paul, Trench, Trübner & Co., 1899), p. 185.

6. Ibid., p. 186.

7. Author's trans., E.A. Wallis Budge, *The Mummy* (New York: Causeway Books, 1974), pp. 197–99.

8. Budge, *Egyptian Magic,* p. 187.

9. Ibid. p. 189.

10. Ibid., pp. 195–96.

11. T.J.C. Baly, "Notes on the Ritual of Opening the Mouth," *Journal of Egyptian Archaeology* 16 (1930): 173–86.

Notes to Chapter 6

1. Ahmed Fakhry, *The Monuments of Sneferu at Dashur,* 3 vols. (Cairo: General Organization for Government Printing Offices, 1959), 1: 3.

2. Ibid.

3. John Ivimy, *The Sphinx and the Megalith* (London: Turnstone Books, Ltd., 1974), pp. 13–14.

4. *Nagel's Encyclopedia Guide: Egypt* (Geneva: Nagel Publishers, 1973), p. 302.

5. George Rawlinson, trans., *The History of Herodotus,* Book II, 133 (Chicago: Encyclopaedia Britannica, 1952), p. 77.

6. I.E.S. Edwards, *The Pyramids of Egypt* (England: Penguin Books, 1972), p. 184.

7. Alexandre Piankoff, *The Pyramid of Unas* (Princeton, N.J.: Princeton Univ. Press, 1968).

8. Ibid.

9. Ibid.

10. Ibid.

11. Ibid.

12. Ibid.

13. Ibid.

14. Ibid.

Notes to Chapter 7

1. R.O. Faulkner, *The Ancient Egyptian Coffin Texts,* 3 vols. (Warminster, England: Aris & Phillips, Ltd., 1977), Spell 535.

2. Ibid. Spell 75.
3. Ibid. Spell 342.
4. Ibid. Spell 239.
5. Ibid. Spell 322.
6. Ibid. Spell 469.
7. Ibid. Spell 573.
8. Ibid. Spell 261.
9. Ibid. Spell 572.
10. Ibid. Spell 316.
11. Ibid. Spell 648.
12. Ibid. Spell 304.
13. Ibid. Spell 657.
14. Ibid. Spell 98.
15. Ibid. Spell 503.
16. Ibid. Spell 554.

Notes to Chapter 8

1. Author's translation from transcription in: E.A. Wallis Budge, *The Egyptian Book of the Dead* (New York: Dover Publications, Inc., 1967), pp. 1–2.
2. Ibid., pp. 112–14.
3. Ibid., p. 84.
4. Ibid., pp. 111–12.
5. Ibid., pp. 118–19.
6. Thomas George Allen, trans., *The Book of the Dead* (Chicago: University of Chicago Press, 1974), p. 159.
7. Budge, *The Egyptian Book of the Dead*, pp. 198–203.
8. Ibid., p. 170.

Notes to Chapter 9

1. F. Ll. Griffith and Herbert Thomson, eds., *The Leyden Papyrus* (New York: Dover Publications, 1974), p. 139.
2. Ibid., pp. 139–41.
3. Ibid., p. 141.
4. Ibid., pp. 141–43.
5. Author's translation from hieroglyphs in: E.A. Wallis Budge, *The Mummy* (New York: Causeway Books, 1974), pp. 237–38.
6. Thomas George Allen, *The Book of the Dead or Going Forth by Day* (Chicago: University of Chicago Press, 1974), pp. 154–55.
7. Sir W.M. Flinders Petrie, *Amulets* (Warminster, England: Aris & Phillips, Ltd., 1972), p. 23.
8. E.A. Wallis Budge, *Amulets and Talismans* (New York: University Books, 1961), p. 137.

9. Petrie, *Amulets,* p. 15.

10. T. Eric Peet, "A Remarkable Burial Custom of the Old Kingdom," *Journal of Egyptian Archaeology* 2, Part 1 (January 1915): 8–9.

11. Winnifred M. Crompton, "Two Clay Balls in the Manchester Museum," *Journal of Egyptian Archaeology* 3, Parts 2–3 (April–July 1916): 128.

12. I.E.S. Edwards, *Hieratic Papyri in the British Museum,* Fourth Series (London: British Museum, 1960), 1: 29–33.

13. Ibid., p. 57.

14. Ibid., p. 25.

Notes to Chapter 10

1. Howard Carter, *The Tomb of Tut-Ankh-Amen,* 3 vols. (New York: Cooper Square Publishers, 1963), 3: 83.

2. H.E. Winlock, "Digger's Luck," *Metropolitan Museum of Art Bulletin,* summer 1975, pp. 57–58.

Notes to Chapter 11

1. Howard Carter and A.C. Mace, *The Tomb of Tut-Ankh-Amen,* 3 vols. (New York: Cooper Square Publishers, Inc., 1963), 1: 133.

2. Philip Vandenberg, *The Curse of the Pharaohs* (Philadelphia & New York: J.B. Lippincott Co., 1975), p. 20.

3. Carter and Mace, *The Tomb of Tut-Ankh-Amen,* 1: 112.

4. Ibid., 1: 178.

5. Barry Wynne, *Behind the Mask of Tutankhamen,* (New York: Taplinger Publishing Co., 1973), p. 110.

6. Carter and Mace, *The Tomb of Tut-Ankh-Amen,* 1: 178.

7. Thomas Hoving, *Tutankhamun, The Untold Story* (New York: E.P. Dutton, 1978), p. 124.

8. Wynne, *Behind the Mask of Tutankhamen,* pp. 114–15.

9. Ibid., pp. 115–16.

10. Alexandre Piankoff, *The Shrines of Tut-Ankh-Amen* (New York: Pantheon Books, 1955), pp. 32–33.

11. Ibid., pp. 33–34.

Notes to Chapter 12

1. Author's translation of hieroglyphic transcription of hieratic in: A. Piankoff and J.J. Clère, "A Letter to the Dead on a Bowl in the Louvre," *Journal of Egyptian Archaeology* 20 (1934): 157–58.

2. Author's translation from hieroglyphs in: Alan H. Gardiner, "A New Letter to the Dead," *Journal of Egyptian Archaeology* 16 (1930): 19.

3. Author's paraphrase of translation in: A.H. Gardiner and K. Sethe, *Egyptian Letters to the Dead* (London: Egypt Exploration Society, 1928), pp. 8–9.

4. Gardiner, *Egyptian Letters to the Dead*, p. 7.

Notes to Chapter 13

1. James Henry Breasted, *Ancient Records of Egypt* (New York: Russell & Russell, 1962), 2: 241.

2. Ibid., p. 116.

Notes to Chapter 14

1. Sir Alan Gardiner, *Egypt of the Pharaohs* (New York: Oxford University Press, 1972), p. 347.

2. E.A. Wallis Budge, *Egyptian Magic* (London: Kegan Paul, Trench, Trübner & Co., 1899), p. 216.

Notes to Chapter 16

1. Author's paraphrase of the translation in F. Ll. Griffith and Herbert Thomson, *The Leyden Papyrus* (New York: Dover, 1974), p. 25.

2. Ibid., pp. 26–27.

3. Ibid., pp. 30–31.

4. Ibid., pp. 41–43.

5. Jack Lindsay, *The Origins of Alchemy in Graeco-Roman Egypt* (New York: Barnes & Noble, Inc., 1970), pp. 204–07.

6. W.E. Crum, "Magical Texts in Coptic—II," *Journal of Egyptian Archaeology* 20 (1934): 197.

7. Ibid., p. 256.

8. Ibid.

Notes to Chapter 17

KING CHEOPS AND THE MAGICIANS

1. This is the conclusion of a tale of which the entire narrative section is missing. It concerns a marvel performed by a lector priest in the reign of Djoser, the builder of the Step Pyramid. Perhaps the lector was Iyemhotep himself. There is no way of knowing how much of the composition was lost at the beginning.

2. Nebka of Dynasty 3 is a predecessor of Cheops. Ankh-towy is a designation for Memphis or a part thereof.

3. Evidently the adulterous wife makes a present to the good-looking towns-man and he returns to thank her.

4. A sort of garden pavilion.

5. The cubit measures 20.6 inches.

6. Life, prosperity, health—used in references to the pharaoh.

7. Philippe Derchain, in *RdE* 21 (1969): 19–25, calls attention to the parallel of the maidens rowing and the goddess Hathor as a rower. The sense of the outing in his view is that of a sort of parody, with the king taking the place of the sun god Re navigating the heavens with the Hathors. The author of our tale would then have stressed the importance of the rulers of Dynasty 5 as the real adherents of Re, in distinction to Snefru as a ruler who merely parodied the god. See H.G. Fischer, in *Fragen an die altägyptische Literatur, Studien zum Gedenken an Eberhard Otto* (Wiesbaden, 1977): 161–165.

8. Evidently a proverb with the sense that she wants the full account of the same thing. See Wm. Spiegelberg, in ZÄS 64 (1929): 90–91.

9. This familiar form of address places Snefru in a good light.

10. The Egyptians often wished for 110 years as a life span.

11. Nobles are sometimes shown in such carrying chairs in relief sculpture in the Old Kingdom. A carrying chair much like this one was found in the tomb of Snefru's queen Hetepheres, the mother of Cheops. The chair is now in the Cairo Museum, with a replica in the Museum of Fine Arts in Boston.

12. Formal greetings are exchanged on both sides. The Ka and Ba are spirits of the dead man and manifestations of his personality. The One Who Clothes the Weary One is the embalmer.

13. Again a signal favor in that a prince condescends to raise up a commoner.

14. The sense of the shrines or number of the secret chambers is entirely unclear. Possibly they were the architectural plan for a part of the pyramid complex of Cheops, as suggested by the text. In any case, the question of the chambers serves to introduce the matter of Reddedet and the future kings.

15. In Dynasty 5 a particular emphasis is placed on the sun god Re as the dynastic god. His chief place of worship was On (Greek Heliopolis); Re, Lord of Sakhbu, is a local variant. Sakhbu is in Lower Egyptian Nome 2.

16. Evidently an abbreviated version of history in which only the builders of the Giza pyramids, Chephren and Mycerinus, are considered as coming between Cheops and the first king of Dynasty 5, Weserkaf.

17. Four goddesses associated with childbirth and the ram god Khnum, regarded as the creator of man on a potter's wheel in one myth.

18. A graphic list of the usefulness of the kings to the gods.

19. Lit. "upside down." E. Staehelin, in ZÄS 96 (1970): 125–39, discusses this passage at length. In her view, Rewosre has his apron untied (unknotted) and hanging down as a sort of sympathetic parallel to the untied garments of his wife during childbirth; parallels in other cultures are cited.

20. As each child is born, Isis makes a pronouncement involving a pun on the king's name. Weserkaf means "his Ka is strong"; Sahu-Re probably means "one whom Re has well endowed," but there is a pun on *sahu*, "to kick." In Neuserre Kakai there is a pun involving Kakai and Keku, "darkness." H. Altenmüller, in *Chronique d'Egypte* 45 (1970): 223–35, suggested that Reddedet is a pseudonym

for Khentkaus, a queen of the end of Dynasty 4, and that she was the mother of the first three kings of Dynasty 5. He further suggests that she may have been the daughter of the same prince Hardedef who introduces the tale. Hence she and her sons would have been descendants of Cheops through a junior branch of the family.

21. As opposed to faience or glass with this color.

22. The goddesses leave magical tokens of the kingship for the children in the sack of grain. They invent the storm as an excuse to return.

23. An attitude of mourning or sorrow.

THE SHIPWRECKED SAILOR

1. A quarrying, mining, or military expedition has returned by Nile from the south, and its commander appears to be downcast at the prospect of facing the king after an unsuccessful mission. His chief aide tries to cheer him up. Wawat is northern Nubia, and Senmut is the island of Biggeh, just south of Aswan in the First Cataract region. The mission took place in the eastern desert or on the Red Sea. The expression, "our land," is not otherwise attested in Egyptian literature and may in fact have a patriotic nuance.

2. Here begins the story within the story.

3. The word for sea is literally, "the great green," and is used of the Mediterranean as well as the Red Sea. Since the mining country is either the Sinai peninsula or the eastern desert, since the serpent speaks of the land of Punt (a southern region in Africa or on the Red Sea), and since the produce is African (giraffe tails, etc.), the sea in our story is clearly the Red Sea.

4. The cubit is the Egyptian measurement of length, about 20.6 inches or .523 meters. The ship is about 204 by 68 feet.

5. Perhaps an idiom with the sense, "we traveled onward."

6. This passage difficult in the original.

7. Possibly the cabin of the boat, but conceivably a natural or man-made shelter.

8. E. Lucchesi, in ZÄS 103 (1976): 148–149; Henry G. Fischer, in *Fragen an die altägyptische Literatur, Studien zum Gedenken an Eberhard Otto* (Wiesbaden, 1977): 155–158. A human-headed serpent.

9. This kind of repetition of an entire section is frequent in all ancient literature.

10. An island of the spirit or enchanted island.

11. Burial in a foreign land was abhorrent to the Egyptians, a theme developed in Sinuhe as well.

12. Here begins the story within the story within the story.

13. M. Th. Derchain-Urtel, in SÄK 1 (1974): 98–99.

14. A meteor? In the historical text of Thutmose III from Gebel Barkal there is a description of a falling star. (See Vittmann, *Göttinger Miszellen* 29 (1978), 149–152.

15. Here the serpent's story ends. Like the sailor, he was a sole survivor.

16. These are the commander's only words. See M. Gilula, in SAOC 39 (1977): 75–82. B. Bryan, in *Sarapis* 5 (1979), 1–13, regards the sailor as a fool upbraided by the commander by this saying.

Selected Bibliography

Chapter 1: Egypt

Breasted, James Henry. *A History of Egypt.* New York: Charles Scribner's Sons, 1909.

Gardiner, Sir Alan. *Egypt of the Pharaohs.* 1961. Reprint. New York: Oxford University Press, 1972.

Hayes, William C. *Most Ancient Egypt.* Chicago: University of Chicago Press, 1965.

———. *The Scepter of Egypt.* 2 vols. New York: The Metropolitan Museum of Art, 1953, 1959.

Herodotus. *The Histories.* Translated by Aubrey de Sélincourt. Revised. New York: Penguin Books, Ltd., 1972.

Kees, Herman. *Ancient Egypt.* Chicago: University of Chicago Press, 1961.

Ludwig, Emil. *The Nile.* New York: The Viking Press, 1937.

Mertz, Barbara. *Red Land, Black Land.* New York: Coward-McCann, Inc., 1966.

———. *Temples, Tombs and Hieroglyphs.* New York: Coward-McCann, Inc., 1964.

Montet, Pierre. *Eternal Egypt.* New York: Praeger Publishers, 1969.

Murray, Margaret A. *Egypt.* New York: Philosophical Library, 1957.

Chapter 2: Hieroglyphs

Budge, E.A. Wallis. *An Egyptian Hieroglyphic Dictionary.* 2 vols. 1920. Reprint. New York: Dover Publications, Inc., 1978.

———. *Egyptian Language: Easy Lessons in Egyptian Hieroglyphics.* 1910. Reprint. New York: Dover Publications, Inc., 1973.

Callender, John B. *Middle Egyptian.* Afroasiatic Dialects, Vol. 2. Malibu: Undena Publications, 1975.

Champollion, Jean François. "Expedition to Egypt: Letter from M. Champollion." *Journal of Humanity and Herald of the American Temperance Society.* Vol. 1 (1829), Nos. 11, 12; p. 44, p. 48.

De Buck, A. *Egyptian Readingbook: Exercises and Middle Egyptian Texts.* 3rd ed. Leiden: Nederlands Instituut Voor Het Nabije Oosten, 1970.

Doblhofer, Ernst. *Voices in Stone: The Decipherment of Ancient Scripts and Writings.* Translated by Mervyn Savill. 1961. Reprint. New York: Collier Books, 1971.

Englund, Gertie. *Introduction to Pharaonic Egyptian.* 1969. Reprint. Uppsala: Uppsala University, 1975.

Faulkner, Raymond O. *A Concise Dictionary of Middle Egyptian.* 1962. Reprint. London: Oxford University Press, 1972.

Gardiner, Sir Alan. *Egyptian Grammar: Being an Introduction to the Study of Hieroglyphs.* 3rd ed., revised. London: Oxford University Press, 1957.

Lenormant, M. "Egyptian Antiquities: Extracts from a Letter by a Companion of Champollion in the Egyptian Expedition." *Journal of Humanity and Herald of the American Temperance Society.* Vol. 1 (1829), No. 13, pp. 49, 50.

Mercer, Samuel A.B. *An Egyptian Grammar with Chrestomathy and Glossary.* London: Lunzac & Co., 1927.

Renouf, P. Le Page. *An Elementary Grammar of the Ancient Egyptian Language.* 3rd ed. London: Samuel Bagster and Sons, 1893.

Salt, Henry. *Essay on Dr. Young's and M. Champollion's Phonetic System of Hieroglyphics.* London: Longman, Hurst, Reis, Orme, Brown, and Green, 1825.

Sharpe, Samuel. *Egyptian Hieroglyphics: An Attempt to Explain Their Nature, Origin, and Meaning. With a Vocabulary.* London: Eduard Moxon and Co., 1861.

Chapter 3: Magicians

Budge, E.A. Wallis. *Egyptian Magic.* London: Kegan Paul, Trench, Trübner & Co., 1899.

Erman, Adolf. *Life in Ancient Egypt.* Translated by H.M. Tirard, 1894. Reprint. New York: Dover Publications, Inc., 1971.

Herodotus. *The Histories.* Translated by Aubrey de Sélincourt. Revised. New York: Penguin Books, 1972.

Petrie, William Flinders. "The Royal Magician." *Ancient Egypt* 10 (1925): 65–70.

Quibell, J.E. *The Ramesseum.* Egyptian Research Account, 1896. London: Quaritch, 1898.

Sauneron, Serge. *The Priests of Ancient Egypt.* New York: Grove Press, 1960.

Chapter 4: Medicine

Breasted, James Henry. *The Edwin Smith Surgical Papyrus.* 2 vols. Chicago: University of Chicago Press, 1930.

Bryan, Cyril P., trans. *Ancient Egyptian Medicine: The Papyrus Ebers.* 1930. Reprint. Chicago: Ares Publishers, Inc., 1974.

Dawson, Warren R. "Studies in the Egyptian Medical Texts." *Journal of Egyptian Archaeology* 18 (1932): 150–54.

————. "Studies in the Egyptian Medical Texts—II." *Journal of Egyptian Archaeology* 19 (1933): 133–37.

————. "Studies in the Egyptian Medical Texts—III." *Journal of Egyptian Archaeology* 20 (1934): 41–46.

————. "Studies in the Egyptian Medical Texts—IV." *Journal of Egyptian Archaeology* 20 (1934): 185–88.

Ghalioungui, Paul. *Magic and Medical Science in Ancient Egypt.* Amsterdam: B.M. Israël, 1973.

Kamal, Hassan. *Dictionary of Pharaonic Medicine.* Cairo: The National Publication House, 1967.

Chapter 5: Mummification

Budge, E.A. Wallis. *The Mummy.* 1894. Reprint. New York: Causeway Books, 1974.

————. *Osiris: The Egyptian Religion of Resurrection.* 2 vols. 1912. Reprint in one vol. New Hyde Park: University Books, 1961.

Dawson, Warren R. "Making a Mummy." *Journal of Egyptian Archaeology* 13 (1927): 40–49.

————. "On Two Mummies Formerly Belonging to the Duke of Southesland." *Journal of Egyptian Archaeology* 13 (1927): 155–61.

————. "Pettigrew's Demonstrations upon Mummies. A Chapter in the History of Egyptology." *Journal of Egyptian Archaeology* 20 (1934): 169–82.

Dreadstone, Carl. *The Mummy.* Adapted from the screenplay by John L. Balderston. New York: Berkley Medallion Books, 1977.

Herodotus. *The Histories.* Translated by Aubrey de Sélincourt. Revised. New York: Penguin Books, Ltd., 1972.

Lucas, A. " 'Cedar'-tree Products Employed in Mummification." *Journal of Egyptian Archaeology* 17 (1931): 13–21.

————. "The Use of Natron in Mummification." *Journal of Egyptian Archaeology* 18 (1932): 125–40.

Pace, Mildred Mastin. *Wrapped for Eternity: The Story of the Egyptian Mummy.* New York: Dell Publishing Co., Inc., 1974.

Reisner, George Andrew. *Canopics.* Catalogue Général Antiquités Égyptiennes du Musée du Caire. Cairo: Imprimerie de l'Institut Français d'Archéologie Oriental, 1967.

Spielman, Percy E. "To What Extent Did the Ancient Egyptians Employ Bitumen for Embalming?" *Journal of Egyptian Archaeology* 18 (1932): 177–80.

Winlock, H.E. "Materials Used at the Embalming of King Tut-Ankh-Amun." *The Metropolitan Museum of Art Papers*, No. 10 (1941): 5–26.

Chapter 6: The Pyramids

Davidson, D., and Aldersmith, H. *The Great Pyramid, Its Divine Message: An Original Co-ordination of Historical Documents and Archaeological Evi-*

dences. Pyramid Records, Vol. 1. London: Williams and Norgate, Ltd., 1946.

Ebon, Martin, ed. *Mysterious Pyramid Power*. New York: New American Library, Signet Books, 1976.

Edgar, Morton, and Edgar, John. *The Great Pyramid and The Bible*. Glasgow: private printing, 1910.

Edwards, I.E.S. *The Pyramids of Egypt*. Harmondsworth: Penguin Books, 1947.

Fakhry, Ahmed. *The Monuments of Sneferu at Dahshur*. 3 vols. Cairo: General Organization for Government Printing Offices, 1959.

——. *The Pyramids*. Chicago: University of Chicago Press, 1961.

Farag, Nagib, and Iskander, Zaky. *The Discovery of Neferwptah*. Cairo: General Organization Government Printing Offices, 1971.

Goedicke, Hans. "An Egyptologist Looks at the Pyramids: Letters to the Editors." *American Scientist* 59 (1971): 671–72.

Goneim, M. Zakaria. *Horus Kekhem-khet: The Unfinished Step Pyramid at Saqqara*. Vol. 1. Excavations at Saqqara. Cairo: Imprimerie de l'Institut Français d'Archéologie Oriental, 1957.

Jequier, Gustave. *La Pyramide d'Abu*. Fouilles à Saqqarah. Cairo: Imprimerie de l'Institut Français d'Archéologie Oriental, 1935.

——. *Les Pyramides des Reines Neit et Opoint*. Fouilles à Saqqarah. Cairo: Imprimerie de l'Institut Français d'Archéologie Oriental, 1933.

Labrousse, A.; Lauer, Jean-Philippe; and Leclant, J. *Le Temple Haut du Complexe Funérarire du Roi Ounas*. Mission Archéologique de Saqqarah. Vol. 2. Cairo: Publications de l'Institut Français d'Archéologie Oriental, 1977.

Lauer, Jean-Philippe. *La Pyramide à Degrés*. Vols. 1–4. Fouilles à Saqqarah. Cairo: Imprimerie de l'Institut Français d'Archéologie Oriental, 1936–1959.

Mendelssohn, Kurt. "A Scientist Looks at the Pyramids." *American Scientist* 59 (1971): 210–20.

——. *The Riddle of the Pyramids*. New York: Praeger Publishers, 1974.

Nour, Mohammad Zaki; Iskander, Zaky; Osman, Mohammad Salah; and Moustafa, Ahmad Youssof. *The Cheops Boats*. Part 1. Cairo: General Organization for Government Printing Offices, 1960.

Ostrander, Sheila, and Schroeder, Lynn. *Psychic Discoveries Behind the Iron Curtain*. Englewood Cliffs, N.J.: Prentice-Hall, Inc., 1970.

Peiss, Joseph A. *A Miracle in Stone: or The Great Pyramid of Egypt*. Philadelphia: Porter & Coates, 1877.

Piankoff, Alexandre. *The Pyramid of Unas*. Bollingen Series XL, Vol. 5. Princeton: Princeton University Press, 1969.

Smyth, C. Piazzi. *Life and Work at the Great Pyramid*. 3 vols. Edinburgh: Edmonston and Douglas, 1867.

Tompkins, Peter. *Secrets of the Great Pyramid*. New York: Harper and Row, 1971.

Chapter 7: The Coffin Texts

Budge, E.A. Wallis. *An Account of the Sarcophagus of Seti I. King of Egypt, B.C. 1370*. Sir John Soame's Museum. London: Harrison and Sons, 1908.

De Buck, Adriaan, and Gardiner, Alan *The Egyptian Coffin Texts: Texts of Spells 355–471.* Vol. 5. Chicago: University of Chicago Press, 1954.

Faulkner, R.O. *The Ancient Egyptian Coffin Texts.* 2 vols. Reprint. Warminster: Aris & Phillips, Ltd., 1978.

Terrace, Edward L.B. *Egyptian Painting of the Middle Kingdom.* New York: George Braziller, 1967.

Chapter 8: The *Book of the Dead*

Allen, Thomas George. *The Book of the Dead or Going Forth by Day.* Studies in Ancient Oriental Civilization, The Oriental Institute of the University of Chicago, No. 37. Chicago: University of Chicago Press, 1974.

Budge, E.A. Wallis. *The Chapters of Going Forth by Day or, The Theban Recension of the Book of the Dead.* 3 vols. Books on Egypt and Chaldaea. Vol. 28. London: Kegan Paul, Trench, Trübner & Co., Ltd., 1910.

———. *The Egyptian Book of the Dead: The Papyrus of Ani.* 1895. Reprint. New York: Dover Publications, Inc., 1967.

Champdor, Albert. *The Book of the Dead: Based on the Ani, Hunefer, and Anhai Papyri in the British Museum.* Translated by Faubion Bowers. New York: Garrett Publications, 1966.

Davis, Charles H.S. *The Egyptian Book of the Dead: the Most Ancient and the Most Important of Two Extant Religious Texts of Ancient Egypt.* New York: G.P. Putnam's Sons, 1901.

Chapter 9: Amulets

Aldred, Cyril. *Jewels of the Pharaohs: Egyptian Jewellery of the Dynastic Period.* London: Thames and Hudson Ltd., 1971.

Budge, E.A. Wallis. *Amulets and Talismans.* Reprint. New Hyde Park: University Books, 1961.

Edwards, I.E.S. *Oracular Amuletic Decrees of the Late New Kingdom.* 2 vols. Hieratic Papyri in the British Museum, 4th series. London: Published by the Trustees of the British Museum, 1960.

Fraser, George. *A Catalogue of the Scarabs Belonging to George Fraser.* New York: Attic Books, 1979.

Heinrich, Bernd, and Bartholomew, George A. "The Ecology of the African Dung Beetle." *Scientific American* 241 (1979): 146–56.

Howes, Michael. *Amulets.* New York: St. Martin's Press, Inc., 1975.

Newberry, Percy E. *Ancient Egyptian Scarabs: An Introduction to Egyptian Seals and Signet Rings.* Reprint. Chicago: Ares Publishers, Inc., 1975.

Petrie, William Flinders. *Amulets.* Reprint. Warminster: Aris & Phillips, Ltd., 1972.

Pratt Collection: Egyptian Amulets. Hanover: Dartmouth Publications, 1964.

Reisner, M.G.A. *Amulets.* Vol. 2. Catalogue Général des Antiquités Égyptiennes du Musée du Caire. Cairo: Imprimerie de l'Institut Français d'Archéologie Oriental, 1958.

Rowe, Alan. *A Catalogue of Egyptian Scarabs, Scaraboids, Seals, and Amulets in the Palestine Archaeological Museum*. Cairo: Imprimerie de l'Institut Français d'Archéologie Oriental, 1936.

Sauneron, Serge. *Le Papyrus Magique Illustré de Brooklyn*. Wilbour Monographs, Vol. 3. Brooklyn: The Brooklyn Museum, 1970.

Van Dine, S.S. *The Scarab Murder Case*. New York: Charles Scribner's Sons, 1930.

Wilkinson, Alix. *Ancient Egyptian Jewellery*. London: Methuen & Co., Ltd., 1971.

Chapter 10: Magical Servant Statues

Clayton, Peter A. "Royal Bronze Shawabti Figures." *Journal of Egyptian Archaeology* 58 (1972): 167–75.

Dunham, Dows. "Royal Shawabti Figures from Napata." *Bulletin of the Museum of Fine Arts* (Boston) 49 (1951): 40–48.

Hall, H.R. "Notices of Recent Publications: *Les Figurines Funéraires Égyptiennes* by Louis Speleers." *Journal of Egyptian Archaeology* 10 (1924): 176–78.

———. "Three Royal Shabtis in the British Museum." *Journal of Egyptian Archaeology* 17 (1931): 10–12.

Newberry, Percy E. *Funerary Statuettes and Model Sarcophagi*. Catalogue Général des Antiquités Égyptiennes du Musée du Caire. Cairo: Imprimerie de l'Institut Français d'Archéologie Oriental, 1957.

Peck, William H. "A Shawabti from the MSU Art Collection." *Kresge Art Center Bulletin of Michigan State University* 1, No. 6 (1968).

Petrie, William Flinders. "Funeral Figures in Egypt." *Ancient Egypt* 3 (1916), part 4: 151–62.

———. *Shabtis: Illustrated by the Egyptian Collection in University College, London*. Reprint. Warminster: Aris & Phillips, Ltd., 1974.

Phillips, Dorothy W. "A Sculptor's Shawabty Box." *The Metropolitan Museum of Art Bulletin* (1948): 207–12.

Ransom, Caroline L. "The Egyptian Ushebtis Belonging to the New York Historical Society." *The New York Historical Society Quarterly Bulletin* 1 (1918): 91–102.

Thomas, Elizabeth. "The Four Niches and Amuletic Figures in Theban Royal Tombs." *The Journal of the American Research Center in Egypt*. 3 (1964): 71–78.

Winlock, H.E. "Digger's Luck." *The Metropolitan Museum of Art Bulletin*. Reprinted. New York: The Metropolitan Museum of Art 33 (1975): 55–72.

Chapter 11: Magical Objects in Tutankhamen's Tomb

Assaad, Harry, and Kolos, Daniel. *Hieroglyphic Inscriptions of the Treasures of Tutankhamun Translated*. Mississauga, Canada: Benben Publications, 1978.

Budge, E.A. Wallis. *Tutankhamen, Amenism, Atenism and Egyptian Monotheism.* 1923. Reprint. New York: Bell Publishing Company, n.d.

Carter, Howard. *The Tomb of Tutankhamen; Discovered by the Late Earl of Carnarvon and Howard Carter.* 3 vols. 1923–1933. A.C. Mace coauthor of Vol. 1. Reprint. New York: Cooper Square Publishers, Inc., 1963.

Carter, Michael. *Tutankhamun: The Golden Monarch.* New York: David McKay Company, Inc., 1972.

Denoches-Noblecourt, Christiane. *Life and Death of a Pharaoh: Tutankhamen.* New York: New York Graphic Society, 1963.

Edwards, I.E.S. *The Treasures of Tutankhamun.* Harmondsworth: Penguin Books, Ltd., 1972.

Giles, F.J. *Ikhnaton: Legend and History.* Rutherford, N.J.: Fairleigh Dickinson University Press, 1970.

Hoving, Thomas. *Tutankhamun: The Untold Story.* New York: Simon and Schuster, 1978.

Piankoff, Alexandre. *The Shrines of Tut-Ankh-Amon.* Bollingen Series 40–42. New York: Pantheon Books, 1955.

Vandenberg, Philip. *The Curse of the Pharaohs.* Translated by Thomas Weyr. Philadelphia: J.B. Lippincott Company, 1975.

Wynne, Barry. *Behind the Mask of Tutankhamen.* New York: Taplinger Publishing Company, 1972.

Chapter 12: Letters to the Dead

Gardiner, A.H. "A New Letter to the Dead." *Journal of Egyptian Archaeology* 20 (1934): 19–22.

Gardiner, A.H., and Sethe, K. *Egyptian Letters to the Dead.* London: Egypt Exploration Society, 1928.

Piankoff, A., and Clère, J.J. "A Letter to the Dead on a Bowl in the Louvre." *Journal of Egyptian Archaeology* 20 (1934): 157–69.

Simpson, William Kelly. "The Letter to the Dead from the Tomb of Meru (N 3737) at Nag' El-Deir." *Journal of Egyptian Archaeology* 52 (1966): 39–52.

Chapter 13: Oracles

Blackman, Aylward M. "Oracles in Ancient Egypt." *Journal of Egyptian Archaeology* 11 (1925): 249–55.

———. "Oracles in Ancient Egypt—II." *Journal of Egyptian Archaeology* 12 (1926): 176–85.

Breasted, James Henry. *Ancient Records of Egypt.* 5 vols. 1906. Reprint. New York: Russell & Russell, Inc., 1962.

Budge, E.A. Wallis. *Egyptian Magic.* London: Kegan Paul, Trench, Trübner & Co., 1899.

Gardiner, Alan H. "The Dakhleh Stella." *Journal of Egyptian Archaeology* 19 (1933): 19–30.

Parker, Richard A. *A Saite Oracle Papyrus from Thebes.* Providence: Brown University Press, 1962.

Thomas, Ernest S. "Oracular Responses." *Ancient Egypt* 6 (1921): 76–78.

Chapter 14: Dreams

Gardiner, Alan H., ed. *Hieratic Papyri in the British Museum.* London: British Museum, 1935.

Gunn, Battiscombe. "Interpreters of Dreams in Ancient Egypt." *Journal of Egyptian Archaeology* 4 (1917): 252.

Chapter 15: An Egyptian Horoscope Calendar

Bakir, Abd El-Mohsen. *The Cairo Calendar.* Cairo: General Organization for Government Printing Offices, 1966.

Chapter 16: Greco-Roman and Coptic Magic

Apuleius. *The Metamorphoses.* 2 vols. Translated by H.E. Butler. Oxford: Oxford University Press, 1910.

Bonner, Campbell. "Magical Amulets." *Harvard Theological Review* 39 (1946): 25–55.

———. "The Numerical Value of a Magical Formula." *Journal of Egyptian Archaeology* 16 (1930): 6–9.

Budge, E.A. Wallis. *Egyptian Magic.* London: Kegan Paul, Trench, Trübner & Co., 1899.

Černý, J.; Kahle, P.E.; and Parker, R.A. "The Old Coptic Horoscope." *Journal of Egyptian Archaeology* 43 (1957): 86–91.

Crum, W.E. "Magical Texts in Coptic—I." *Journal of Egyptian Archaeology* 20 (1934): 51–53.

———. "Magical Texts in Coptic—II." *Journal of Egyptian Archaeology* 20 (1934): 195–200.

Griffith, F.Ll., and Thompson, Herbert. *The Leyden Papyrus.* 1904. Reprint. New York: Dover Publications, Inc., 1974.

Hunt, Arthur S. "An Incantation in the Ashmolean Museum." *Journal of Egyptian Archaeology* 15 (1929): 155–57.

———. "The Warren Magical Papyrus." *Studies Presented* to F.Ll. Griffith. London: Oxford University Press, 1932.

Lindsay, Jack. *The Origins of Alchemy in Graeco-Roman Egypt.* New York: Barnes & Noble, Inc., 1970.

Nock, A.D. "Greek Magical Papyri." *Journal of Egyptian Archaeology* 15 (1929): 219–35.

———. "Magical Notes." *Journal of Egyptian Archaeology* 11 (1925): 154–58.

Thompson, R. Campbell. *Semitic Magic*. 1908. Reprint. New York: KTAV Publishing House, Inc., 1971.

Worrell, W.H. "A Coptic Wizard's Hoard." *The American Journal of Semitic Languages and Literature* 46 (1930): 239–62.

Chapter 17: Tales of Magic

Lichtheim, Miriam. *Ancient Egyptian Literature*. 2 vols. Berkeley: University of California Press, 1975, 1976.

Maspero, Gaston. *Popular Stories of Ancient Egypt*. Translated by A.S. Johns. New Hyde Park: University Books, 1967.

Petrie, W.M. Flinders. *Egyptian Tales*. 1899. Reprint. New York: Benjamin Blom, Inc., 1971.

Simpson, William Kelly, ed. *The Literature of Ancient Egypt*. 2nd edition, revised with corrections. New Haven: Yale University Press, 1977.

Chapter 18: Spells for All Occasions

Allen, Thomas George. *The Book of the Dead or Going Forth by Day*. Studies in Ancient Oriental Civilization, The Oriental Institute of the University of Chicago, No. 37. Chicago: University of Chicago Press, 1974.

Bryan, Cyril P., Trans. *Ancient Egyptian Medicine: The Papyrus Ebers*. 1930. Reprint. Chicago: Ares Publishers, Inc., 1974.

Budge, E.A. Wallis. *The Chapters of Going Forth by Day or, The Theban Recension of the Book of the Dead*. 3 vols. Books on Egypt and Chaldea. Vol. 28. London: Kegan Paul, Trench, Trübner & Co., Ltd., 1910.

———. *The Egyptian Book of the Dead: The Papyrus of Ani*. 1895. Reprint. New York: Dover Publications, Inc., 1967.

———. *Egyptian Magic*. London: Kegan Paul, Trench, Trübner & Co., 1899.

Faulkner, R.O., Trans. *The Ancient Egyptian Coffin Texts*. 2 vols. Warminster: Aris & Phillips, Ltd., 1973, 1977.

Griffith, F.Ll., and Thompson, Herbert. *The Leyden Papyrus*. 1904. Reprint. New York: Dover Publications, Inc., 1974.

General Index

Name Index

Egyptian Word Index